Dangerous Sexualities

Dangerous Sexualities

Medico-moral politics in England since 1830

Frank Mort

ROUTLEDGE & KEGAN PAUL
London and New York

First published in 1987 by
Routledge & Kegan Paul Ltd
11 New Fetter Lane, London EC4P 4EE

Published in the USA by
Routledge & Kegan Paul Inc.
in association with Methuen Inc.
29 West 35th Street, New York, NY 10001

Set in Imprint
by Inforum Ltd, Portsmouth
and printed in Great Britain
by The Guernsey Press, Guernsey, Channel Islands

Library of Congress Cataloging in Publication Data

Mort, Frank.
    Dangerous sexualities.
    Bibliography: p.
    Includes index.
    1. England—Moral conditions. 2. Sexual ethics—
England—History. 3. Hygiene, Sexual—England—
History. 4. Public health—England—History. I. Title.
HN398.E5M67   306.7'0942   87–4679

British Library CIP Data also available
ISBN 0 7102 0856 1

CONTENTS

Contents

Contents

ACKNOWLEDGMENTS

This book took many years to write, years in which its arguments were discussed with friends and colleagues and presented at countless conferences and seminars. These collective contributions are evident on every page. The Social Science Research Council funded the first three years of the project as a doctoral thesis at the Centre for Contemporary Cultural Studies, University of Birmingham. Thereafter, research at the Open University and teaching at Bristol Polytechnic and West Midlands College of Higher Education provided me with the income to finish it. Students at those institutions were remarkably patient when I used them as a sounding board for my ideas. Libraries and librarians loomed large in the research, especially the staff at the British Library, the Public Record Office and the Fawcett Library. David Doughan, the Fawcett's Assistant Librarian, has been a mine of information and a source of encouragement and I owe him a special thanks.

Many of my early ideas came out of discussions with past members of the Centre for Contemporary Cultural Studies, and in particular the state group. Jane Beckett, Deborah Cherry, Philip Derbyshire, Stuart Hall, Rachel Harrison, Sheila Henderson, Stuart Marshall, Lynda Nead, Roy Peters, Adrian Rifkin, Bill Schwarz, Simon Watney, Christine Weedon, Jeffrey Weeks and Bruce Wood also commented at various stages on my ideas or on sections of the manuscript and I am grateful for their help. Nikolas Rose and Maureen McNeil were sympathetic examiners when the material was presented as a thesis and I have acted on much of their good advice. My parents, Lillian and James Mort, were generous with financial support and encouragement, and Gwenllian Rhys was meticulous in typing the manuscript.

Finally, I owe a special debt to three friends. Richard Johnson provided me with much of the initial impetus for the book, sustained me with help and advice, and taught me how to be a historian. Lucy Bland discussed almost every stage of the research with me in joint articles and projects. Her critique and

Acknowledgments

intellectual stimulation has added a major dimension to my approach. Nicholas Green has lived with the book (and with me) almost as long as I have. Without his intellectual support and practical help it might never have seen the light of day.

INTRODUCTION: NARRATIVES OF SEX

To begin at the end of our story. In May 1982 the medical journal *The Lancet* front-paged an article called 'Risk Factors for Kaposi's Sarcoma in Homosexual Men'.[1] The piece reported on an American study of twenty gay men in New York and California with a particularly rare form of skin cancer. Symptoms included sores, coupled with weight loss and low fever. Pointing to significant links between the spread of the disease and promiscuity, the article drew medics' attention to alarming differences between the sex life of the infected homosexuals and a control group of non-infected heterosexuals. Fifty per cent of the gay patients admitted to having sex with ten or more partners in an average month. The most promiscuous 'confessed' he had had intercourse with ninety different partners in the weeks before succumbing to the virus. Conclusions were tentative, but an initial hypothesis was clearly spelt out – 'deviant' sex was an important factor in spreading this potentially killer disease.

The previous December studies published in the prestigious *New England Journal of Medicine* had signalled the appearance of even more drastic symptoms, again among American gay men.[2] Medics were at a loss in the face of an unidentified virus, which attacked the natural capacity of blood cells to defend themselves against infection. Physical symptoms included respiratory problems, glandular fever, a virulent form of pneumonia (*pneumocystis pneumonia*) and Kaposi's sarcoma. Patients had already died from the syndrome. All known broad-spectrum antibiotics proved useless in checking its career. Research teams concluded that they had identified a new form of acquired cellular immunodeficiency, AIDS. Again they made connections between high rates of 'deviant' sex and the rampant growth of the disease. Doctors concluded that given the abnormally high promiscuity of gay men, some form of sexually transmitted virus or exposure to a common lifestyle played a critical role in establishing immunodeficiency.

Cases of AIDS began to be reported in Britain towards the end of 1982. Almost immediately medical journals, TV and the popular press fuelled speculation about the link between promiscuity and killer diseases. Positions were staked out. The medical profession warned gay men against sex. In the absence of any known cure, the best means of prevention was to avoid frequent contacts and reconsider their whole lifestyle. Gay men's self-help groups attacked the lurid press coverage of AIDS, and began to mobilize in the face of government lethargy. Fund-raising and health education has been to the fore in their fight back. Since then, mortality rates have risen dramatically. Successive waves of panic have drawn in heterosexuals, without shifting the burden of blame from gay men. Currently effective treatment is still some way off. Despite the barrage of prestige medical research into the structure of the virus, AIDS represents the front-line of sexual politics.

This book is about unravelling the narratives which link our beliefs about health and disease to moral and immoral notions of sex. AIDS and all that follows from it cannot be contained by official medical explanations. Nor is it simply a conspiracy, fuelled by the moral right and press sensationalism. AIDS is the contemporary moment in a much longer history, the extraordinarily complex interweaving of medicine and morality with the surveillance and regulation – even the very definition – of sex. The disease has produced gay men as its victims and their sexuality as the problem. This is part of the norms, protocols and procedures written into the history of medico-moral discourse.

The book has a double axis. First, a detailed account of the relation between systems of medical knowledge and power. Second, an analysis of the way medical and other discourses have produced a distinct regime of sex, targeting sensitive or dangerous groups and generating forms of resistance. Historically, our main focus is on the nineteenth and early twentieth century, but in conclusion we shall return with some urgency to our own situation now. It is therefore a history of and for the present; an attempt to use history writing both to understand why our current dilemmas have arisen and to shape future political demands. This means seeing the present as historical, as the product of a particular combination of structural forces.

What perspectives have suggested the most fertile and incisive questions to break open the area? The introduction is not in the business of providing a 'general theory', either of sexuality, or of professional experts. Indeed, the book as a whole argues that such concepts can only be grasped within historically specific structures, ranging from the detailed and the immediate to problematics pitched at a much higher level of abstraction. Nevertheless, we are concerned with providing a self-conscious account of the politics and theories which have informed the making of our history. Two influences have been paramount. The revival of marxist and marxist-influenced theory and history, and the impact of the feminisms – both as ways of thinking about the world and with their specific injunctions to men over sexual politics. Feminist interventions have meant that in writing about sexuality as a man I have been made very much aware of the gender-specific access to the questions we ask and the knowledge we seek. This, I believe, should not imply that men abandon the field. But without a recognition that sexuality has constructed men and women in terms of difference – a difference shot through with power relations – the very nature of the struggles confronting us remains distorted or obscured. Like all historical accounts, the narrative is deliberately, though thoughtfully, selective in its choice of material; choices which are made on the back of current concerns. All students of social movements stand in a definite relation to the historical developments they describe, not outside them. Hence we have 'taken sides' and have not held back from explicitly arguing for political and intellectual preferences. Wilful exclusion of these criteria from history-writing not only contributes to the discipline's mystique – and confusion! – but also closes off many of the possible associations between historical understanding and progressive politics.

The base-line insistence underpinning our account is the historical construction of sexuality. An emphasis in the broadest sense on sexuality as historically specific and culturally variable still radically challenges those other accounts of sexual definitions which dominate the field. Since the late nineteenth century, anatomy, physiology and psychology, projecting sex as central to our personality and bodily functions,

Introduction

have exerted a powerful influence on official programmes and political positions. Although now under challenge, they still hold sway over commonsense ideas about what we mean by sex. A history of sex raises a number of expectations. We expect it to cover things like the sex act, procreation, the family, birth-control, motherhood, prostitution, homosexuality. At some level or other we also anticipate the personal or experiential – questions of identity more intimate than in other forms of social or cultural history.[3] This account is primarily concerned with neither. It does not start from lived experience, nor from a set of pre-given objects called sexuality. Rather it explores one par-ticular field of official knowledge; the linked areas of social medicine and moral politics. The book argues that this domain has been instrumental in producing some of the central mean-ings and power relations around sex.

Why study the official area at all? The personal dimensions of power are now high on the political agenda, and rightly so – the power of men over women in lived relations, sexual authority within the family, attempts to forge new personas and plea-sures. So why study public policy? Because official program-mes are not neatly sealed off from more intimate forms of social relations. The whole paraphernalia of government reports and professional knowledge does set the broad conditions for the way we experience our sexual identities. Official discourses do have concrete, if complex and often bizarre, effects on the sexuality of constructed men and women. Unless we hold to a spontaneist or libertarian politics, changing sexual relations must involve transforming the institutions and practices which fix our personal life. This is not to imply that there is any direct, one to one, relation between dominant social structures and the personal. Nor is it to suggest that as soon as we accept our sexuality as constructed the personal comfortably evaporates – an argument frequently used by socialist men to get their private life off the hook! But any encounter with officialdom does pose the sharp end of awkward questions which won't go away with the hoped-for installation of a new regime of sex. Questions about legislation, about the power of science and medical knowlege – these issues will continue to be high on the agenda. Used self-consciously, a historical encounter with the official can prove a political education in itself.

4

Introduction

It may come as something of a surprise to find that many of the accounts which have opened up the area – histories of state policy and the professions, theories of the state – do not deal explicitly with sexuality at all. In large part this is due to the widely held belief, especially among male academics, that sex is not a fit subject for serious study. We will not spend a great deal of time outlining these theories. Instead we will concentrate on saying what has proved most useful or problematic about them for us.

One way into the medico-moral complex is via the official problematic itself; to go straight to the big histories and sociologies of public health, state administration and government, together with more discrete accounts of medicine and its institutions. In the post-war period these have exercised a decisive influence over many areas of what we might term 'the social' – *social* policy, *social* work, even *social* democracy.[4] The main strength of such work is also its most glaring weakness. Written from a standpoint internal to the policy-making process itself, we are ushered into the more obviously generative social processes – government departments, the world of formal politics, etc. Here we encounter the most immediately responsible persons and organizations – politicians, professionals, articulate interest groups. In doing so, terms like 'morality', 'medicine', or 'education' are taken as given. We are not encouraged to analyse their social meanings and frame of reference. Moreover, politics tends to be treated only as a specialist or expert field. Wider movements of popular and feminist protest go unacknowledged, or are seen as constraints on the policy makers. In short, such accounts work hand-in-glove with the professionals, and write out the whole history of contesting forces beyond their focus.

Recent marxist sociologies of the professions and theories of the state, together with marxist informed social history, have provided a more structural and politically engaged approach.[5] Here, policy and expertise has been probed much more critically, not so much for what is said, as for the underlying ideological problematic, which functions as social control or class regulation. In writing this history, marxism has been most useful in its injunctions to think through the big structures organizing conjunctures and social formations. Our main quarrel has been with functionalist and reductionist schools of marxism, and their tendency to lose sight of the particular forms of power and resistance which are not directly related to the needs or interests of capital. At certain key moments, of course, major transformations in the economic forces and relations of capitalist production do set the broad parameters for sexual and moral disciplining. Sanitary politics in the 1830s and 1840s for example cannot be understood without reference to these conditions. What is at issue is whether a general theory of capital's needs and requirements can adequately come to grips with the internal complexities of professionalism and expertise, the production of scientific knowledge and the gendered power relations which have been at the centre of our study.

Much of the initial impetus for tackling the medico-moral domain came from the work of the French philosopher and historian, Michel Foucault. Foucault's classic area of study has been the historical interrogation of objects so often designated as natural, but which he argues, are constructed through particular genealogies and systems of knowledge – 'madness', 'medicine' and 'punishment', as well as 'sexuality'.[6] His radical deconstruction of such objects challenges their conceptual unity. In other words, 'sexuality' is not necessarily what we mean by sex; we find it in the most unlikely places, dispersed across a range of sites and institutions. Foucault's discourse theory is based on a method which scans texts to bring to light their discursive coherence. Under specific historical conditions statements are seen to combine together and, despite even sometimes because of contradictions, they exhibit a systematic organization. Intimate forms of power are produced through these particular regimes of knowledge. Foucault's axiom that power is everywhere in modern societies is complemented by detailed attention to its micro-physics and to the complex mechanisms through which it is exercised. His analysis seeks to understand how power is both regulatory and productive; productive of knowledges and institutions and of bodies, pleasures and desires.

Foucault's paradigm has had most impact on those parts of the book which encounter highly specialized forms of professional expertise, with their own codes, protocols and their own written archive. Discourse analysis works best wherever intellectuals have staked out distinctive monopolies on truth. In this respect Foucault's method usefully preserves linguistic and semiotic emphases on the production of meaning, but now understood much more historically. We have used it as a sophisticated tool to probe the formal character of official representations (and the mechanisms of their 'power effect'), and at moments to grasp how languages of resistance are generated.

There have by now been many critiques of the absences and inadequacies of discourse theory. In putting together this history two related problems have come up time and again: questions about agency and political struggle. What to do about those 'heroes' of official narratives – the great civil servants and sanitarians, Chadwick, Kay and Simon – and the 'heroines' of our history – Butler, Hopkins and Christabel Pankhurst. There are protagonists agitating here; not voluntaristic individuals who stand at the centre of events, but socially constructed subjects, the men and women who people our account as policy makers and leaders of resistance. Any account of medico-moral discourse must occupy this moment in the cycle of power and politics. Programmes are implemented and resistances fought out through ideologies which constructed men as if they really were at the centre of the world, and many women as leaders or missionaries in the vanguard of moral reform. Foucault has little to say about all this. Simplistic, polarized distinctions between voluntaristic notions of human agency on the one hand, and the worst excesses of subjectless structuralism on the other, do little to help the historian. We have understood agents not only as bearers of policy and politics, but also as subjects whose particular formation had effects on the campaigns they were involved in. Letters, biographies and memoirs have provided us with ways into the personal dimensions of agency. They need to be approached with caution, though, for they are not neutral and carry very traditional understandings about individuality and personal life.

A more general point follows from the issue of agency. Shifts and transformations in official power are not generated by their own internal momentum, they are always shaped by negotiations with competing political forces. Large-scale movements of organized revolt, along with more localized though not less significant cultural struggles, have had a major impact on sexual regulation and moral reform. Women's struggles have been central here. In the field of sexuality they were in large part spearheaded by outrage against the medical establishment. From the repeal campaign against the Contagious Diseases Acts in the 1870s, through to the purity feminism of the suffrage movement, successive generations of women put together an alternative strategy – and alternative understandings of sex – which at moments routed the power of male experts. Recent feminist historical work has transformed the way we understand these campaigns. Foucault's sexualization of bodies and subjects singularly fails to get to grips with the way access to knowledge and power was gendered through ideologies of sexual difference. For the opposition between masculine and feminine understandings of sex provided some of the most heavily contested battles in this area. We need accounts of how these resistances were formed just as complex as our work on official discourse. Resistances did not just drop from the sky nor were formed by spontaneous eruptions from below. They were dependent on the languages available, which could endow such struggles with meaning. As we shall see, 'feminine' and feminist appropriations of evangelical religious morality proved especially important in providing women with the voice to resist male professionals.

The two sides of our history need to be worked together, in order to bring out the inter-relations between official networks of power and forms of resistance. Here we come up against some of the most difficult problems of history-writing. For while official history is uninterested in the whole question of struggle, history 'from below' baulks at grasping the structural relations which bind these two moments together.[7] The problem has been acute for us, because so often those who refused medico-moral authority – especially middle-class women – themselves stood with one foot inside the power bloc. Hence, though women are to the fore in the book as the collective subject of a progressive sexual politics, their role is never unproblematic.

Finally, a word about presentation. To begin with a *narrative* – of AIDS – is no accident. Forms of story-telling loom large in the book, from cholera in the 1830s through official wrangles at the Home Office to small-town rivalries over feminism and sex education. This is not to trivialize the seriousness of the political issues involved. Narrative is one very deliberate technique of history-writing. Interspersed with other 'genres', we have used it as a self-conscious way of presenting empirical material. It helps to draw attention to the constructed nature of historical 'facts' and events. But there is more to it than that. Medico-moral politics lends itself particularly well to dramatic treatment. Gruesome stories of moral decay and lurid metaphors of punishment and pestilence are the stock-in-trade of writing in this area. They carry with them distinctive sexual scripts – at once terrifying and titillating – which organize the reader's emotional and erotic experience and produce their own forms of pleasure. In writing about sexuality, we realize how many of these pleasures are highly gendered. Nevertheless, negotiating the pleasures of the text – juggling them alongside more traditional political priorities – is a major challenge for the cultural historian. *Dangerous Sexualities* is an attempt to make sense of some of these stories of pleasure and danger.

PART ONE

MORAL ENVIRONMENTALISM 1830–1860

1   CHOLERA

Asiatic cholera, or *cholera morbus*, spread to Britain from India in a series of epidemics which engulfed much of Europe in the 1820s. The symptoms and the rapacity with which the disease struck must have been alarming even to a population used to the sight of typhus, scarlet fever and smallpox. The Central Board of Health issued a vivid description of the symptomatology:

> The attack of the disease in extreme cases is so sudden, that, from a state of apparent good health . . . an individual sustains as rapid a loss of bodily power as if he were suddenly struck down or poisoned; the countenance assuming a death-like appearance, the skin becoming cold. . . . The pulse is either feeble, intermitting, fluttering or lost; a livid circle is observed round the eyelids. . . . Vomiting soon succeeds; first some of the usual contents of the stomach, next a turbid fluid like whey . . . or water gruel. . . . Spasms, beginning at the toes and fingers soon follow. . . . The next severe symptoms are, an intolerable sense of weight, and constriction felt upon the chest . . . a leaden or bluish appearance of the countenance . . . the palms of the hands and soles becoming shrivelled. . . . At length a calm succeeds and death. . . . The powers of the constitution often yield to such an attack at the end of four hours, and seldom sustain longer than eight.[1]

The epidemic broke out in northern England in the autumn of 1831. In Sunderland, where the approaching threat had become serious as early as April, a local board of health had been meeting to discuss preventive measures.[2] It was chaired by Dr Reid Clancy who, as senior physician to the Sunderland Infirmary, was the closest to an official medical officer of health that the town possessed. On the night of Sunday 16 October twelve-year-old Isabella Hazard was taken violently ill with vomiting, cramps and general fever. At four in the morning the local doctor, Mr Cook, was called. He returned later to find the child weakening. By the following afternoon Isabella was dead. The symptoms seemed unmistakable – Isabella's mother asked the doctor, 'What makes the child so black?' But Cook either missed the diagnosis or tried to ignore it. When William Sport died of similar symptoms on the nineteenth it was clear that cholera had arrived. On 1 November official notification of the presence of the disease in England was sent by Dr Clancy in a special report to the newly established Board of Health at Whitehall. Thereafter the disease spread to Scotland, the North and Manchester and later to the Midlands and London. Mortality for the first outbreak was estimated at 23,000.

There was of course no question of cure; the cholera bacillus was not isolated until 1884. The King's parliamentary speech for 1831 directed that 'precautions should be taken against the introduction of so dangerous a malady.'[3] These amounted to recommendations issued by the Board of Health authorising the creation of local boards, which were to be responsible for the monitoring and control of the disease. Beyond that there were a host of popular remedies, prayers and moral homilies administered by the local clergy. In the summer of 1831 special services of intercession were organized to plead for divine mercy:

> O Almighty God, who has visited the nations with the sudden death of pestilence, spare, we beseech thee, this thy favoured land, the wrath which to our sins is justly due.[4]

The newly founded medical journal, *The Lancet*, along with other leading periodicals, carried numerous articles on the causes of cholera and the steps to be taken for prevention. Evidence was conflicting and contradictory, reflecting current medical divisions on the origins and transmission of disease. But though there was no agreement about causation, medics, clerics and other local officials were all agreed that the *urban poor* were the human agents responsible for spreading the contagion. As more sporadic outbreaks were reported throughout the summer of 1831, medical evidence sent to the hastily constituted Board of Health confirmed that the environment and the physical and moral habits of the poor actively stimulated the disease. In the metropolis it was in Bermondsey, Southwark and among 'those afloat on the river', rather than in stately Hanover Square or semi-rural Kensington, that cholera was seen to be taking the greatest toll.[5]

In July the board had received disturbing accounts of an outbreak at a flax mill in Port Glasgow. Nancy Kitchen, a mill girl, had been living 'very perniciously' with an Irishman named Murray, who habitually spent his his 'idle time' with the girls. Both had been struck down by the disease. The local doctor suggested that the couple's irregular conduct, 'living in the closest intimacy', had acted as a stimulus to infection.[6] When Dr Mahony reported from Hull in August that a soldier serving in the Fusiliers had contracted cholera, Dr Dawn at the central board wrote back: 'You will be good enough to make most explicit . . . as to the habits of the soldier in question, the circumstances immediately preceding his illness.'[7] Mahony reported that the man had been in the regiment for twenty years as an officer's servant and was generally of sober habits. But three days prior to his death he had been absent from camp for two nights and had returned 'not absolutely drunk, yet not sober'.[8] On visiting Hull, Dawn concluded, the soldier had been 'living in debauchery' and his dissolute behaviour had contributed to the onset of the illness. The central board, many of whose members had by now fled to the purer air of the country, minuted ominously: 'should this disease ever make its appearance in the country (which God forbid) its first appearance will be among the squalid parts of the population'.[9]

When reports from the north-east in November forced Whitehall officials to admit to an epidemic, the condensation of immorality, poverty and the spread of disease became even more pronounced. The first case in North Shields involving a 'mendicant of intemperate habits', Dennis McGair, occurred on 10 December. McGair's wife, also intemperate, died a few days later.[10] More alarming still was the discovery that the disease spread from the dissolute to the sober and industrious. At the height of the outbreak in the north, the Mayor of York wrote to Lord Melbourne, Home Secretary, alerting him to the large numbers of vagrants and other disorderly persons who were bringing cholera into the city. They arrived at common lodging houses and began to commit acts of vagrancy and indecency, thereby infecting the native population.[11] Equally, *The Westminster Review* warned the city fathers of the danger of hundreds of starving paupers who came to London for relief, and were compelled to herd together 'in much less cleanliness and comfort than the lowest orders of Indians'.[12] All this was not just the metaphoric evocation of pestilence at a moment of panic. Nor was it a simple search for a scapegoat in the absence of any cure. The logic which twinned poverty and immorality with contagion was made through a specific language – the discourse of early social medicine – and was circulated at key institutional sites within the central and local state. The intentions were clear: greater surveillance and regulation of the poor.

The proposed solution was twofold: to isolate the human sources of infection, subjecting them to a regime of compulsory inspection and detention, combined with propaganda to educate the poor into a regime of cleanliness and morality. In Sunderland the board of health used the by-laws to isolate vagrants and paupers from the community.[13] *The Cholera Gazette*, the weekly bulletin on the disease, stressed a more educative approach. It advised issuing handbills to impress on the poor the importance of clean, temperate and moral habits as the only sure means of prevention.[14] Local residents in London were warned about the dangers of dissipation; they were told to keep regular hours, strict attention to hygiene and a comfortable and nutritious diet.

Yet from the outset the general response to the epidemic was sporadic and revealed how ill-equipped the central and local state were to deal with public health measures. This was not just an effect of rudimentary medical knowledge. The threat of epidemic disease precipitated heated political arguments about the extent of state intervention, which became condensed with wider debates over reform. The new Board of Health had no legislative powers. It was in effect only a consultative committee – one of those peculiarly English bits of nineteenth-century administrative ad hocery, with an unclear relation to Parliament and statutory authority. Designed to avoid accusations of government expansion, and to side-step the full glare of political scrutiny, it was shunted off to the Privy Council. Almost immediately its members came under fire from the radical wing of the medical profession, keen to extend their status and authority. In the campaigns leading up to the 1832 Reform Act, Thomas Wakley, editor of *The Lancet*, had been polemicizing for the wholesale reform of the medical establishment, as part of the more general scheme of parliamentary and social reform to replace the 'tyrannical ruling oligarchy'.[15] The new board, he claimed, was yet another illustration of the way the profession was being led by drones, sycophants and titled imbecility, most of whom had no personal experience of treating disease, nor any understanding of how infection was transmitted.[16] Far from avoiding contention, the new public health machinery was becoming caught fast in the tangled web of professional politics.

Underlying the battle for control of public health was a fundamental argument about the validity of state intervention. The proposals for compulsory local powers and the whole issue of funding were highly contentious. When the disease began to reach epidemic proportions in the winter of 1831, the central board was inundated with desperate letters from local officials demanding clarification of the extent of their powers. Civic dignitaries in Birmingham asked if money from the parish rates could be used to combat the disease. Mine owners in the north-east petitioned for increased state intervention, not on humanitarian grounds but to alleviate losses to capital.[17] The Privy Council replied that they could not authorize the reckless outlay of public money but would apply to the Cabinet for further powers. Whereon they received a piece of cautionary advice from Spring-Rice, financial secretary to the Treasury. He emphasized that while the Exchequer would be ready to assist local efforts, money should be given 'with extreme discretion', lest it repress rather than stimulate voluntary exertions.[18]

State intervention not only meant increased financial expenditure, it also contravened implicit assumptions about the role of government shared by both Whigs and Tories. Pressure from the new professional men, especially medics, for the state to take fuller responsibility for public health was severely qualified by dominant political and administrative ideologies. Government was to be kept cheap, and the central state was not to take on statutory powers for issues which were essentially the province of local authorities and voluntary initiatives.

As the epidemic died down, it became increasingly clear that this new system of health administration was a temporary measure only. There was little notion of a permanent public health network. During 1833 the Privy Council announced that they would not re-apply for the renewal of compulsory powers, advising local medics that henceforward the management of the disease would be left 'to the prudence and good feeling of those communities where it may occasionally show itself'.[19] Voluntary self-help rather than any state-backed public health network remained the watchword.

Britain was again ravaged by cholera epidemics in 1848–1849, 1853–1854 and 1866. The history of the disease is largely preserved within the narrative of the public health and other 'reform' movements in early Victorian Britain. Health, housing, sanitation, the emergence of preventive medicine, the foundations of a national system of education, the reform of industrial conditions – these objects have formed the classic terrain for histories of government and public administration. Official history, whether in its Fabian or Tory variants, has been written as a celebratory progress from the early nineteenth-century origins of the welfare state, to its full flowering in the post Second World War period. Such narratives have been carried by their own heroes, the dedicated civil servants and administrators, and by an unswerving commitment to the ideology of professional expertise. But there is another history to be written here. Official transformations at the level of the state defined a new field of social intervention and consolidated a particular regime of moral disciplining. Representations of sexual immorality were constructed through institutional programmes which linked the habits and environment of the urban poor with medico-moral concepts of health and disease. It is this specific domain of sexuality – of sensitive social groups targeted by professional experts and their knowledge – which forms the basis of our history.

2   JAMES PHILLIPS KAY

When cholera reached Manchester in the early summer of 1832 James Kay was senior physician at the Ardwick and

Ancoats dispensary, in an area chiefly inhabited by Irish labourers and textile workers. Kay was typical of the new type of expert who was instrumental in co-ordinating plans for state intervention. Like many of his contemporaries he came from a strong nonconformist background, with direct links to the industrial bourgeoisie – the family's capital was in cotton, calico, printing and blacking.[20] Trained as a medical practitioner, in 1826 he was appointed assistant at the Edinburgh New Town dispensary and clerk to the fever hosptial, Queensferry. His early work was characteristic of the way many early nineteenth-century intellectuals combined theoretical research with a commitment both to evangelical religion and to the politics of state administration. In the late 1820s and early 1830s he published research on diseases of the brain and the circulatory system, but like Wakley he saw no division between medical inquiry and politics. Research into the causes of infection led inexorably to a wider field of action. As Kay put it, the development of a strategy for the 'mitigation of suffering', had to take in fundamental questions of economic, political and moral causation. He was personally motivated by a nascent professionalism *and* by the culture of his own native dissenting religion, which stressed the importance of practical good works for self-validation and eventual salvation. In a typical passage from his 'autobiography', written in 1877, Kay showed how he moved from the particular concerns of physical health, through mental and moral considerations, to a full conception of social intervention:

I came to know how almost useless were the resources of my art to contend with the consequences of formidable social evils. It was clearly something outside scientific skill or charity which was needed. . . . Very early therefore, I began to reflect on this complex problem. Were this degradation and suffering inevitable? Could they only be mitigated? Were we always to be working with palliatives? Was there no remedy? Might not this calamity be traced to its source, and all the resource of a Christian nation devoted through whatever time, to the moral and physical regeneration of this wretched population? Parallel therefore with my scientific reading I gradually began to make myself acquainted with the best work on political and social science, and obtained more and more insight into the grave questions affecting the relations of capital and labour and the distribution of wealth, as well as the inseparable connection between the mental and moral condition of the people and their physical well-being.[22]

The sets of relations posed here were recurrent in Kay's work, as they were in the writings of many early social reformers. Physical degeneracy and mental and moral deterioration demanded scientific solutions, but they were also framed in relation to questions of Christian morality, political economy and social science. Moving beyond mere palliatives, Kay became convinced that it was necessary to intervene in the arena of social and political debate – to abandon 'the purely scientific spirit' in favour of a career in public administration.[23] This change of direction was backed by a utilitarian belief that the health and strength of the great mass of the population was the key to good government, and the indispensable basis for preserving social and political order. In 1833 Kay was appointed an assistant commissioner to the new Poor Law Board, and the following year he served as a major witness to the Select Committee on the Education of the Poorer Classes in England and Wales. As secretary to the new Privy Council committee on education from 1839, he was central to implementing the new programme for public education.

A number of distinct elements are brought together in Kay's biography. Through his family background he was linked with industrial capital. But in no sense was he a direct representative of its interests; his specific formation was within the field of preventive medicine. It was this professional discourse which provided Kay with the impetus to scrutinize the physical and moral health of the labouring classes. Here was a programme which was simultaneously medical and moral; directed both to the reform of the environment and the training of the mind. Sexual immorality was integral to these concerns.

Kay's own early contribution to the debate on the immorality of the urban poor was set out in his pamphlet *The Moral and Physical Condition of the Working Classes Employed in the Cotton Manufacture in Manchester*, 1832. Written in direct response to the problems of cholera, it was dedicated to his mentor, the Scottish political economist the Rev. Thomas Chalmers. Chalmers, drawing on his work as a Glasgow minister, always stressed the supremacy of the moral over the physical.[24] Kay's plan for the improvement of the population twinned material *and* moral reform since, as he pointed out, 'the purely physical condition of the people seemed to me to be incapable of permanent improvement without an increase of their intelligence and virtue . . . through the influence of education and religion.'[25]

Reform of sexual conduct was an important part of Kay's schema. Sexuality – always referred to by Kay as sexual *immorality* – was constructed in direct relation to the themes of disease, filth and material squalor, depravity, political sedition and the perceived threat of an oppositional culture:

> No event is more painfully calculated to excite the public mind, than the invasion of pestilence . . . no other can be so well calculated to unmask the deformity of evils which have preyed upon the energies of the community. He whose duty it is to follow in the steps of this messenger of death, must descend to the abodes of poverty, must frequent the close alleys, the crowded courts, the overpeopled habitations of wretchedness, where pauperism and disease congregate round the source of social discontent and political disorder in the centre of our large towns, and behold with alarm, in the hot-bed of pestilence, ills that fester in secret, at the very heart of society . . .[26]

Moral intervention arose in personal terms for experts like Kay from an emotive perception of the distance between their own lived culture and the patterns of working-class life. Many of their confrontations with working people were traumatic and intense. Close personal observation of the habits of the labouring poor simultaneously confirmed the absolute separation of the reformers' culture from the habits and morals of those under their scrutiny. Kay's use of specific forms of knowledge was a means of coming to terms with these perceived realities – quite literally putting them into discourse to gain some control over them:

There is however a licentiousness capable of corrupting the whole body of society, like an insidious disease, which eludes observation, yet is equally fatal in its effects. Criminal Acts may be statistically classed . . . but the number of those affected with the moral leprosy of vice cannot be exhibited with mathematical precision. Sensuality has no record.[27]

These passages articulate many of the major themes which will concern us in a detailed unpacking of early nineteenth-century social and moral reform. For the moment it is enough to note the particular combination of elements and the heightened, dramatic language. Gothic images of horror, Old Testament style narratives of pestilence and pollution, dramatized through personal encounters and heavily resonating metaphors – all this was commonplace. The language of moral frisson, combined with the methodology of scientific inquiry, constructed sexuality at the heart of its concerns.

3 EIGHTEENTH-CENTURY SOCIAL MEDICINE AND PHILANTHROPY

This medico-moral discourse was not wholly new. Many of the issues foregrounded in Kay's scrutiny of the labouring classes had their antecedents in earlier theories of social medicine. The 1830s and 1840s marked the crystallization of debates dating back at least half a century over medical and philanthropic perceptions of the poor. In the eighteenth century a system of hygienics, directed at the improvement of specific institutional populations (prisoners, workhouse inmates and hospital patients) was as much a moral as a medical crusade. As early as the 1750s two London physicians, John Pringle and Stephen Hales, had drawn attention to medical and sanitary hygiene as a means of reducing the rising prison mortality rates. Similar medical programmes were drawn up for deployment within other closed populations such as the workhouse and the navy.[28]

I Moral environmentalism 1830–60

The sustained crisis over the dual problems of criminality and punishment in the 1770s and 1780s produced not just the stark exercise of legal power but condensed new technologies of social disciplining. The planned system of incarceration implemented under the new penal regime was simultaneously medical, hygienic and moral. It involved the surveillance and regulation of minds as well as bodies.[29] John Howard, the nonconformist squire turned prison reformer, laid down rules of prison discipline which combined 'compassion' with a rigid system of regulation. Howard was part of an intellectual and scientific circle of dissenting clerics and medics who sought a hygienist solution to the linked problems of the diseased state of the prisons, the rising tide of crime and wider threats of social and political upheaval. The polluted state of the prison and hospital populations – and by extension the poor in general – were defined in a direct relation to their mental and moral condition. The absence of any desire for self-improvement was ascribed to the fact that prisoners were 'inured to misery, by the depravity of their minds; and vice rooted in their hearts'. Filth and disease were as natural to them 'as cleanliness and health are to the virtuous and the industrious'.[30] Corrupt institutions were identified as the breeding ground for physical and moral depravity, precisely because closed communities encouraged contamination of 'the healthy, strong, vigorous and decently habited' by 'the infirm, weak, feeble, filthy and naked'.[31] Daniel Layard, one of Howard's philanthropic circle, was alarmed that the clean and decent were preyed on by the immoral and the depraved, producing a situation 'which daily grows more pestilential as the healthy grow more corrupt'.[32]

This early equation between physical deterioration and a depressed moral condition was not just based on the empirical inquiries of doctors and physicians. It also had its intellectual foundations in the Hartleian and Lockean forms of materialism prevailing among reforming and philanthropic groups of the period. Mind and body – the domain of mental and moral behaviour and physical functioning – were equally material according to the philosopher David Hartley. Disease produced its own moral or immoral sequence.[33] At the same time immorality was identified as an important factor in the breakdown of the body's resistance and in the subsequent production of contagion.

Hence, in the practical implementation of prison and hospital reform there was a consistent attempt to link forms of physical and mental regulation. The penal regime introduced at Gloucester Penitentiary after 1784 subjected incoming prisoners to a hygienic ritual of bathing, shaving, medical inspection and the donning of prison uniform. It combined explicit humiliation with rituals of symbolic purification, designed to initiate the inmates into a new moral order. But all this was not a simple case of 'the language of social and moral condemnation veiled as the language of medicine', as one historian has suggested. It was not medicine developing the scientific legitimacy for a general social and political offensive against the poor, the impetus for which came from 'class fear.'[34] These early medical concepts had an internal dynamic and history which was *not reducible* to economic and political class relations. Social medicine did not merely reflect pre-given class interests. Rather, through its theories of health and disease and systems of prevention, this discourse staked out the claims of a new domain of expertise. It was this specific regime of professional competence which not only validated the claims of an emergent group of experts but also became critical to forms of social regulation.

Sexual immorality and sexual disease were classic targets for these early medical campaigns. Lettsom's collaboration with James Neild, the prison reformer, led to a national survey of English prisons published in the *Gentleman's Magazine* between 1803 and 1813. In these articles the authors frequently singled out sexual immorality as a major problem for prison discipline. Promiscuous mingling of prisoners – men and women, young and old, debtors and felons – was the main anxiety. The answer lay in a system of hospital police and in the enforcement of broad principles of urban hygiene.[35] For Thomas Percival, a medic prominent in these debates, the cleansing virtues of the hospital restored to virtue and religion those votaries whom pleasure had seduced or villainy betrayed. The lock hospital in particular, designed for the treatment of venereal disease, promoted 'benevolent principles consonant to sound policy, and favourable to reformation or to virtue'.[36] Percival's medical code laid down a strict set of rules to be followed by the hospital physician, who was to eliminate filth, encourage personal neatness and monitor standards of sexual decency. Recovery from disease was also seen to exercise a beneficial moral influence, because convalescence prompted patients to review past offences which were the consequence of vice.

In practice of course these crusades remained relatively localized; dependent on the efforts of particular institutions and professional coteries, especially in the metropolis. Nevertheless, they do point to the early formation of a discourse of social medicine with sexual immorality as one of its component concerns. The expansion of medico-moral politics at the time of the first cholera epidemic formed part of a more extensive network of social policing. Here the strategic aim was much broader, namely the regulation of urban working-class culture in the first stages of industrial capitalism.

4   EXPERTS AND THEIR CONCEPTS

The 1830s and 1840s need to be considered as a key moment in the formation of official concerns over morality. In comparison with the late eighteenth century the perception of problems as well as their solutions had radically changed. The official campaign against cholera, though ad hoc and piecemeal, pointed to the way moral strategies were now promoted by the state in response to the social and cultural dislocations of early industrial society. Qualitatively as well as quantitatively, there were quite fundamental transformations in those government structures broadly concerned with the rubric of 'reform'. These involved the expansion of existing departments and the creation of new apparatuses, together with the crystallization of the procedures of social inquiry. Central here was the empirically based royal commission, with its blue-book evidence heralding intervention and orchestrating a wide range of professional knowledges. Many of the investigations had their discursive roots in eighteenth-century medicine, evangelical religion and philanthropy. But such inquiries were articulated on a transformed social field. The rapid development of a distinct urban working-class politics and culture, along with the shifting balance of forces within the state after 1832, set the broad conditions for almost all the social reforms of the period. Rather than fixing on the localized scrutiny of the poor or particular closed populations, they now targeted the habits and morals of the labouring classes.

Blue-book investigations into health and sanitation, reports from the new poor law commissioners and factory inspectors and the abstracts of the Registrar-General, all precipitated a medico-moral debate about the relation between the individual and the environment and between physical and mental processes. Edwin Chadwick, doyen of the sanitary movement, in his circular letter to assistant commissioners in the Poor Law Commission's inquiry into sanitary conditions, 1842, authoritatively spelt out its environmentalist terms of reference: 'The Commissioners wish to observe that the state of the dwellings occupied by the labouring classes exercise an important influence upon their health.'[37] But the state of the urban or industrial environment was always understood to produce moral as well as physical results. Local officials of the Children's Employment Commission, 1842, were ordered to examine the effects of industrial employment on both moral and bodily health.[38]

'Morals' here condensed a plethora of meanings all jostling for attention. The term served as a synonym for culture, or cultural lack, and to impute blame. Under its rubric were subsumed the terrifying catalogue of barbarous habits which Kay had measured: the collapse of family life, drunkenness, prostitution and political sedition. It was through this nexus of concerns that a specific domain of sexuality was produced. The domain constructed a distinctive repertoire of representations of the sexual around the linked themes of ill-health and immorality. It actively shaped and regulated definitions of class and gender by deployment in key institutional programmes. Mapping this field first takes us deeper into the moral discourses of environmentalism, and to the institutions, forms of knowledge and intellectual agents underpinning the particular construction of sexuality.

A major component of this domain was the social medicine typified by Kay. The medical profession was an influential pressure group campaigning for moral reform, providing the intellectual rationale for state intervention into working-class culture. This statist putsch was intimately bound up with medics' own desire for enhanced status and authority. The 1830s witnessed the beginnings of a distinctive professionaliza- tion of medicine, which was enhanced by members' large scale involvement in the new apparatuses of the state.[39] The exact position of the local doctor, in terms of class and professional status, remained economically and culturally ambiguous until well into the mid-nineteenth century. He was caught between the trade origins of the barber-surgeons and the superior ranking of lawyers and barristers.[40] Many came from relatively humble origins, like Wakley, the son of a West Country farmer and William Farr, a central figure at the General Register Office, who was from a family of agricultural labourers.[41]

The period witnessed early attempts by the profession to carve out a distinctive space of expert knowledge within the emergent culture of the bourgeoisie. The appearance of local medical associations from the 1830s, like Charles Hastings Provincial Medical and Surgical Association (forerunner of the BMA), reflected growing self-recognition of the importance of professional structures, as did campaigns for the reform of qualifications taken up in Parliament by Wakley.[42] Prominent medics also played a central role in radical bourgeois politics. Thomas Southwood Smith was friend and physician to the founding father of utilitarianism, Jeremy Bentham. Both Smith and Kay forced a passage into formal politics through their contacts with leading Whig and Tory philanthropists in Parliament. But it was in the state institutionalized programme of reform of the labouring classes that medics first secured large-scale professional representation. Here they worked to advance their staus – as commissioners in the new poor law administration, as local medical officers and as part of the Home Office team of factory inspectors.

Yet medics secured their ascendancy not just through institu- tional politicking. They also claimed intellectual monopoly over key explanations of human affairs and social progress, notably over the rapid cultural transformations taking place within urban society. As a result, medical research rubbed shoulders with moral philosophy and political economy.

Nowhere was this clearer than in the early debates over the causes of contagious disease.

The heated arguments over the origins of infection prompted by the first cholera epidemic continued unabated until the 1870s. As late as 1853 *The Lancet* comically listed the range of competing explanations: 'Is it a fungus, an insect, a miasma, an electrical disturbance, a deficiency of ozone, a morbid off-scouring from the intestinal canal? We know nothing; we are at sea in a whirlpool of conjecture.'[43] Three rival theories promoted by medical research were seriously considered by early social reformers. Both the germ theory of infection by a living organism (which stressed that disease was relatively independent of the immediate social environment) and the explanation which maintained that cholera was produced by spontaneous chemical combustion within the blood, were generally dismissed as lacking substantial proof.[44] It was the 'atmospheric' or 'miasmatic' approach which was favoured. Members of the profession like Kay and Southwood Smith, along with prominent sanitarians such as Chadwick and Florence Nightingale, established miasma as the orthodoxy within the public health movement. This theory held that under certain unpredictable circumstances the atmosphere became charged with an epidemic influence, which turned malignant when combined with the effluvia of organic decomposition from the earth. The resulting miasma produced disease within the body.

The 'choice' of miasma theory was influenced both by the internal logic of medical discourse and by wider cultural and political considerations. Miasma fitted well with the scientific materialism of early social medicine. At the level of public debate it was graspable – effluvia could be pointed to and graphically illustrated. But like the concepts of the eighteenth-century hygienists, miasma also targeted the *human agents* of infection – now defined as the labouring classes. The theory was elastic and capable of infinite variation; its environmentalist logic ranged from insanitary conditions to immoral practices.

Southwood Smith's early *Treatise on Fever*, 1830 was typical. He argued for further research into the diffusion and propagation of infection, together with a survey of the material conditions and habits of life of the poor:

> The room of a fever patient, in a small and heated
> appartment of London, with no perflation of fresh air, is
> perfectly analogous to a stagnant pool in Ethiopia full of the
> bodies of dead locusts. The poison generated in both cases
> is the same; the difference is merely in the degree of its
> potency. Nature, with her burning sun, her stilled and
> pent-up wind, her stagnant and teeming marsh,
> manufactures plague on a large and fearful scale. Poverty in
> her hut, covered with her rags, surrounded by her filth,
> striving with all her might to keep out the pure air and to
> increase the heat, imitates Nature but too successfully; the
> process and the product are the same . . . penury and
> ignorance can thus, at any time in any place, create a mortal
> plague.[45]

The language here constructed the familiar equation between
poverty and disease. But the quasi-Gothic images of squalor,
personified in the 'small and heated appartment' of the fever
patient, introduced a comparison with primitive society which
would have been familiar to Southwood Smith's scientific
audience. 'Ethiopia', like the culture of the urban poor and
especially the Irish, signified precisely the animalism and lack
of civilization which was in danger of pulling the whole of
civilized society back into the abyss. This pre-Darwinist understanding of the nature of progress and decline worked with a
comparative historical sociology, which consistently juxtaposed representations of the primitive and ancient world with
the problems of contemporary society. Like ancient Greece and
Rome, modern commercial enterprise was under attack from
barbarous forces.

As in Kay's *Manchester* pamphlet, the range of cultural
meanings condensed in Smith's account point to the expansive
logic of early social medicine. Immoral conduct was the direct
result of the filth, squalor and disease of the urban working-
class environment. But immorality – conceived as a general lack
of self-reliance and improper habits – was also cited as one
of the principal *causes* of disease. It was no accident that
Chadwick placed his weight firmly behind miasma theory,
despite his contemptuous dismissal of the whole medical con-
troversy over the origins of infection. Although implacably

opposed to medics gaining control of the public health movement, he was not adverse to drawing on this type of grandiose scientific pronouncement to bolster arguments for his practical programme of reform, precisely because it had an immediate social field of reference. Miasma served the early sanitarians well.

5   SCIENCE AND RELIGION

For Kay, as for many medics, the cholera epidemic demonstrated scientifcally that a 'mighty source of moral causation' was at work in society. Epidemic disease was a providential intervention, and the transgression of God's law through immoral acts brought forth dire consequences.[46] We have seen how Kay mobilized Old Testament language to argue that cholera was a messenger of death, which had been sent to punish the corruption of the people and a flawed system of government. At the time of the second outbreak in 1848, the surgeon John Liddle claimed that doctors were as much Christian philanthropists as scientists, and had a duty to interpret God's message to his children.[47]

Recurrent images of retribution drew heavily on religious language which informed medical pronouncements on disease. The clergy were the other key intellectual grouping in the public health alliance, particularly at a local level as poor law officers and members of the new health boards. Many of these men were Anglicans, sharing a traditional paternalist concern about the industrial town. But it was evangelicals in the established church, together with Congregationalists, Methodists and Baptists, who provided the strongest input into the sanitary movement. For these religious fundamentalists cholera was a divine plan of providential intervention, designed to punish the nation for wickedness and wrong-doing. At the time of the 1832 epidemic *The Evangelical Magazine and Missionary Chronicle* pointed to the multiple evils besetting the country. Trade slump and the reform bill crisis, secularism among the middle-classes and infidelism among the poor, all fuelled the conviction that general moral decline precipitated divine vengeance:

violence hath been rampant in our cities – wasting and destruction have entered into all our borders – the church languishes – its vintage faileth – fanaticism and speculation like a wrathful bolt from the skies, have scattered some of the Cedars of Lebanon.[48]

In the industrial parishes of the midlands and the north, cholera was a favourite subject for Sunday sermons, when local vicars used lurid metaphors of disease to demonstrate that sickness was God's chastisement for sin. In the mining district of Sedgley in south Staffordshire, Charles Girdlestone, a low church Anglican vicar, preached his *Seven Sermons* on the fixed equation between physical and moral laws:

Whatsoever evil we see around us, whatsoever evil we feel within us, is, we know, the consequence of sin. By sin came death. And by sin came that which brought the evil on us. It is Satan that first tempted us to sin, and now works on us this miserable consequence.[49]

Girdlestone noted with satisfaction the general improvement in moral habits among his parishioners under threat of God's wrath. More shops were closing on Sunday, there was a decline in bull-baiting and other barbarous pastimes, while marriages were on the increase along with a general improvement in morals. He was emphatic that ministers of religion – 'they who are most conversant with man and his interests in a spiritual aspect' – needed to take their place beside medics in the battle for moral reform.[50] Within the public health movement there was little antagonism between religious principles of morality and scientific observation. The evangelical commitment of many medics may itself have been linked to their attempts to define a new professional ethic which was at once distinctive and serious.[51] William Cooke, a fellow of the Royal College of Surgeons, noted in 1839 that in earlier periods science and religion had 'seemed mutually to dread approximation', but in recent years 'reciprocal confidence has been growing, and so far from being now ashamed of each other's company we often see them in the most loving harmony'.[52]

This interleaving of medicine and religion was underpinned

by the fundamentally deistic conception of early nineteenth-century science. Scientists had a duty to validate the religious and moral order of the universe. God had granted men the power of rational inquiry to explain the harmonious organization of the world. Archdeacon William Paley's *Natural Theology*, 1802 – subtitled 'evidence of the existence and attributes of the deity collected from the appearances of nature' – was still required reading for all students at Oxford and Cambridge in the 1830s. Paley's popular reading of Newtonian science maintained that scientists who studied the natural world were participating in God's creation, because their inquiries always verified the existence of the Designer, thereby combating atheism.[53] Trees, flowers, plants, animal life *and* the providential organization of human society all displayed the hand of the great architect of nature.

This was the dominant Anglican conception of scientific inquiry. It partly explains why the ranks of the clergy mustered such a strong contingent of amateur scientists. Local vicars embarked on a wide range of studies and were especially involved in promoting the nascent sciences of geology, botany and biology.[54] Within their conservative framework, scientific arguments could be used to bolster traditional moral and political sermonizing on the virtues of a fixed hierarchy of order and authority. Some dissenting ministers challenged such a comfortable integration of science and religion. At least one Congregationalist preacher used the first cholera outbreak to attack the cold and dreary materialism of medics, who, while busily promulgating scientific laws, roundly ignored the principles of God's moral government.[55] Much more characteristic, though, was the call for increased dialogue between the two arms of social reform.

6   MEDICO-MORAL POLITICS IMPLEMENTED?

Practical alliances between scientists, clerics and other political forces were forged through the various pressure groups campaigning for public health in the 1840s. Such coalitions cut right across class and party lines. The Health of Towns Association, formed in 1844, was especially representative of the diverse class and intellectual coteries pushing for moral reform. It was led by the Marquis of Normanby, Whig Home Secretary, while its committee members included Lord Ashley and R.A. Slaney (both reforming Tories), and the evangelical Girdlestone, as well as the medics John Simon and Southwood Smith. The aims and objects of the association made the characteristic move from environmental reform – sewage, drainage, water-supply, air and light, building construction – to the inevitable moral reforms confidently predicted to follow in its wake. Decent material conditions would:

> yield increased facilities to the practice of Devotion . . . and to attendance on public worship, and . . . in promoting health of the body and cleanliness of person . . . will thus at the same time clear the way for the Purifying and Healing of the Soul.[56]

The creation of the General Board of Health under the Public Health Act, 1848, marked a high-water mark for medico-moral politics. It seemed as if the plans for state-backed hygienics had at last come to fruition. Yet the limited powers of the new board showed just how far removed early public health administration was from the grandiose ambitions of sanitarians like Chadwick. He had campaigned for a nationwide system of sewers, drains and public burial grounds. The new legislation largely left control of public health in the hands of local authorities. It was founded on the voluntary principle, whereby towns were empowered rather than forced to establish public health administration. But the act did set up a central commission appointed for five years and composed initially of three active members: Lord Ashley, Chadwick and the First Commissioner of Woods and Forests as President.

Almost immediately there were familiar cries of outrage from medics over what they saw as their wilful exclusion from the new board. It was deeply insulting, they complained, to comprise a 'medical board of two noblemen who are perfectly innocent of medical information and a lawyer'.[57] Even at this stage, medical representation within the state was not a foregone conclusion – though Southwood Smith was hastily appointed to stave-off further criticism. Organized opposition was also being mounted from other quarters. Anti-statist groupings, bitterly opposed to what they perceived to be 'prussianism' by big landlords, private drainage and water companies all blocked any move into full-blooded sanitary statism and effectively preserved the balance between voluntary effort and central control.[58]

It was Lord Ashley's membership of the new board which consolidated the medico-moral alliance. As a committed evangelical and social reformer he had long attached 'immense and unparalleled importance to the sanitary question, as second only to the religious and in some aspects inseparable from it'.[59] Chadwick himself was quick to see the benefits of securing Ashley's co-operation, bringing with him the religious and moral wing of the public health movement.[60] Ashley's reaction to his appointment was characteristic, trembling at first with the weight of responsibility but then pledging a firm commitment to God's mission in the world. His work for the board between 1848 and 1851 promoted the continuing alliance between science and religion. He fervently believed that rational sanitary measures were the practical enactment of God's law on earth. It was the evangelical message that was paramount in Ashley's sanitary politics; even in the midst of disease and suffering God's work was manifest. The cholera epidemic of 1848 had brought good out of evil, because religion had made 'visible progress among the poorer sort and many of the wealthy are turning their minds to the improvement of society'.[61] Ashley's main worry as the cholera abated was that the spirit of physical and moral regeneration would also diminish. Fearful, he wrote to Chadwick in October 1849: 'The cholera thank God has passed – is not the wholesome fear passing also?'[62]

The strong religious and ethical presence in all the reform movements checked any purely mechanistic theorization of the individual/society equation common among secular Benthamites. They were pushing for a fully blown materialism in tackling the social domain. But in all campaigning groups there was a continual dialectic over the precise importance awarded to moral responsibility as against environmental influences. The tension between the two elements resulted in neither a victory for pure environmentalism nor for moral individualism. What occurred was the relative privileging of one element or another in different fields of intervention, according to different political priorities and different visions of social order. While the new poor law placed emphasis firmly on individual self-improvement, public health tended to stress that material advancement would produce beneficial changes in modes of living and beliefs.[63]

It was this tension which fed into the differing conceptions of the moral duties of the new secular state held by the reformers. All groups were agreed that state intervention into public health was necessary to promote personal morality. But though 'morality' was the ether which all of them breathed it was composed of different elements for different constituencies; utilitarian discipline as opposed to liberal philanthropy, benevolent paternalism as compared with hard-edged professional expertise.

As an improving Tory aristocrat, Lord Ashley fervently hoped that a properly administered state could embody the values of benevolent paternalism and play the role of a faithful and pious parent. Medics and clerics on the other hand favoured a conception of the ethical state. For Kay, morally humane state intervention was necessary to counteract the inadequacies of pure Benthamism and the laissez-faire fallacy. Political economy was not designed to deal with the problems facing the social body which could not be constructed on abstract principles like a machine, ignoring the promotion of happiness and the cultivation of religion and morality.[64] Kay's offensive here was aimed at the 'immorality' of sections of the big bourgeoisie, who blocked all attempts at intervention into the social as well as the economic sphere.

As a purer Benthamite, Chadwick's understanding of the role of government was much more utilitarian and secular. The state promoted the health and happiness of individuals, while at the same time delivering important moral and economic benefits to capital. Sickness was a costly thing, especially to the nation state, and hence public health administration needed to form a central plank of the art of government. Health reform would secure real commercial and industrial rewards. A clean, healthy and morally ordered workforce increased the efficiency

of labour-power, reduced manufacturers' costs and so promoted a general increase in comfort and wealth for all classes of
society.[65]

Despite their internal differences, at no time did the reformers mount a direct attack on the manufacturing system itself
as the *source* of physical and moral deterioration. Such a logic
was outside their framework and points to the limits of their
analysis. Explanations of the underlying causes of depravity
frequently worked with an evils extrinsic argument. The
national social body, conceived as fundamentally healthy and
morally virtuous, had been subjected to invasions from without, or to divine vengeance which followed in the wake of
wickedness. Demoralization from the Irish, or disease as God's
punishment were characteristic forms of explanation. Kay's
pronouncements were typical: 'the evils . . . so far from being
the necessary consequences of the manufacturing system, have
a remote and accidental origin, and might by judicious management, be entirely removed.'[66] There was also a characteristic
distinction between *types* of evil; those that were avoidable and
those seen as inevitable. Economic crises were often depicted
using imagery drawn from the natural world. The periodic
fluctuations of the business cycle were attributed to physical
causes. The social order itself, and the fundamental inequalities
betwen capital and labour were understood as fixed and immut-
able.

Preventive medicine, philanthropy and religion advanced a
scientific and moral critique of the effects of nascent industrial
capitalism. But these professional and religious principles did
not undermine the basic political and economic assumptions on
which capitalist social relations were based. Ultimately, the
majority of reformers identified the commercial system as a
force whose movement was inexorable. Though tensions between the experts and other political forces were often acute,
the product of real fractures and oppositions within the ruling
bloc, they were resolved by this over-arching logic.

7   DE-CODING MORALITY: THE DOMAIN OF THE SEXUAL

We have established that moral reform was a key component in the overall programme aimed at the disciplining of the early industrial working-class. But the loose and expansive use of the term 'moral' often makes it difficult to deconstruct its fields of reference. This is not merely a problem of historical interpretation, it points to the fact that the concept was subject to a wide number of connotative meanings, which were continually being condensed and which are incapable of precise differentiation. Morality at once referenced a series of codes and practices regulating individual conduct, and a range of protocols and procedures about the art of government. Immorality signified all the practices of working-class life leading to ungovernable and disruptive behaviour: lack of individual self-reliance, ignorance, criminality, the threat of political sedition and of course sexual impropriety. The multiple points of reference condensed here point to the grandiose and all-embracing approach to reform, involving as it did a general onslaught on the culture of the poor. In a period in which economic crises and working-class political agitation were an ever-present threat, the majority of social problems were seen to be inter-related, though later they were to become differentiated as distinct pathologies. It was these broad conjunctural factors which set the conditions for the strong professional and intellectual alliances at work within environmentalism.

In what ways did the reformers stake out a particular construction of the sexual as part of their programme. First, the image of sexuality was almost invariably negative – sexuality was always referenced as *sexual immorality*, an integral part of all the other immoral and ungovernable habits of working-class life. As always, Ashley was explicit about the evil. In a parliamentary speech in 1843 he put before the house a picture of 'an accumulated mass of squalid wretchedness'. Leeds, for example, boasted of a:

beer-shop where there are rooms upstairs, and the boys and girls, old people, and married of both sexes, go up two by two, as they can agree, to have connection . . . the most revolting feature of juvenile depravity is the early contamination from the association of the sexes. The outskirts of the town are absolutely polluted by this abomination.[67]

'Abomination', 'depravity', 'pollution' – there were no positive representations of sexuality in this discourse. Debauchery and licentiousness stood at the opposite pole to those forms of social and civilized behaviour – cleanliness, sobriety, industriousness, the structures of home and family – which made up the vision of a disciplined working-class. Further, given the constant interplay of moral and material factors within early social reform, sexual debauchery was understood both as a product of material squalor and a causal factor in the decline of the urban environment.

These themes were to the fore in all the official inquiries, but they were particularly dominant in the blue books on sanitary reform. The wretchedness of the working-class environment, the state of the dwellings, non-existent sanitation, lack of concern over personal decency and hygiene were seen to encourage irregular sexual conduct. There were constant references to the effects of overcrowding and bad housing on sexual behaviour throughout the official investigations. In the sanitary report it was a sense of horror and ritual denunciation which predominated:

How they lay down to rest, how they sleep, how they can preserve common decency, how unutterable horrors are avoided, is beyond all conception. . . . It shocks every feeling of propriety to think that . . . civilized beings should be herding together without a decent separation of age or sex.[68]

Then the narrative moved to a more precise classification of specific immoral acts:

In a cellar in Pendleton I recollect there were three beds in

the two apartments . . . in one of which a man and his wife
slept; in another, a man, his wife and child; and in the third
two unmarried females. . . . I have met with upwards of
forty persons sleeping in the same room, married and
single, including, of course, children and several young
adult persons of either sex. In Manchester . . . I found such
promiscuous mixture of the sexes in sleeping-rooms . . . I
have met with instances of a man, his wife, and his wife's
sister, sleeping in the same bed together. . . . In Hull . . . I
found in one room a prostitute, with whom I remonstrated
on the course of her life . . . she stated that she had lodged
with a married sister, and slept in the same bed with her and
her husband; that hence improper intercourse took place,
and from that she became more and more depraved.[69]

Incest was the most common source of moral anxiety, precisely because it dramatically disrupted middle-class norms of
family propriety.[70] But these representations contained rather
more than the perception that sexual immorality resulted from
an impoverished and over-crowded environment. Sexual immorality was defined through the significations of dirt, disease,
squalor, corruption and the political and cultural threat of an
urban working-class populace. When Chadwick pointed out
that the habits of labouring families soon became 'of a piece'
with the dwellings, he evoked precisely that type of
condensation.[71] Filthy habits of life were never separated from
the moral filthiness for which they were the type and the
representative. Local medical officers and poor law officials
compared the factory operatives, sunk 'into sensual sloth' or
revelling in even 'more degrading licentiousness', against their
idealized vision of the rural poor. Dr Alison of Tranent was
reassured by his visits to the cottages of Scottish agricultural
labourers:

With very few exceptions, the condition of the interior of
the houses of the hind population is excellent, most pleasing
to the eye and comfortable. These respectable people, in
spite of the defective construction of their cottages, manage
to throw an air of comfort, plenty and neatness and order
around their homes. I have often been delighted to observe

these characteristics, and not less so to mark the co-existence of pure, moral, and religious principles in the inmates, the presence of practical religion and practical morals.[72]

Such descriptions of the more 'natural', and the more moral, relations of rural society were always intended to evoke their opposite. Urbanization had produced a cultural miasma; for public health reformers dirt stood as the grand metaphor for all forms of urban disorder. It was this powerful cloacal imagery of pollution, excretion and disease which lay at the heart of the depictions of sexual immorality. It was reinforced by evangelical religion, which possessed an elaborate language for discoursing on bodily pleasures and animal appetites.

In the 1830s and 1840s evangelical religious language, part visionary, part denunciatory, was mobilized by groups right across the political spectrum, from feminists within the Owenite socialist movement through to professionals and religious reformers. Many women reworked evangelical discourse to advance their political demands or to discuss their sexual and emotional experience. But conservative preachers like Girdlestone used the vivid Pauline oppositions of flesh and spirit, God and mammon, as part of their repertoire for morally disciplining the poor:

> we must not pretend, in affectation of humility, not to see, and know, and feel the difference between serving God, and serving mammon, between walking by faith in love, and living selfishly and sensually, between being brethren of Christ, and being children of Belial.[73]

His rhetoric of moral denunciation was not silent on the issue of immorality; he painted a lurid and explicit picture of lewdness and sensual pleasure, framed by the terrors of the final judgment. Girdlestone appealed to children and parents, his sermons always mounting to a climax of emotional frisson and terror:

> The next idol against which I have to warn you is sensual pleasure. . . . Other sensual pleasures will beset your souls

hereafter, with snares most alluring, with poison the most deadly. . . . Oh, when we think how many souls are lost by forbidden indulgence.[74]

Yet though medics and clerics were vituperative in their condemnation of the sexuality of the labouring poor, their moralizing was not wholly negative and prohibitive. It held out the promise of definite satisfactions to their patients and congregations who observed the dictates of morality. For some evangelicals, satisfaction lay in the knowledge of having fought the battle between flesh and spirit and ultimately won through, but other reformers promised material rewards to those who heeded their warnings: good health, longevity and a prosperous, settled existence. These were comfortable, homely pleasures, but for a working-class dependent on the vagaries of an unstable economic system and subject to extreme social dislocations they must have offered a tempting vision of security. The Health of Towns Association promised the weary labourer returning from his work an end to the crowded, dirty, damp and cold washed-out cellar shared with other families. Cheerful society in a cheerful place was what the working man was thought to yearn after. Order, beauty, sweetness and health, with women returned to their rightful place as domestic helpmates, would flow logically from sanitary reform.[75]

In the discourse on the urban poor, reformers constructed the sexual through the class-related polarities which were central to their programme: physical health/non-health, virtue/vice, cleanliness/filth, morality/depravity, civilization/animality. The binary oppositions were organized in such a way that each polarity functioned to reinforce the other. Bourgeois cleanliness was impossible without the image of proletarian filth, middle-class propriety could not be defined without the corresponding representations of working-class animality, and so on. All this was not wholly new; as we know it had continuities with eighteenth-century social medicine and with earlier religious constructions of sexuality across the spirit/flesh divide. What was new was that these definitions were now incorporated into a variety of official knowledge as part of a broad programme of state intervention into the culture of the industrial labouring classes. This discourse on sexuality now had distinctive *class articulations*. Hence, though these representations did not originate in the economic, political and cultural transformations of early industrial capitalism, in this period they increasingly became annexed to class-cultural relations.

It is also important to be clear in what sense this configuration around sexuality was a *discursive construction*, a construction within and by very specific sets of power-knowledge relations, and in what sense it was a product of concrete environmental conditions. To speak of its discursive formation is not to deny that this construction of the sexual was grounded in particular historical conditions and social relations. But discourses did not simply reflect these. We are not dealing with practices either rendering a 'true picture of reality' (i.e. sexuality constructed as filthy and diseased because filth and disease were the realities of the working-class environment) or as neatly representing pre-given forms of class power and knowledge whose origins lie elsewhere. We are dealing with specific social practices – religion, medicine and sanitary science – whose organization was an active force in the production of the sexual meanings in play. They neither transparently reflected reality nor did they passively represent class relations. They were active in the construction of both.

8   HYGIENICS AND BOURGEOIS HEGEMONY

If the labouring classes were portrayed as possessing an immoral sexuality, then the cultural identity of the bourgeoisie was formed around its opposite; in relation to the linked themes of health, hygiene, procreation and inheritance. It is tempting to follow Foucault and designate this nexus of concerns 'bourgeois sexuality', but within official discourse the sexual was so strongly identified with the urban working-class that it is more accurate to describe it as a code of personal hygiene, moral restraints and procreative ethics.[76] The medical profession acted as powerful ideologues for the professional gentry and sections of the industrial bourgeoisie, laying claim to a middle-class monopoly over the issues of health and hygiene. They endowed these groups with a distinctive cultural repertoire, separate both from the perceived debauchery of the aristocracy and the disease-ridden working-class. For Kay, health was the 'precious jewel of life,' to be guarded against the proverbial 'thief walking in darkness' who might 'rifle the casket' while one slept.[77] The thief was cholera and the working-class threat personified, but it was also an image of self-destruction brought about by sensual indulgence and voluptuousness.

Specific warnings on the dangers of sexual excess figured prominently in numerous tracts and pamphlets on personal and domestic health which appeared from the 1830s. Almost invariably these injunctions were addressed to men. According to one popular writer offering *Twenty Minutes Advice on Diet, Regimen and all other matters connected with health*, those who followed the downward path of the voluptuary were always 'cut off in their prime.'[78] *The Lancet* spelt out the dangers forcibly; the 'sexual sensualist' pursued a course which led inevitably to moral degradation, mental and bodily infirmity and even madness.[79] One medic claimed he had isolated a specific form of consumption – *Tabes Dorsalis* or *Spermatic Plethora* – which occurred in 'young men of salacious dispositions' who had indulged in an immoderate use of the sexual function.[80] The physical excitation accompanying 'venereal enjoyments' acted like a convulsion, destroying the nerve tissue, sapping the body fibres and thinning the blood. Moderate exercise of the male sexual appetite was the best possible safeguard against ill-health. Behind these arguments lay the teachings of contemporary physiology, which insisted on the ill-effects of all forms of bodily excess. But in the hands of some medics the notion of moderate sexual indulgence was used to justify occasional but necessary lapses by the bachelor or frustrated husband. Total abstinence was as detrimental to health as over-indulgence.[81]

Moderation was the keynote in the professional advice offered to the bourgeoisie on all aspects of their personal habits and behaviour. Physicians prescribed a careful physical and moral regimen for patients, encompassing sleep, ventilation of rooms, diet and control of the sexual appetitite:

The good secret of health is simply this – Regulate your bowels by taking mild aperients when necessary: Be

careful not to eat what disagrees with you: Be regular and
temperate in your habits: Refrain from the use of Spirituous
Liquors: Retire to rest early, and rise betimes in the
morning.[82]

Such a self-conscious code of rituals and restraints was designed
to display a set of inner moral qualities, as part of a wider
middle-class bid for cultural hegemony over key areas of personal and domestic life. According to William Cooke, only
among the middle-classes were regular and temperate habits
strictly observed; it was 'one of the great causes why the middle
classes of society have more of real soundness of mind, as well as
body, than either the highest or the lowest'.[83]

Regular habits were a real asset in the successful pursuit of a
business or professional career. But for middle-class wives and
daughters a regime of sobriety and healthy living was essential if
they were to reproduce sound offspring and thereby transmit
personal reputation, property, legitimacy and life to the next
generation. A spate of medical tracts on marriage and childbirth
laid down strict guidelines for 'maternal hygiology' and the
management of women during pregnancy, parturition and
lactation. The medic Michael Ryan gave detailed instructions
on the organization of the labour chamber: the need for absolute cleanliness, the role of the obstetrician and the duties of the
midwife, while Cooke, the surgeon-accoucheur, was concerned
with the 'moral management of childbirth', especially the correct medical etiquette to be observed by the doctor in treating
his female patient.[84]

This scheme of moral hygienics was carried into official
discourse through the programme of population assessment,
developed by the early statistical societies and the newly created
General Register Office. 'Moral statistics', or as they were often
termed, 'vital' or 'life statistics', comprising 'population distribution, consumption, divisions of life, health and public or
private charity', formed an important sub-domain of the Royal
London Statistical Society, founded in 1834.[85] The Manchester Society produced similar studies on *The Relative Proportion
of Male and Female Population*, 1840, on puberty and early
marriages and on the physiology of particular racial groups.[86]
With the setting up of the General Register Office under the

provisions of the Births, Marriages and Deaths Registration Act, 1836, there was a specific government agency to address the population issue.[87] With the appointment of William Farr as head of the office's statistical branch, the department had acquired one of the chief protagonists of population politics.

Farr had been pressing throughout the 1830s for more detailed knowledge on the health and moral habits of individuals and groups within the population. His French-influenced system of hygiology, outlined in a series of articles in *The Lancet*, argued that the health of individuals (promoted by the medical practitioner) and the vitality of the general population (the domain of public health administration) were inter-linked. Both were concerned with increasing the strength and stamina of the nation state, by raising the health of the population to the greatest degree:

> The true object of hygiene . . . is to increase the *sum of vitality* by extending individual life to its full term (averting death); by obviating sickness; and by increasing the energy of all the vital forces, whether nutritive, formative, locomotive, or sensitive and intellectual.[88]

At the Register Office Farr worked to implement his plans through a skilful mixture of bold polemic and detailed statistical evidence. Refuting the overpopulationist panic of the Rev. Thomas Malthus, by arguing for the benefits of an expanding mode of production, Farr hoped to see an increase in the marriage rate and the legitimate birth rate. These factors, he asserted, 'ensured the perpetuity of life and nations', in the midst of the antagonistic forces of disease and death.[89] It was the middle-classes above all who held the key to the future prosperity of the country. Through his appendices to the annual reports of the Registrar-General – more statements of policy than mere statistical commentaries – Farr called for greater attention to the rules of maternal hygiene and the medical supervision of childbirth. His main aim was to promote quantitative and qualitative increase among the middle ranks of society. The local medical practitioner could play a central role in disseminating the principles of procreative hygiene to women of the better classes. The well-informed sections of the community,

Farr claimed, owed their enlightenment to the teaching of their medical attendants. It was essential that doctors lost no opportunity of 'laying down the rules of health, and enforcing them, by drawing the attention of families to the sad and often striking consequences of neglect'.[90]

Farr's plans were not implemented in any large scale immediate policy initiatives. Rather, what occurred were piecemeal elements of legislation throughout the century governing solemnization of marriage and the divorce laws, which were designed to promote sound and legitimate offspring.[91] Nevertheless, his arguments were articulate statements about the links between personal moral hygiene, the health of the population and the power and puissance of the middle-class.

What is the relation between this hygienist enterprise and the domain of sexuality staked out by the sanitarians and clerics? Foucault has convincingly argued that the regime of sex instituted in this period was not characterized by negative repression. The bourgeoisie were constantly inciting and evoking the sexual through modes of control which were productive of new identities, pleasures and desires.[92] While pointing usefully to the productive nature of regulation, Foucault's account leaves a number of important questions unanswered about the class articulations in play. First, it would be more accurate to say that it was the new *professional experts*, working in conjunction with clerics, philanthropists and improving employers, who staked out the new field of sexuality – not the bourgeoisie in general. What this cadre of male intellectuals continually incited were representations of *working-class sexuality*. When it came to their own culture, their public polemic (and we shall come to their private fantasies shortly) was concerned with something quite different. Not 'sexuality' but bourgeois hygienic; the health-giving rituals of moderation and ordered living which led to population increase and promised cultural and economic ascendancy.

9   WORKING-CLASS FEMALE SEXUALITY AND PROFESSIONAL MASCULINITY

Early social reformers identified the great mass of the urban working-class as the major cultural threat. Yet they did mark out specific gender distinctions and divisions as part of their programme. For not only were the polarized representations of health and hygiene, dirt and disease bound up with class assumptions, they were also overlaid by middle-class notions of sexual difference. Working-class men had been brutalized through the state of the workplace environment and through their own inherent lack of morality as men; they were often described as semi-barbarous and closer to nature. Official representations of the morals of working women were more complex and contradictory, shifting across the health/disease, morality/ immorality oppositions according to the focus of the male investigators. The moral judgments made by the experts were heavily determined by their own class specific expectations of femininity. Working-class women were both eroticized and condemned as immoral pollutants, the cause of the decline of whole communities, *and* heralded as the agents of moral reform. In the dramatic local incidents, where experts encountered women colliers and factory operatives, we can see this double axis at work.

The factory commissioners believed that women had become depraved under the improper conditions of heavy manual labour and industrial employment in the mines and factories, where they worked in close and indecent proximity to men:

I have no doubt the debauchery is carried on, for there is every opportunity; for the girls go constantly, when hurrying, to the men. . . . I think it scarcely possible for girls to remain modest who are in pits, regularly mixing with such company, and hearing such language as they do. I dare venture to say that many of the wives who come from pits know nothing of sewing or any household duty, such as women ought to know.[93]

And the 1842 factory report concluded that:

all classes of witnesses bear testimony to the demoralizing effect of females underground . . . the girls and boys and the young men and even married women and women with child, commonly work almost naked.[94]

The subcommissioners pursued their quest for immoral behaviour with vigour. Young women operatives were summoned to testify to the extent of the problem, and their accounts give important insights into the gendered dimensions of early factory culture. 'Lads and lassies' arrived at the spinning mills and took off their overclothes. It was then that the big boys 'spied' the big lassies taking off their stockings and shouted naughty and pert obscenities.[95] It seems that sexual harassment has not changed all that much over a hundred and fifty years. Women had their clothes pulled up while asleep in the rest periods, together with other forms of ritual humiliation. The lads called it practical jokes, but one seventeen-year-old girl was adamant: 'a lass stands no chance with so many boys'.[96]

Yet it was the perception of female depravity which filled the page after page of the subcommissioners' evidence, intruding into all aspects of their inquiries. Questions about the women's physical suffering, or the specific division of factory labour (issues central to the concern with the male workforce) were subordinated to this obsession. In the male-defined culture of these blue-book reports there was space for officials to indulge, *sotto voce*, their own sexual fantasies. Their moralizing diatribes on female behaviour carried a heavily sexualized, erotic sub-text. Detailed descriptions of the girls' physical appearance – their clothing, habits and even their jewellery – tell us much about the sexual desire of these professional men.

Take the lawyer, Jelinger Symons. Symons was from the clerical gentry, a sub-commissioner in the Yorkshire coalfield and an early educational expert. Prefacing his report with the pompous statement that it was his official duty to 'direct . . . attention to the deplorable outrage of introducing females into the collieries', he went on to concentrate on the depraved, filthy and animal-like appearance of the pit girls:

> One of the most disgusting sights I have ever seen was that
> of young females, dressed like boys in trowsers, crawling on
> all fours, with belts round their waists, and chains passing
> between their legs, at day pits at Hunshelf Bank, and in
> many small pits near Holmfirth and New Mills.[97]

In his report from one New Mills mine Symons lingered over the
fact that 'the chain, passing high up between the legs of two . . .
girls, had worn large holes in their trowsers, and any sight more
disgustingly indecent or revolting can scarcely be imagined
than these girls at work.'[98] His intention may have been to
shock but it also drew attention to his own sexual preoccupa-
tions. As he put it: 'No brothel can beat it.'[99] Symons inter-
viewed nearly three hundred witnesses, many of them pit girls.
His particular fixation was that they dressed in boys' clothes
and thereby became 'unsexed'. He described one ten-year-old
as a 'nice-looking child, but of course as black as a tinker, and
with a little necklace round her throat'.[100] Similarly, Edward
Newman, a Barnsley solicitor, salaciously reported that on
more than one occasion he had seen pit girls 'washing themselves naked much below the waist as I passed their door'.[101]
    Several aspects of this construction of male sexual desire are
significant. First, it worked through the sexualization of the
physical traits of working-class women's appearance. Dirty
clothes, tawdry jewellry, nakedness, all functioned as potent
emblems, registering the cultural distance between the male
investigator and his female object. This process of objectifica-
tion involved a particular sexualized way of looking which bore
close relation to the protocols of official knowledge shaping the
public inquiries of these men – the rules of detailed observation
and classification central to the empirical method. But when
applied to working women this discourse eroticized the cultural
distance between observer and observed. For these professionals, sexual desire was produced at the interface of class and
gender oppositions set up by environmentalism. Here was male
sexuality constructed through the erotic mechanism of a
voyeuristic gaze and the fetishization of cultural difference.
    Yet men like Symons also regarded these women as central to

the reform of working-class habits. Their innate but dormant moral qualities needed to be cultivated by sanitary science and religion. This could only be achieved by returning them to their proper sphere of influence – the family. Pit women were judged to be moral if they possessed key domestic virtues such as bakery and cookery, needlework and a knowledge of family economy. Instructions sent out from the Central Board of the Children's Employment Commission to the regions noted under the category 'moral condition':

> In regard to female workers, you will inquire how far their employment during Childhood has prevented them from forming the domestic habits usually acquired by women in their station, and has rendered them less fit than those whose early years have not been spent in labour for performing the duties of wives and mothers.[102]

Sub-commissioners made frequent comparisons between the manufacturing districts and the mining communities of the north-east. The improved moral condition of the colliers of Northumberland and Durham was due to the more feminine, i.e. more domestic, habits of the women:

> In their habits they partake of much of those which prevail in the house; cleanliness and sobriety are much more common traits than the reverse. The young are more feminine than females in a manufacturing community.[103]

Similarly, evangelicals painted their picture of hell with images of domestic chaos, filth and by implication female immorality. Christian virtuousness on the other hand was evoked through feminine metaphors of sweeping, cleansing and garnishing. Girdlestone's sermonizing employed this language to appeal directly to women in his congregations: 'When the soul of a sinner has been arrested . . . how truly it is described as being swept and garnished. For how like unto filth in habitation is profligacy in a Christian.'[104]

What were the connections between the experts' double-edged perceptions of working-class women and their own personal and professional culture? Of course intellectuals and administrators were not the source or origin of this sexual iconography in a psychological sense. Their language was always socially produced. But the experts' lived experience of their constructed personal lives did have effects on their public personas and official actions.

The biographies of men like Symons, Kay and Chadwick point to the beginnings of the male career, organized around an increasingly rigid division between the public world of professional life and the private sphere of women, home and domesticity. The formation of professions like medicine and public administration in this period produced a stricter differentiation of gender roles, which was part of the general separation of spheres and duties for men and women within the bourgeoisie. Professional masculinity was a mixture of scientific, hard-edged expertise, unflinching in its attack on all forms of amateurish incompetence, and an ideology of dedication to public service. This male identity was forged through the new intellectual knowledges which endowed the experts with a caste-like mode of cohesion. A number became related through inter-marriage, creating an informal cultural network where ideas could be turned over and disagreements aired. Chadwick married Rachel Kennedy, daughter of John Kennedy, vice-president of the Manchester Statistical Society, while another daughter was married to Samuel Robinson, the brother-in-law of the educationist and industrialist Benjamin Heywood.

It was of course a male-defined culture, working systematically to marginalize women. Women figured in this world as objects of grace and adornment and as efficient household managers. They were also expected to oil the wheels of their husbands' careers through the extension of kinship and by organizing the social round of entertainment. Rachel Chadwick described her husband's soirées as 'sanitary parties', and it is clear that Chadwick himself viewed his private life as secondary and inferior. On marriage at the age of thirty nine he was amazed and irritated to discover that domestic affairs involved administrative politics quite as complex as public health law. Writing to a friend in 1839, he complained that this 'new experience in household matters' had brought much annoyance from workmen and domestics. His reponse was characteristic: 'I intend to make these experiences of . . . indolence and inattention . . . the subject of some remarks on popular education.'[105] When his wife was recovering from childbirth, Chadwick apologized for his non-appearance at public meetings with the comment: 'Mrs Chadwick has had a child and I have had a fever and I have recovered first.'[106]

Not all the private lives of these professional men conformed to the Chadwickian pattern. Half a generation younger than the Chadwicks, John and Jane Simon negotiated a more progressive personal relationship, organized around companionship and cemented by 'mutual affection' and respect.[107] This arrangement gave the wife a considerable degree of informal influence over her husband's public career. We know that Jane Simon was intellectually formidable, competing as a relative equal with men like Ruskin, Darwin and Chadwick at the regular salons and dinner parties the couple organized.[108]

It is difficult to map the structures of personal and sexual experience which these men and women lived out. What is clear is that middle-class men, dependent on the ministrations of their wives for emotional support and domestic management, transferred the same needs onto working-class men and a disproportionate burden onto their partners. At the same time the experts' erotic perceptions of working-class women were structured in opposition to norms of middle-class femininity. The Kay household provides us with a particularly incisive account of personal relations within the professional middle-class, and of what happened when they went wrong.

Kay's marriage to Janet Shuttleworth in 1842 brought him a connection with the established gentry. As an heiress in her own right, his wife's dowry was considerable, including estates in Lancashire and a large personal fortune. The couple's engagement was the subject for celebration. Symons, a personal friend, penned three pages of rhyming doggerel celebrating the joys of companionate marriage. Kay's own experience of early married life seems to have been bound up with the perception of his wife as both emblem of cultural status and mute confidante. She was a decorative object, the 'most good pure beauty', the guiding principle of his public deliberations and the most precious adornment of their two beautiful houses.[109] He infantilized Janet, constantly referring to her as 'my sweet little wife', and using her as an audience for his social philosophising –

though there was no notion that the relation was reciprocal. For her part, Janet Shuttleworth's understanding of married love, as for so many women of her class and generation, was expressed in quasi-religious terms. She felt herself happy in Kay's 'strong and holy affection', giving thanks to Him who had bound them together in mutual trust and confidence.[110]

But in the early 1850s the Kays' marriage went disastrously wrong. The couple were estranged and the ensuing litigation hinted at sexual 'difficulties' and Lady Shuttleworth's suspected adultery. From then on Kay's perception of his wife altered dramatically. Structurally she was shifted across the polarities demarcating respectable as opposed to unrespectable womanhood. Kay pathologized her, implying that she was mentally unbalanced. The death of his mother in 1858 occasioned some bitter comparisons between the two women. His mother had been 'an upright prudent matron' with 'remarkable firmness of mind' who had lived a simple, pure, religious life. All this was in contrast to his own wife.[111] When middle-class women disrupted the boundaries policing their personal conduct, the moral opprobrium was as great as that directed at mill girls and colliers' wives.

10 HIERARCHIES OF EXPERTISE: FEMALE PHILANTHROPHY AND THE GENDERED POLITICS OF REFORM

There was a reverse side to the gendered dimensions of professionalism. For though the reformers defined all women in terms of the private sphere of the family, these male experts were not without female allies and competitors in the public domain. The early nineteenth century witnessed the growth of the male professions but the period also saw the emergence of their female counterpart, namely charity and philanthropy as fit work for middle-class women. Sanitarians, medics and clerics were anxious to forge alliances with lady philanthropists, especially at a local level. The growing dialogue between male experts and female social reformers, particularly from the 1850s, is important to our argument. This gendered alliance both cemented the programme of social disciplining and became a major factor in the political struggles over sexuality in the later nineteenth century. Philanthropy was to act as a springboard for the early women's movement, aiding the development of a full-scale feminist critique of male power and expertise. The contradictions which erupted between these two élites over sexual regulation constitute a major strand of our subsequent history. First it is important to outline the specific position occupied by middle-class women within the discourse of environmentalism.

Like early social medicine, philanthropy was deeply influenced by the culture of evangelical and dissenting religion. Between 1790 and 1830 the new evangelicism, with its emphasis on the regeneration of national morality through the purity of domestic manners and an ethic of practical Christianity, was a major factor in the growing participation of women in philanthropic work.[112] Clapham Sect evangelicals like Hannah Moore and William Wilberforce were early polemicists for the separate spheres ideology, laying down rigid distinctions between the private female domain of the family and the male-defined world of industrial and professional enterprise. But evangelical definitions of women as moral regenerators opened up an area of considerable power and influence for bourgeois women. Philanthropic work was seen as a natural and socially justifiable extension of women's domestic role into the public sphere.

Philanthropic charities grew rapidly in the early years of the nineteenth century. In the metropolis the London City Mission founded in 1835, the Ragged School Union begun by Ashley in 1844 and the Young Men's Christian Association started in the same year were the most prominent examples. Much of their work was organized around personal contact with the poor, often centering on visits to working-class women by charity workers, who brought moral and material relief and sought to bridge the growing political and social divisions between classes. The most striking feature of the expanding charity network was the dramatic rise in the numbers of women members. They acted as non-participating financial patronesses, or more usually as the backbone of the system of district visiting, as

helpers in lying-in hospitals and asylums and as the organ-
izers of clothing clubs, soup kitchens, village shops and
chapels.[113]

From the 1850s medics and clerics began to grasp the
potential importance of this network of female philanthropy for
the sanitary movement. Though public health campaigns were
male dominated, at a local level it was women who became
reponsible for the day-to-day supervision of working-class
health and morality. Farr saw possibilities for an alliance
between medics and a reformed nursing profession, which
would put working wives and mothers in touch with sanitary
science.[114] In 1855 the Rev. Frederick Maurice organized a
series of lectures for middle-class women as part of his scheme
to found a college for training charity workers. Maurice, a
leading figure in the Christian socialist movement, had recently
set up the London Working Men's College. The lectures, given
by prominent sanitary reformers, harped on as usual about
the dual principles of medico-moral improvement. But they
sounded a new note by arguing that middle-class women were
especially suited for sowing the seeds of sanitary knowledge.
Edward Sieveking, fellow of the Royal College of Physicians,
quoted the recent shining example of Florence Nightingale in
the Crimea to prove that women's involvement in sanitary
reform was a natural extension of their domestic role; for 'what
we claim for the woman in the house we would also claim for her
beyond its walls'.[115] Medical men, he suggested, more than any
other group of social reformers, urgently needed to enlist the
co-operation of lady philanthropists. These women could 'help
to elucidate much that is otherwise enigmatical with regard to
the relation of mind and body', showing that there is a correlation on the one hand between 'temperance, equable temper,
and other moral virtues' and on the other between 'intemper-
ance, vice and misery'.[116] Maurice found that the middle-class
lady's presence in the wards of poor law hospitals provided such
a 'softening, humanizing, health-giving influence', teaching all
men that 'in whatever abyss he might be sunk, he is still capable
of health and resurrection'.[117] Lady hospital visitors could
supervise and reinforce the medical regime, administering
medicines, scrutinizing the nurses, reporting their behaviour
and above all inquiring into the moral habits of poor patients –

factors which were now known to play such a crucial role in the spread of disease.

All the contributors to Maurice's lecture series stressed the social and political benefits to be gained from female philanthropy. These were re-affirmed in numerous tracts and handbooks on charity work. Rapid industrialization and urbanization had produced new and chaotic forms of urban society, no longer held together by personal ties of paternalism and defence. The better classes were deserting the inner city areas for the healthier and more exclusive suburbs. Middle-class women could provide the missing link between classes and help promote social and political stability.

More unusually, Maurice felt the need to anticipate criticisms of lady philanthropists as proto-feminists. He acknowledged that many male professionals were suspicious of these women. Not only were they challenging the monopoly of male experts but they also seemed to be at the centre of campaigns for female suffrage, women's higher education and entry into the medical profession.[118] Yet Maurice insisted that if men would only recognise the importance of female philanthropy this would stem the growing demand for women's emancipation. The founding of a ladies' college for work among the poor would 'remove the slightest craving for such a state of things, by giving . . . a more healthful direction to the minds which entertain it'.[119] In short, Maurice saw philanthropy as an effective means of constraining middle-class women, by channelling their energy into a minor form of expertise subservient to male professionals.

Maurice's anxieties about the inter-relation between philanthropy and feminism anticipated class and gender contradictions which were present in almost all the charity organizations in the mid-Victorian period. For while middle-class women were active agents in the regulation of working-class behaviour – especially of working-class women – philanthropic work did provide them with an enlarged social role, employment opportunities and the experience to reflect on their position which often fed into feminist campaigns. Many prominent figures in the movement for women's higher education, suffrage and medical reform had a history of involvement in charity work.[120]

Ellen Ranyard embodied many of these contradictions in the

1850s and 1860s. Her story illustrates the cross-class relations between women played out in the personal dialogue of philanthropy. As a young single woman she had begun work in south London as a collector and distributor for the Bible Society. After marriage she had settled in Kent, but in 1857 moved to Bloomsbury, living in an area which bordered on the notorious rookeries of St Giles Parish, Holborn.[121] It was here that she began to recruit poor biblewomen for work in districts considered impenetrable by many male reformers.

In her published tracts and pamphlets Ranyard stressed that it was vital for women to take the lead in missionary work. She had become convinced that female workers were often more successful than clerics and medics in establishing a foothold in working-class areas and gaining an influence over the women. This, she claimed, was because lady philanthropists were capable of 'getting down, down, deeper down into the hearts of the poor':

> Why are they so wretched in their circumstances and in their habits in our great metropolis of civilization? Because the middle-class which ought to civilize them, has known so little of them. This knowledge is now being daily attained *in a womanly way*. The women make their homes – and it is these who must be influenced. . . . The Lord, in this day of mercy and power, is now awakening Christian Women of all classes to a sense of duty to their sisters – erring and outcast – and especially directing them to those measures which shall prove preventive as well as curative.[122]

The stress on knowledge 'gained in a womanly way' represented an implicit challenge to the routine methods of the male social investigators, backed as they often were by statutory coercion and the full panoply of the state. Ranyard's use of the term 'sisters' condensed a range of meanings – sisters in Christ, but also sisters joined together for mutual help and assistance. She felt that religion not only provided a common bond between women of different classes, but could also awaken the consciences of middle-class and aristocratic ladies who had been taught since birth to be 'lovely butterflies who float and glitter in the fairyland of wealth and fashion'.[123] Charity work, she claimed, could provide these women with a religious vocation, extending their sphere of influence beyond the empty world of dinner parties and morning calls. By drawing on a vocabulary of missionary vanguardism, women like Ranyard not only developed cross-class notions of sisterhood but also established their position as moral leaders among women of their own class.

Injunctions like these came close to arguing for a genuinely *public* role for middle-class women. But Ranyard was at pains to close off such potentially disruptive implications, insisting that philanthropy did not contravene the separate spheres ideology. Far from it, the charity worker was 'safe under the shadow of the Bible and the Home' and was fully justified in her activities: 'She forsakes no quiet, womanly aim in dealing with individualities, and in seeking to bring souls one by one to Christ.'[124] Man's power and intellect fitted him to deal with generalities and masses while woman as his helpmate filled in the smaller details!

Ellen Ranyard was instrumental in setting up the London Bible and Domestic Mission in 1857. City missions had played a prominent part in the network of charity and poor relief in London and other urban centres since the 1830s. Ranyard believed that the system lacked 'sisters' who could serve as 'native agents' to the destitute. Her plan for recruiting poor but respectable biblewomen provided the 'missing link' between the lady philanthropist and the urban poor.[125] The mission scheme expanded rapidly in the 1860s, especially in the East End, fielding over two hundred workers by 1868. Ranyard's 'native agents' were selected from local neighbourhoods: 'good women, middle-aged, pious and humble', who had been trained in what she termed the 'school of affliction'.[126] The system needed both a worker and a watcher – the 'link' and the 'rivet' as Ranyard called them. Lady superintendents brought money, food and clothing for distribution by the biblewomen. But they also came to watch and supervise. The main weekly activity was the mothers' meeting, chaired jointly by the superintendent and her assistant, when classes were given in sewing, cookery, elementary domestic hygiene and child-care.

The power structures linking the lady superintendent, her biblewomen and the poor women in the locality reveal that while philanthropic work contributed to the widening of middle-class women's sphere of influence, it was often directly opposed to the interests of women in the classes beneath them. Scrutiny and supervision characterized the relation between the lady and her assistant. Biblewomen were initially taken on for one month's probationary period and were always under the vigilant eye of the superintendent. Ranyard counselled that it was unwise to trust them with the actual purchase of clothing or the management of accounts. Moreover, the programme these assistants were trained to carry out was one of traditional sanitary improvement, for Ranyard firmly believed that the immoral state of the poor lowered their resistance to disease. Teaching the rudiments of domestic management delivered the usual sanitary and moral benefits. Cleaning, sewing and domestic economy sanctified the home and discreetly encouraged respectable womanhood. Like the factory commissioners, missionaries were alarmed that poor women were losing all semblance of femininity and were leading independent and hence unnatural lives as petty criminals and prostitutes. Ranyard recounted that in the 'unreformed muddy streets' women of the lowest class stood openly on the path, not hiding from the daylight but advertising their trade.[127] Against these manifestations of recklessness and ignorance she posed the subservient domestic ideal: 'instead of finding her at the gin-shop, he (the husband) finds her in prayer, and his meal ready and the place clean, and a tract or chapter in the Bible, waiting for him too.'[128] Religious conversion, conversion to domestic respectability and female dependence on men went hand-in-hand.

Despite the adherence of many male professionals to a separate spheres ideology, they did see the importance of an alliance with lady philanthropists as critical to the success of sanitary politics at a local level. The domestic position of women, the promotion of hierarchies of discipline and authority between husband and wife and parents and children, the relation of the family to wider questions of social order and stability, all these issues were taken up by women visitors and charity workers. But equally significant was the way in which this system marked the potential entry of middle-class women into the public arena of social reform. It was the political contradictions embedded here, and the hostility women provoked from male professionals, which generated key conditions for the feminist campaigns around sexuality in the later nineteenth century.

11   CONCLUSION

How then do we characterize this early moment of official intervention into sexuality. We have not been concerned here with an inclusive history of ideas about sex, nor with a 'sanitary ramble' through early Victorian social reform. Rather with the way in which a particular domain of sexuality was produced. In the period of nascent industrial capitalism it was the systematic forms of knowledge of sanitary science, social medicine, evangelical religion and philanthropy which staked out a specific regime of sexuality. Historians ignore this discursive dimension of cultural analysis at their peril. Statements by sanitarians and social investigators on the sexuality of the labouring classes were not the official reflection of a pre-given social reality. They were the active product of specific regimes of knowledge and their power relations. Sexual meanings were constructed at the interface of the class and gender related polarities laid down by moral environmentalism. They marked out distinctive cultural identities for middle-class men and women and crystallized dominant images of the labouring poor.

This domain was not some purely ideational creation, put together through the discursive combination of concepts free-floating in society. It was deployed by specific historical agents and underwritten by a strategic set of political alliances. These were at work both inside the apparatuses of an expanding state and in the newly enfranchised professional groups within civil society.

Much of moral environmentalism had its broad conditions set by the social and political transformations attendant on the economic expansion of capital and the reorganization of productive forces and relations. But it was not reducible to those structures, nor were its effects. The distinctive formation of masculine professional expertise is crucial here, with its concepts and procedures of inquiry, its particular cultural experience and its self-conscious distance from industrialists and politicians alike. Injunctions by Kay and Chadwick on health, morality, sexual behaviour and the position of women were not mere marginalia in the expansion of industrial capitalism. This repertoire began to emerge in the period as an important site of control and political struggle in its own right. Nevertheless, in the 1830s and 1840s we can still map out remarkably clear lines of convergence between different fields of intervention. By the mid-Victorian period these connections were becoming more difficult to establish as forms of knowledge and political positions hardened and generated their own momentum. It is this second stage of sexual and sanitary politics which we now need to consider.

PART TWO

THE SANITARY PRINCIPLE IN DOMINANCE: MEDICAL HEGEMONY AND FEMINIST RESPONSE 1860–1880

1   MEDICAL HEGEMONY AND SOCIAL POLICY 1850–1870

The medico-moral strategy was consolidated in the period after the initial reforms of the 1830s and 1840s. Environmental medicine, working in conjunction with religious principles of moral education, formed a dominant response to the problems posed by the working-class in the period between 1850 and 1870. But the history of mid-century educational reform or the public health movement shows how partially the sanitary principle was actually enacted. The solutions, across a variety of fields of intervention, were the product of complex compromises between the various political forces in play. The radical programmes drawn up by the experts were severely qualified. Experts were themselves 'educated' into the political realities lying outside their own specialist domains. Central government intervention into public health, sanitation and housing was cautious and piecemeal in comparison with Chadwick's conception of a centralized supervisory network. It is tempting, but completely illegitimate, to slide from analysis of the *production* of official solutions to their *implementation*. The two elements need to be understood as distinct and often disjointed moments of state policy.

The Board of Health was disbanded in 1858 amid a welter of political intrigue and orchestrated opposition. Chadwick himself had been forced out of office four years earlier by a powerful lobby of anti-centralizers, private drainage and water authorities and those with a personal antipathy to the 'wizard of Whitehall'.[1] *The Times*, once an ardent supporter of Chadwick, was particularly vicious in its appraisal of his administrative career, chortling that Mr Chadwick would receive his final reward 'when he falls at last a sanitary martyr to a choked two-inch pipe drain and is carried by policemen . . . to an extramural cemetery'.[2] The board was replaced by a Medical Office within the Privy Council – that refuge for unpopular branches of government which needed shielding from the glare of parliamentary scrutiny. Changes in personnel reflected shifts in overall public health strategy. The appointment of John Simon as first Medical Officer heralded the replacement of the grandiose principles of sanitary engineering by preventive medicine. Chadwick had always insisted that ultimate sanitary authority needed to remain with non-medical administrators. Simon was a medic, with a background in medical research and a proven record against cholera as Medical Officer to the City of London between 1848 and 1855. His approach to public health combined effective administration (involving a team of inspectors, control of the water-supply and the removal of nuisances) with an emphasis on research into the causes of infection. Simon worked for discreet administrative transformations within government, avoiding until late in his career clashes with ministers over contentious issues of policy and principle. Through skilful manoeuvering he was able to build up a research department which concretized the new importance awarded to scientific inquiry in public health campaigns.[3] His annual reports beteen 1859 and 1871 were exemplary statements of this dual focus on sound administration and pioneering research.

Like Chadwick, Simon saw public health as an important asset for an industrial nation. But the new Medical Officer gave this conception a more ethical and humanitarian gloss. The improvement of the physical and moral health of individuals was one of the prime duties of a Christian country, for the level of national health reflected the degree of civilization attained by the state.[4] Simon's public health philosophy was informed by his commitment to Christian socialism, a strong current among many social reformers in mid-century. He formed part of a loose network of clerics, philanthropists and intellectuals, including Ruskin, Charles Kingsley, Louisa Twining, campaigner for workhouse improvement, and Octavia Hill, the housing reformer.

Simon's burgeoning career at the Medical Office in the 1860s coincided with the consolidation of the status of the medical profession, both as a privileged domain of expertise and as a distinctive cultural grouping within the middle-class. The new Medical Officer, a highly visible public figure, was instrumental in pushing for increased professional status, especially in the campaigns over the Medical Act of 1858, the single most important measure governing medicine. The act established for the first time the statutory definition of a medical practitioner, together with a register and a General Medical Council to watch over conduct and education. The growth of experimental science, with the new technology of the microscope and the more rigid principles of research established in the laboratory, also contributed to medical ascendancy within social policy.[5] Following the recent work of Pasteur and other European scientists on the micro-organic causes of disease, Simon embarked on major programmes of research into the chemistry of morbid processes and the aetiology of contagion. He attached his team's findings to his own reports, as quiet but conclusive proof of the steady advance of scientific progress and its ultimate conquest over infectious disease. On the wider political stage, in the face of continuing opposition to public health, these statements were designed to promote the image of the doctor as a serious and high minded questor after truth:

> Every step in the physiological sciences, every better knowledge of the origins of the living body, and of their material and functional fluctuations under whatever influences is of actual or potential gain to us; and such knowledge constantly gives more and more success to the provisional practice which it enlightens. As regards the anatomical studies of late times, with very varied utilization of the microscope, and the otherwise greatly improved means of minute structural investigation, I need hardly say that, by them during the last thirty years, great parts of the science of disease have been completely transfigured.[6]

This quasi-evolutionary conception of painstaking scientific progress, with its stress on technical control over human life, proved a powerful input into the work of Simon's new department.

Administratively, growing medical prestige and authority was visible in the series of mid-century acts addressing the health, housing and sanitary condition of the urban working-class.[7] In practice, the net result of these medically directed reforms was often to exacerbate the housing and sanitary conditions of the urban poor, especially in London. Local medical officers were usually committed to a purely profession-al radicalism, transfixed with the reduction of their magic figures, the disease and death rates, in local sanitary areas. All the statutes lacked compulsory clauses to enforce rebuilding schemes and the temptation was to 'shovel-off' the poor onto neighbouring districts.[8] Conceptually, the acts continued to be underpinned by a dual commitment to physical improvement and moral regulation. Simon, concluding his report for 1870, staked out the familiar equation between lack of sanitation, immorality and the depressed quality of working-class life:

> where grievous excess of physical suffering is bred, large parts of the same soil yield, side by side with it, evils of another kind . . . in some of the regions of insanitary influence, civilization and morals suffer almost equally with health . . . education . . . is little likely to penetrate, unless with amended sanitary law, nor human life to be morally raised while physically it is so degraded and squandered.[9]

It was this sanitary principle which exerted a major structural influence on the Contagious Diseases Acts of 1864, 1866 and 1869.[10] This was the single most important legislative interven-tion addressing sexuality throughout the nineteenth century. Extensive state-backed medical involvement in the regulation of venereal disease and female prostitution crystallized an approach which had its origins in the public health programme of thirty years before. It was these acts, together with the resistance they provoked, which resulted in the growing speci-fication of the sexual within official discourse and a marked polarization of political positions.

2   THE CONTAGIOUS DISEASES ACTS AND MID-VICTORIAN SOCIAL REFORM

In an immediate sense the legislation was a response to growing official pressure among medics and military chiefs for some form of sanitary scrutiny of the armed forces. Military returns had reported a steady increase in venereal infection among the men since the 1820s.[11] A series of government inquiries in the 1850s and 1860s, precipitated by the Crimean War, testified to the seriousness with which the dual problems of VD and sexual immorality among the lower ranks was regarded in official circles.[12] From the 1840s public anxiety had also been focused on prostitution, the 'great social evil', by studies from evangelical clerics and medics, and by rescue and reform societies campaigning for a police crackdown on the London streets.

The jurisdiction of the 1864 Act applied to a number of naval ports and army garrison towns in England and Ireland. Under its schedules, both police personnel and medical practitioners (acting under the direct supervision of the War Office and the Admiralty, rather than the local constabulary) were empowered to notify a justice of the peace if they suspected a woman of being a common prostitute. The woman would then be taken to a certified hospital for medical examination, where she could be detained for up to three months. Infringement of the hospital rules, or quitting without medical consent, carried penalties of up to two months imprisonment. There were also penalties for brothel keepers. The acts of 1866 and 1869 extended the geographical locations covered by the regulations, while the Admirality and the War Office were now mandated to provide hospital facilities for inspection and treatment. Provision was also made within hospitals for adequate moral and religious instruction of the women and for the regular fortnightly inspection of former detainees, while the period of compulsory detention was extended to six months.

II   The sanitary principle in dominance 1860–80

What concerns us is not so much a detailed account of the politics which led to the passing of the acts and to their eventual repeal in the 1880s. These aspects have received sustained analysis from recent feminist and social historians.[13] Rather, the purpose here is to build on that recent research in order to situate the debates on sexuality and disease in the light of the longer-term history of medico-moral regulation. Within this context the acts represented a high point of sanitary interventionism.

From the 1850s the sanitary principle had been used to justify demands for state intervention regulating sexual disease and immorality. As *The Lancet* declaimed, the state interfered in the case of a diseased woman on the same grounds and by the same right that it interfered with the typhus fever or smallpox patient – to avert the spread of disease.[14] In 1850 *The Westminster Review* urged that the newly created Board of Health should establish a system of periodic inspection of prostitutes, enforceable at law.[15] Twelve years later, Sir John Liddel, Director-General of the Naval Medical Department, justified arguments for the hygienic control of diseased prostitutes by invoking the general principles of state medicine.[16] Medical authorities on venereology, like William Acton, pointed to the longstanding concern of French medics and social reformers with the health threat posed by prostitution.[17] Much impressed with the continental system of state hygiene, they were determined to implement a similar programme in Britain. Here was a new putsch for compulsory state action on sexual and moral issues, backed by specialist medical expertise.

The medical profession was the most significant group in support of the new legislation. Numerically, medics were dominant on all the parliamentary inquiries into the working of the acts between 1867 and 1881, pushing hard for their extension to a national system of inspection and detention of prostitutes. In 1867 a report of a committee of the Harveian Medical Society of London called for the expansion of the 1866 legislation to London and other large towns.[18] The enthusiasm generated by this investigation led to the formation of the Association for Promoting the Extension of the Contagious Diseases Acts to the Civilian Population. Its membership was drawn from the ranks of the Tory Party, the Anglican clergy and the aristocracy, but it was dominated by the intellectual voice of the medical profession.

The growing hegemony of state medicine written into the new regulations bore witness to a substantial shift in the balance of forces within the sanitary movement. Men like Acton used the twin issues of prostitution and venereal disease to insist that medics rather than moralists now had far greater claim to authority on social and environmental issues. At a meeting of the Royal Medical Society in 1860 he gave his own gloss on the prostitution debate. Philanthropists and clergymen had to admit that their own reforming schemes had completely failed. The problem needed to be handed over to scientific investigation.[19] Moral intervention was by itself at best a mere palliative unless co-ordinated by official sanitary regulation. Prayer and lamentation would not arrest the deterioration of national fibre. Schemes of reformatories and maids' protection societies were but 'paltry, peddling scratches on the surface of evil'.[20] Statements such as these reflected growing confidence and optimism among members of the profession; the conviction that state-backed medicine, as opposed to voluntary and charitable effort, provided the ultimate solution to pressing social problems. *The Lancet*, smug from recent public health victories, captured the new mood of medical optimism in 1871 when it claimed success for the recent improvements in working-class habits. Medics were the true friends of the labouring classes, for they knew more about the genesis of poverty and the needs of the working man than any other groups in the community.[21] It was a confidence borne of a quarter-of-a century of growing medical ascendancy, which was to have far-reaching effects on the sanitary alliance.

Supporters of the acts did not see the principles of state hygiene as contradicting the moral emphases of the public health movement. Far from the state sanctioning male vice by providing men of the forces with a clean supply of women, it was claimed that the acts were essentially moral in aim and intention. Campaigners against the regulations were working to undermine the time-honoured alliance between medicine and morality but the healer who deployed his art 'honourably and fully' could never be in antagonism with divine law.[22] It was believed that the curative functions of medicine provided their own *moral* guarantee. Medics presented glowing testimonies to successive government inquiries on the marvellous conversion worked by the acts; where before the conduct of prostitutes was miserable in the extreme, now they had common decency and self-respect. The *Report from the Royal Commission on the Administration and Operation of the Contagious Diseases Acts*, 1871, pointed out that the 'decorous and wholesome' improvement in the manners and habits of the people was a direct result of expanded sanitary regulations. In the same way, the contagious diseases legislation would both sanitize and moralize the people, by purging towns and encampments of those 'miserable creatures who were mere masses of rottenness and vehicles of disease'.[23]

Many of the medical supporters of the legislation had a history of involvement in hospital and sanitary work among the poor, as local medical officers and poor law doctors – work which reinforced their commitment to the acts as part of the wider politics of public health. Their biographies provide us with access to the professional and class alliances which fed into the politics of mid-Victorian social reform.

John Brendon Curgenven, joint secretary to the extensionist association, was typical of the newly professionalized medic who spearheaded the regulationist campaign. From a provincial background, outside the ranks of the medical élite, Curgenven characteristically sought increased professional status by a series of official posts rather than through private practice. In 1852 he was appointed medical officer to the Royal Free Hospital, Hampstead, where he handled the local offensive against cholera during the 1854 epidemic. Later he served in the Crimea, officially as medical attendant to Lord Ward but enlisting as a volunteer surgeon with Florence Nightingale. In addition to his work promoting the Contagious Diseases Acts, in the 1860s he also served on the Parliamentary Bills Committee of the British Medical Association, helping to draft legislation on habitual drunkenness, infant mortality and the examination and registration of midwives. A member of the sanitary committee of the Paddington Vestry, he was influential in forming a local section of the Charity Organization Society in 1869 and was medical representative on a number of philanthropic bodies.

II The sanitary principle in dominance 1860–80

Curgenven represented one type of medical supporter; Matthew Berkeley Hill, his colleague as joint secretary on the extensionist association, came via a different route.[24] Hill was the third generation of a family of prominent educationalists and social reformers, who had their origins in the radical Unitarian culture of eighteenth- and early nineteenth-century Birmingham. It was the same sort of low church dissenting background which had produced many first generation medics like Kay and Wakley. But by the 1860s Berkely Hill had become integrated into the culture of London's professional gentry, where experts rubbed shoulders with the leaders of upper middle-class and aristocratic society. Hill was professor of surgery and pathology at University College, London, with strong links to the military hierarchy through his marriage to the daugher of Sir Thomas Howell of the War Office. Rising professional status involved a negotiation of establishment culture, and Hill dropped many of the public trappings of his evangelical background – embracing Anglicanism and sending his son to Eton and Oxford. For him, regulationism meant adherence to the values and ordered hierarchy of the governing élite as much as to sanitary reform. Hill must have been typical of many mid-Victorian medics who reorientated their social and political allegiances as a result of a shift in class and professional status.

The Contagious Diseases Acts not only involved a subtle shift in the balance of forces within moral environmentalism, they also marked a new and more particular specification of sexuality within sanitary discourse. Early nineteenth-century environmentalism had focused on sexuality as part of a general concern with the habits and morals of the urban working-class. Legislation on public health, sanitation and industrial conditions did not contain prescriptions for the *direct* regulation of sexual conduct. We have seen that it was often difficult to isolate the various sub-domains condensed and subsumed under the general categories of morality and immorality. In contrast, the acts implicated the state and medical expertise in a much more precise and extensive discourse on sexuality – inciting and crystallizing representations, especially around female sexuality. This was quite new. It involved the co-ordination of a number of government departments which was extensive by the standards of nineteenth-century administration. But such a phenomenon cannot be explained by recourse to general principles of 'bureaucratization' or administrative expansion. It was part of the intensified scrutiny of female behaviour and the sexual habits of the urban poor, under the impact of social and political conditions in mid-nineteenth-century Britain.

The process represented a refined and more detailed application of the principles of environmentalism. Environmentalism in its first phase had advanced its hegemony through a grandiose moral and scientific logic. But at the level of implementation such as totalizing conception of social disciplining often lacked precision when it came to dealing with specific problems. Simon's shift of approach away from Chadwick's grand sanitary plan was not only an administrative necessity in the face of political opposition, it was also an acknowledgment of this difficulty. From the early 1850s environmentalists began to define social questions and their solutions in much more specific terms. There was a gradual move away from insistence on the inter-related nature of all social, political and economic problems and a shift towards specialization. Medical research into the causes of contagion, secular and religious education, charity and philanthropic schemes, moral reclamation of prostitutes, the work of the temperance movement, all signalled this change of direction, as did the growing tendency towards the pathologization of recalcitrant individuals such as criminals, prostitutes and the insane.[25] It was facilitated by the transformations within the administrative process itself. Legislation now produced separate apparatuses and spheres of activity, with distinctive forms of knowledge and expertise. Simon himself was a product of the first phase of this process, while reform of the civil service structure outlined in the Northcote-Trevelyan report of 1854 proposed a new tier of secular administration within the state.[26]

The move towards specialization was encouraged by changes in the overall economic and political situation from the 1850s. The relative stabilization of the economy after the wild fluctuations in the business cycle in the previous decade, together with the defeat of Chartism and early militant trade-unionism, assisted social reformers in their attempts to treat issues as discrete and separate, rather than interdependent. The National Association for the Promotion of Social Science, founded in 1865, typified the new problematic. A loose umbrella reform group, whose members in the early years included both regulationists and their opponents, it embraced an ameliorist approach to social problems, shying away from any attempt to see them as structurally related. Patient and painstaking empirical investigation would reveal the optimum measure of reform. It was a belief backed by the conviction that society was essentially a good order, and that there existed a general professional consensus on the treatment of social ills.[27]

Passing through Parliament with little immediate opposition, the contagious diseases legislation was a significant manifestation of consensus politics, marking the application of precision social engineering to the domain of sexuality. The acts were concerned with the regulation of the sexual and moral habits of two particular groups within the urban poor – female prostitutes and the lower ranks of the armed forces. But the tactics used to discipline these two groups were very different. For what lay behind the assumptions of the legislators were the gender-specific, male-defined norms which had been embedded in the reforming programmes of the 1830s and 1840s. These were now crystallized in an expanded discourse on male and female sexuality.

As an intervention into the health of the army and navy the legislation developed a new 'enlightened' approach to the lower ranks, advocated by the 1857 Royal Commission and in part the outcome of the Crimean War débâcle.[28] Witnesses to the Select Committee on Venereal Disease, 1867 testified to the environmental and sanitary improvements which had already been adopted. Healthy exercise, rational recreation, better living conditions and temperance campaigns were all designed to morally arm the men against temptation. On the vexed question of how far soldiers and sailors should themselves be subjected to compulsory periodic genital inspection, medics and military chiefs were divided. Some like William Hickman, the Royal Navy's Secretary and Paymaster, put the case for compulsory ablution on sanitary and moral grounds. Yet he acknowledged that 'any thorough examination . . . would be an extremely difficult thing to carry out on account of the prejudice of the men'.[29] Others, like Dr Barclay, a staff surgeon-major, argued that such a system would destroy the men's self-respect and counteract the good effects of environmental reforms, a position upheld in the report of the 1871 Royal Commission.[30]

It was *women* who were defined as the human agents of infection, threatening national health and security and challenging the social order by their active and autonomous sexuality. The acts introduced a more coercive form of medico-legal regulation of prostitutes, together with an intensified system of police surveillance. When, flushed with success, pro-regulationists pressed Gladstone's government to extend the statutes in the late 1860s, many supporters made the traditional connection between the threat of the prostitute and wider anxieties about public order and moral habits among the unrespectable poor. In a paper to the Social Science Association in 1868, Curgenven insisted that the acts not only promoted the moral reform of fallen women but also raised the standard of public order on the streets.[31] The newly established *British Medical Journal* was quick to stress the general benefits to public morality if the legislation were imposed on the northern cities.[32]

Prostitution, drunkenness, vagrancy and other 'unrespectable' manifestations of urban popular culture had long been a headache for local borough councils. Increasingly, local government used its legal powers to separate out specific groups as targets for police intervention. As early as the 1850s Plymouth City Council embarked on this new tack, passing a series of by-laws to promote police control of the streets and common lodging houses, with explicit reference to prostitutes.[33] In the following decade many local police forces were given new powers to discipline drunk and disorderly street-walkers, powers strengthened under the Licensing Act, 1872. Central to this coercive policing was a concerted effort to isolate the prostitute from working-class culture. A new and powerful medical ideology, crystallizing definitions of normal and deviant female sexuality was the cornerstone of this process.

3   FEMALE SEXUALITY

Before the passing of the acts prostitutes were relatively integrated into the cultural and economic life of the casual poor in the garrison towns. As Judith Walkowitz has demonstrated, prostitution was used by many working women as a temporary move to supplement the pitifully low wages gained from needlework, dressmaking or domestic service.[34] A move back to respectable status through marriage was still possible; it was often the route taken by many women in mid-career. The medical and clerical inquiries of the 1840s had frequently complained about precisely these difficulties of identifying 'immoral' women.[35] Medical definitions implemented in the Contagious Diseases legislation made visible the perceived threat of the prostitute, by focusing on her sexuality and isolating it as unnatural and deviant.

Acton typified this new medical discourse. Like that of Curgenven, his own rising professional career was bound up with a commitment to expansionist sanitary reform. Son of a provincial clergyman, with a background of work among the poor at the Islington Dispensary, he specialized in venereology as medical consultant to the London Lock Hospital and as an *externe* to the Female Venereal Hospital in Paris. A vigorous campaigner in support of regulationism, and a major witness on all the parliamentary inquiries, his studies *Prostitution* and *Functions and Disorders of the Reproductive Organs*, both published in 1857, were key contributions to the new medical discourse on sexuality. The whole tenor of Acton's approach was to insist on the primacy of medical knowledge – dismissing popular beliefs, especially those put forward by midwives, as dangerous quackery. Sexuality, he pontificated, was one of 'the areas of social life that are revealed only to medical men, in the hope that they may be in a position to suggest some mode of relief'.[36] Drawing heavily on French physiological science, Acton premised his theory on a belief in the absolute difference between male and female physiology and their related forms of sexuality. Male sexuality was defined as an instinctual force which, while needing constant medical supervision, was an essential attribute of masculinity. It was a power and a privilege, giving man 'his dignity . . . his character as head and ruler, and . . . his importance'.[37] Pre-Darwinist concepts of comparative natural history were used to show certain fundamental connections between man's physical organization and that of the lower mammals. The strength of the male instinct was proof of this biological link.

The other central feature of this early sexology was its stress on the direct relation between mind and body. Here Acton followed the general materialist principles of contemporary physiology, in which ideas and sensations were conceived as the direct product of physical processes or environmental influences. Male 'sex passion' was either the result of stimulation from external sensations, or of involuntary influences coming from the sexual organs themselves. Sensations were conveyed from the brain through the nervous system, resulting in erection. Men could only achieve full physical and mental gratification by discharging their semen in the act of copulation.

There was a constant tension in Acton's writing between his assertion that the male sexual instinct was capable of intellectual and moral control and his stress on male sexuality as a powerful, inevitable expression of basic physiological processes. Acton did advise restraint for men, both inside and outside marriage, as a solution to the problem of promiscuity and infection. Restraint was also necessary because of the massive drain on the body which occurred during intercourse. This was especially dangerous for the urban, professional paterfamilias, 'the hardworked, intellectual married man residing in London', whose health was at risk from the cumulative strain of metropolitan life and frenetic mental labour.[38] These formulations were grounded in the early hydraulic model of the circulation of energy derived from fluid mechanics; the body possessed only a fixed quantity of semen, once expended it was lost forever. Implicitly, the emphasis on conserving energy registered the austere virtues of hard work and cultural restraint which were the hallmark of the professional gentry.[39] Control was possible by exerting the power of the intellect and those 'moral capabilities' which distinguished man from the animals.

In the practical application of his theory Acton became much more pragmatic. Here medical theory intersected with wider class and gender assumptions about sexual behaviour. While male continence was *necessary*, it could not be *guaranteed*, because of the strength of the male urge. When this logic was applied to the lower ranks of the armed forces it also carried the gloss that these men were less capable of intellectual control, being more animal and closer to nature.[40]

In contrast, women were defined in terms of the norm of asexuality and the absence of sexual desire. Acton again explained this as a biological phenomenon, present in all forms of the female species. He noted approvingly that 'in a state of nature wild female animals will not allow the approach of the male except when in a state of rut'.[41] Motherhood, marriage and domesticity were basic female instincts which Acton compared to the 'unnatural' sexual desire of the prostitute, the nyphomaniac and the courtesan. Once more the argument was physiological; maternity and suckling made such vital demands on a woman's organs that 'sexual desire is almost annihilated'.[42]

Acton's work is usually represented as the highpoint of mid-Victorian distinctions between the asexual bourgeois lady and the sexually depraved working-class prostitute. What is less often recognized is that it was distinctly innovatory, marking important breaks with earlier theories of female sexuality and helping to generate an intellectual climate favourable to regulationism. His polarized oppositions between pure and impure women connected with a whole range of representations regulating female behaviour in the 1850s and 1860s. These were present in literature and art as well as in medicine. The growth of an overtly moralizing genre of English painting from the 1840s staked out similar representations of female purity and immorality. Pre-Raphaelite artists like Holman Hunt and Dante Gabriel Rossetti, whose work was popular with the northern bourgeoisie, juxtaposed images of the middle-class home against a range of social outcasts. Representations of fallen women, or images of women as fatal seductresses, were central to these didactic narratives. Often such paintings pointed to the maxim that prostitution led to death, confirming the prostitute as the member of an outcast group.[43]

II   The sanitary principle in dominance 1860–80

The extent of the shift registered by these approaches becomes clear when compared with its antecedents. Earlier accounts of prostitution by Congregationalist ministers like William Bevan, Ralph Wardlaw and Robert Vaughn, physicians such as Ryan and Tait and the temperance and moral reformers William Logan and John Talbot had worked to define the prostitute as a distinctly pathological female type. But she was not juxtaposed against an *asexual* image of respectability. Moreover, in the handbooks on marriage, reproduction and bourgeois hygienics of the 1840s the respectable woman was defined through marriage and the family but female asexuality was not the guiding principle. Rather, what was emphasized was the family as the source of conjugal love, happiness and companionship, within which sexual and emotional relations between husband and wife played a valid part. Procreation was of course the ultimate goal, but sexual satisfaction in marriage was important for *both* partners.[44]

The importance awarded to sexual fulfilment within marriage owed much to the rationalist dissenting tradition of Quakers, Unitarians and Congregationalists. Bevan, Wardlaw and Vaughn were themselves all Congregationalist ministers, defining marriage as a civil and religious contract – the basis of a stable and well-ordered society in a world disrupted by industrialization. But for Wardlaw and other dissenters marriage was also the perfect compact between men and women 'by which they engage in mutual love and friendship for the purpose of procreation'. Pleasure and enjoyment were seen as natural, legitimate and God-given, provided they were not excessive and were linked to the desire for procreation. Morality was contravened only when pleasure was sought 'independently of the end which pleasures are only meant to subserve'.[45] Equally for Ryan, a moderate exercise of the sexual function for both marriage partners was essential to good health as well as conjugal happiness regulating 'the functions of the brain or nervous system and consequently of the whole body'.[46] He condemned the practice of marital chastity as highly dangerous, leading to infertility in women, impotence in men and even to death. Bourgeois hygienics, at least for these male reformers, had some conception of acceptable pleasure for women.

In the 1860s medical interventions into the contagious diseases debate polarized earlier representations of female sexuality. They marked out clear distinctions between the asexual respectable married woman on the one hand and the depraved prostitute on the other. In Acton's famous phrase 'the majority of women . . . are not very much troubled with sexual feeling of any kind'.[47] Those few women who shocked public feeling with a display of sexual desire were branded either as prostitutes, nymphomaniacs or lunatics. Schemes put forward by regulationists for the reform of prostitutes in the lock hospital institutionalized the distinction between 'pure' and 'impure' women. Once inside the hospital, prostitutes were subjected to a programme of physical and moral disciplining, which reinforced their distance from respectable women. Lessons in personal hygiene and ablution were combined with a stress on class deference and a belief that 'fallen women' needed to re-learn their femininity through moralizing domestic labour. Needlework and laundrywork provided an effective class and gender strategy, designed to prepared the prostitute for her correct place in the female labour force and to re-educate her into an approved feminine role.[48]

Medical isolation of the prostitute in the 1860s went hand-in-hand with a range of related social demarcations. These included the respectable/unrespectable divisions made by many philanthropic organizations, distinctions drawn by the newly founded Charity Organization Society between the deserving and undeserving poor and the healthy/diseased oppositions employed by medical officers of health to identify the carriers of contagion.[49] All such pathologies registered the move towards the particularization of social problems and their solutions. The new medical polarizations clearly worked to regulate the sexuality of *all* women. They visibly sharpened at the end of the decade as medics were forced onto the defensive by a growing feminist campaign demanding the repeal of the acts – itself part of the wider upsurge of the mid-Victorian women's movement. In his defence of the legislation before the Association of the Medical Officers of Health in 1869, Acton countered opposition by resorting to increased extremism. The public needed to be made aware that prostitutes were not 'soiled doves', but were a class of women who were almost 'unsexed' and had lost all 'womanly feeling', consorting with as many as 'eight to twelve different men in the same night'.[50]

Medics also responded to the feminist challenge by drawing on their new sexual ideology to label the 'shrieking sisterhood' as immoral and impure for daring to speak publicly about sexuality. Acton's 1875 edition of *The Functions and Disorders of the Reproductive System* carried a diatribe against the revolting and intolerable insubordination now suffered by husbands from their wives.[51] Parliamentary speeches opposing women's emancipation singled out feminist repealers – 'a defiant sect who would have nothing sacred, nothing veiled, nothing hidden' – as the precursors of what was to come if women were to enter the public arena.[52] Similar dirty tactics were employed in other medical debates. *The Lancet*'s sustained opposition to the first women doctors, the 'advance guard of the Amazonian army' as it dubbed them, was argued on the grounds that young ladies would be rendered indelicate, and by implication immoral, by attending lectures and dissections on human anatomy and pathology.[53]

This strategy of imputing impurity to women who challenged medical hegemony had its effects. In the 1870s leaders of the women's movement, particularly teachers working for the extension of educational opportunities, were caught over support for the repeal campaign. Practically all of them felt it was impossible to back the repeal movement publicly for fear that involvement would jeopardize their own campaigns.[54] When Annie Besant was prosecuted with Charles Bradlaugh for publishing *The Fruits of Philosophy*, a book of contraceptive advice in 1877, she faced public abuse and insinuations about the immorality of her private life, culminating in the successful attempt to deprive her of the custody of her young daughter. As she confessed much later, it was not the thought of failure which made Bradlaugh and herself pause at the outset:

> It was the horrible misconception that we saw might arise; the odious imputations on honour and purity that would follow. . . . To me it meant the loss of the pure reputation I prized, the good name I had guarded – scandal most horrible a woman could face.[55]

It was no accident that medical misogyny, with its powerful definitions of moral and immoral female behaviour, reached a peak at precisely the moment when middle-class women were beginning to challenge the hegemony of the male professions.

4   MALE DESIRE

If the mid-nineteenth-century witnessed the increasingly polarized representations of women around the definitions of asexual purity/immorality, these oppositions also had a profound impact on class-specific forms of male sexuality. We have already noted the erotic fantasies of men like Jelinger Symons over the appearance and behaviour of the pit girls. Turning to the private letters, diaries and pornography of aristocrats and professional men we can see how their sexual desire was structured around notions of private debauchery, lust and licentiousness. Here desire was incited and pleasure produced through transgression of the sanctioned norms of middle-class marriage and domesticity. More often than not it was the 'depraved', sexualized and socially inferior female prostitute who was seen to condense these aspects of male fantasy.

The most elaborate and highly wrought codes in this area were of course those of contemporary pornography. Here the new physiological theories of the uncontrollable male instinct were incorporated into erotic fantasy. 'Walter's *My Secret Life*, the fictional narrative of a debauchee, constructed male desire as an illicit but physiologically based animal appetite, which drove men on to fresh excess. The growing market in visual pornography, with the improvement of photographic techniques, provides the most striking illustration of the way male sexuality was being socially shaped. By mid-century, many scientific and professional groups had grasped the value of the new medium as an aid to empirical verification. According to *The Lancet* in 1859 photography was so 'essentially the art of truth – that it would seem to be the essential means of reproducing all forms and structures which science seeks for delineation'.[56] This realist definition of photography as truth and evidence was reworked in pornographic texts to consolidate the notion of male sexual desire as instantly aroused and requiring constant relief. Visual codes, with their deeply embedded resonances of actuality, reinforced the immediacy of the male urge, responding spontaneously to sensory stimuli.

Both written and visual pornography represented women for the male gaze across the virtue/vice, innocence/depravity oppositions. The clearest examples were in the early photographic studies of child prostitutes dating from the 1860s and 1870s, where childhood innocence was erotically framed against visible signs of immoral sexuality, such as exposed genitalia or the depraved stare. Similarly, in *My Secret Life* sexual pleasure was signified in total opposition to the norms of bourgeois married life and sexual relations with one's wife:

> I tried to love her (my wife). It was impossible. Hateful in day, she was loathsome to me in bed. Long I strove to do my duty, and be faithful, yet to such a pitch did my disgust at length go, that laying by her side, I had wet dreams nightly, sooner than relieve myself in her.[57]

In such accounts 'duty', 'faithfulness' and conjugal union were defined as innately unpleasurable. In contrast, the perceived coarseness and animality of working-class women was the focus for male arousal, producing an experience of sex as illicit and furtive, breaking the boundaries of class and gender:

> Never did a woman enjoy a poking more. . . . She'd lost of course all modesty, if she ever had any, but she must have been reared like a pig . . . her language was indescribably common and coarse, and whether eating, drinking, speaking, washing or even pissing, her vulgarity and idiocy were intolerable. She was a magnificent bit of fucking flesh and nothing more.[58]

These male fantasies reduced working women to a series of purely physical functions organized around sex. They had a continuity with the rites of upper-class masculine culture acted out in the clubs and pleasure haunts of the Haymarket and other areas of the metropolis from the 1840s. When Flora Tristan, the French feminist and socialist, visited London in 1839 she noted not just the extent of prostitution but the complex ritualization of male debauchery. Luxurious private supper rooms in the West-End known as 'the finishes' organized part-orgies part entertainments which centred on the 'erotic' degradation of women by male clients. One of these involved plying a woman with drink until she fell reeling to the floor, where glass after glass of liquor was poured over her until she became 'merely a confusion of filth'.[59]

Arthur Munby's diaries from the 1850s through to the 1870s, point to further examples of middle-class male desire centred on the physical coarseness of working women. Munby was a cultivated lawyer and civil servant, working for the Ecclesiastical Commission in Whitehall. A social investigator and lecturer, he established a cross-class liaison with Hannah Cullwick, a Shropshire servant, in the 1850s. Central to Munby's experience of the relationship was a form of sexual desire structured around the cultural polarities of class. Here is Munby's description of Hannah when she was working as a servant in a Margate boarding house in the early 1860s:

> I presently see a figure approaching from a hundred yards off, up the middle of the street: a tall young woman, in a close white cap, and a short frock of lilac cotton, and coarse sack-cloth apron, and strong boots. Her hair is blown about by the wind, for it is cropped like a charity girl's: her arms are bare servile arms, touched with redness and roughness: she carries a pail in either hand. She is but a servant maid, and one of the lowest kind: yet look at her face, as the light of recognising love spreads over it.[60]

Munby's codes of observation drew on the protocols of official inquiry, with which he was personally familiar from his studies of Wigan colliery girls. Hannah was a thing to be explored, dissected through detailed empirical investigation. But, like Symons' case-studies, the male gaze was eroticized through the cultural distance between observer and observed, exemplified in Munby's fascination with the emblems of Hannah's working-class physiognomy.

We should be cautious in building too many general conclusions from these specific cases. But they do point to the complex inter-relation between official discourses and the domain of constructed personal experience and pleasure. All examples reveal a link between the growing polarization of official definitions of female sexuality and the sexualization of those representations in the fantasies of certain groups of men. It is possible that what we are dealing with here is the experience of sections of the professional gentry, though it was not confined to that group alone. What is clear is that such private desires were not sealed off from the world of public representations. These forms of sexuality were dependent on specific codes and rituals to give them meaning.

5   THE REPEAL CAMPAIGN AND THE COLLAPSE OF THE MEDICO-MORAL ALLIANCE

The expansionism of preventive medicine was severely checked by the political opposition provoked by the Contagious Diseases Acts, resulting in their suspension in 1883 and their final repeal three years later. Recent feminist historians have insisted that the repeal struggle needs to be seen not just as one of the single-issue campaigns which characterized the reform politics of radical liberalism, but as a landmark in the history of the nineteenth-century women's movement and in the development of a feminist politics of sexuality.[61] In terms of our longer history of medico-moral politics the battle over the legislation certainly marked a watershed in mid-Victorian social reform. The combined forces of opposition ruptured the earlier environmentalist consensus, making opponents out of former allies, staking out a new regime of sexual regulation and defining sexuality as a crucial site for feminist intervention. The consequences for state medicine were far-reaching and profound.

How did the women and men of the repeal movement contest the discourses of medical expertise and military authority which underpinned the acts? What languages did they draw on to fracture the earlier consensus and what historical forces ennabled them to orchestrate their campaign as a national protest? Such questions are important because they probe the conditions under which political and cultural resistance is generated. Movements of struggle are rarely spontaneous eruptions from below. Their forms of organization are partly structured by the dominant network of power and authority and they are dependent on specific languages to endow their protests with meaning.

Medical efforts to extend the acts first provoked organized opposition at the Social Science Congress at Bristol in October 1869. The newly founded National Anti-Contagious Diseases Acts Association excluded women from its first meeting. Though the association was quick to change its policy, women, led by Josephine Butler, broke away to form the separatist Ladies' National Association (LNA).[62] Almost immediately, the Ladies' Association issued a strongly worded protest in *The Daily News*, signed by prominent figures like Harriet Martineau and Florence Nightingale, claiming that the acts were not only an attack on the civil liberties of all women but also implicated the state in sanctioning male vice. This women's protest was received with expressions of outrage and puzzlement by men within the dominant political culture. One MP confided to Butler that her manifesto had shaken the house very badly. Politicians, he confessed, knew how to manage organized opposition, 'but this is very awkward for us – this revolt of the women. It is quite a new thing; what can we do with such an opposition as this?'[63]

The women in the repeal movement encountered not only the power and outright misogyny of medical and military chiefs but also the restrictive codes of parliamentary politics, which defined the issues touched on by the acts as indecent and immoral. Divorce, prostitution and women's emancipation were designated as outside the parameters of political discourse, and MPs customarily prefaced speeches on these topics by apologizing to the house for intruding on parliamentary time. Discussion of immorality was particularly problematic, given the strongly held belief that to name it and put it into discourse was a dangerous incitement to further acts of depravity. As early as the 1836 debate on divorce bills, proceedings had been referred to select committee 'to obviate the necessity

of painful and disgusting exhibitions at the bar of the House
. . . calculated to excite feelings of shame and disgust', which
were 'grossly indecent in their character'.[64] Repealers were
forced to adopt similar tactics. In the Commons' debate on the
Contagious Diseases Acts Repeal Bill, 1873, Henry Fowler, the
proposer, prefaced his speech with the usual apology for intruding on members' time with so disgusting a subject.[65]

This parliamentary etiquette was much more than mere
expression of 'Victorian prurience'. The moralization of public
life, under pressure from evangelicals, was producing a new
language of politics and an insistence that men holding public
office should outwardly subscribe to respectable standards of
personal conduct. Prior to the 1830s, personal morality had not
been seen as necessary for political eminence. Sexual intrigues
were almost part of the culture of high politics, and were
commonplace in big Whig and Tory families in the early
nineteenth century. Lord Palmerston was a notorious rake,
having had a long-standing affair with Lady Cowper, whom he
finally married in the late 1830s. The evangelical Lord Ashley
viewed the prospect of marrying into such a family with
trepidation, particularly as it was rumoured that his bride-to-be
was the illegitimate daughter of Palmerston and Lady
Cowper.[66]

Already by the 1830s these aristocratic codes of libertinism
were beginning to be challenged, both by organized evangelical
pressure groups and by the structural shift in the overall
balance of power in favour of the middle-classes. The result was
not so much the realization of Ashley's vision of national
regeneration but a growing acceptance by those holding high
office of the need to subscribe *publicly* to an upright moral
code. At the level of parliamentary discourse the net effect was a
gradual transformation of the field of the political. This involved the crystallization of a grammar of politics which defined a whole range of sexual and moral issues as apocryphal,
irregular and outside the codes of gentlemanly conduct and
civilized political debate.

Repealers quickly grasped that this parliamentary language
surrounding prostitution and venereal disease increased their
difficulties in launching an effective campaign. Thomas Biggs,
in his address to the Social Science Association in 1870, com-

plained that such a 'painful . . . topic is not considered a proper theme for discussion . . . by the great majority of the House of Commons'.[67] In their campaign to rupture parliamentary discretion and medical hegemony, the women and men of the repeal movement drew on the only vocabulary able to bear the moral and intellectual weight of their challenge. This was the militant language of radical dissenting religion. Many other languages fed into the movement and made significant contributions: the secular discourse of anti-statism and personal rights, the tactics of pressure group politics, even the heavily patriarchal morality of the newly enfranchised labour aristocrats in the industrial north. But religious language not only provided a link between different political constituencies, it offered a set of concepts, a rhetoric of resistance and a strength of moral certainty powerful enough to take on the weight of the medical and political establishment. Even more importantly, it supplied many mid-Victorian feminists with a critical perspective on existing social relations. If the growing power of the medical profession was in part derived from the certainty and coherence of its discourse, then the success of repeal opposition was dependent on the mobilization of an alternative language capable of challenging professional power and expertise.

Repealers launched a double-edged assault on medics. One strategy involved tackling the profession on its own terms, refuting statistics and medical claims that the acts led to improvements in morality and public order through a mass of published tracts and pamphlets.[68] The other approach worked with a scathing moral and religious attack on the concepts of hygiene and sanitation embedded in the legislation. For James Stansfield, a prominent repealer, the critique of regulationism was founded on the belief that 'humanity is governed by a providential law which can only come from one source'.[69] A sanitary code which sought to evade fundamental moral principles could never ultimately succeed. Acts which contravened moral law were 'calculated to degrade and debase the manhood and womanhood of this country', entangling them 'in the meshes of its wide and sweeping net'.[70] At the International Congress of Geneva, 1877, attended by Butler and other women repealers, delegates avowed that the hygienic principles governing sexual conduct needed to be steeped in the highest personal morality. The indispensable basis of the health of individuals and nations was 'self-control in the relations between the sexes'.[71] Public health could not be restricted to the surveillance and prevention of specific maladies. Nor, it was argued, could medics pursue a mere blind materialism, for the absorbing devotion to material progress, without the subordination of that pursuit to the highest interests of humanity, had generated a crisis of the utmost gravity for morality. The profession's eagerness for scientific advance had impaled it on the horns of a dilemma, forcing an unnatural choice between science and morality.[72]

Repealers scored a notable success when Simon, in his annual report of 1868, came out against any extension of the acts.[73] As a Christian moralist Simon could not tolerate the seemingly deliberate flouting of principle by the extensionist lobby. He emphasized that respectable ratepayers would object to contributing to the cost of giving artificial security to their neighbours' looseness of life. Moreover, since venereal disease was contracted by a man at his own risk he could not claim protection from the medical arm of the state. The real priority was a greater stress on moral responsibility in the education of the sons of the upper class. More than anything else, Simon's report put an end to any immediate prospect of the acts being extended to civilian towns.

The pervasive influence of a combative religious morality was evident not only in the repealers' language but in the common culture which bound many of them together. Though the group which dominated the executive board of the National Association tended to be drawn from the secularist, radical circles of the metropolis, the women and men who effectively led the repeal movement came from the same provincial backgrounds which sustained many other mid-century reform groups. Living in the northern cities, they had a deep commitment to the radical wing of the Liberal Party and were overwhelmingly nonconformist in religion. More specifically, it was the radical and fundamentalist sects in the dissenting tradition (Quakers, Unitarians and Congregationalists), with their long-standing opposition to the power of the established church and their vigorous anti-statism, which produced the majority of leaders.

Mary Priestman and Margaret Tanner, prominent in the LNA, were strict Quakers, in touch with reforming politics via their elder sister's marriage to the Quaker politician John Bright. Butler herself had rather different origins. Aristocratically connected, she came from a Northumberland background of prominent agricultural landowners with strong Liberal and reforming links. Though an Anglican, she was very much an adherent of the evangelical, low church wing of her religion. Many of the men had direct connections with northern industrial capital. Stansfield, one of the few prominent radicals in Gladstone's cabinet of the early 1870s, was from a Unitarian brewing family. Henry Wilson from Sheffield typified the northern male repealer. A self-made industrialist, with capital in smelting and spinning, both he and his wife Charlotte were Congregationalists, involved in the anti-slavery and temperance movements. Elected to Parliament in 1885, Wilson was able to bring pressure to bear on the Liberal Party, both for repeal and for a wider programme of moral reform and social disciplining.

In their private lives, many of the repealers sought to live out the ideal of companionate marriage. This was seen as an equal union between husband and wife, founded on a strong sense of religious purpose and cemented by the power of human love. Butler described her marriage as 'a perfectly equal union with absolute freedom on both sides for personal initiative in thought and action'. Her husband, the Rev. George Butler, understood it as a true reflection of divine love.[74] The Wilsons' daughter, Helen, testified to a similar if more patriarchal version of the same model in her own parents' marriage.[75]

Repealers were at pains to stress the immense cultural distance which separated them from their opponents; they positioned themselves as wholly outside the political and military élite which upheld the acts. For Butler, medics were always 'those terrible aristocratic doctors' who violated women and were destroying English civil liberties.[76] In fact, the lines of demarcation between the two camps were much less distinct. Many repealers and regulationists shared a common culture and held similar positions on class and social behaviour – one of the characteristics of mid-Victorian consensus politics. Throughout the 1860s feminists like Martineau and Elizabeth

Wolstenholme worked together with their future antagonists in the Social Science Association. The repeal campaign effectively heralded a deep split within the medico-moral consensus over the regulation of sexuality, fracturing the earlier discourse of sanitary interventionism. But in class terms it marked a split *within* the ruling bloc, not the totalizing rupture from without that repealers claimed. The growth of the middle-class women's movement was central to this break in ruling alliances.

6   RELIGION, MORALITY AND REPEAL FEMINISM

Butler, in her retrospective account of the repeal campaign, insisted that the movement had been characterized less as 'the revolt of a sex' than by 'the depth and sincerity of the moral and religious convictions of the mass of the population'.[77] Her analysis may have been inflected by the upsurge of a new wave of militant feminism in the early twentieth century from which she felt distanced. For in looking back she underplayed the impact of feminist discourses on the repeal struggle.

The use of the term feminism here requires explanation. In a strict linguistic sense the concept is anachronistic, since it was not referenced in England until the 1890s. Yet the majority of women repealers clearly identified, if not with feminism, then with a body of ideas and aspirations variously known as the woman question, the emancipation of women, the rights of women and so on. This points to the existence of a distinctive women's politics and culture prior to the entry of the term feminism into linguistic usage.

But Butler was correct in her insistence that moral and religious conviction was central to the repeal campaign. Moral and feminist discourses were absolutely inseparable. Religious language provided women with a powerful critique of male sexuality, a language of outrage which gave them their means of representation into the male world of public political debate. This was not the first time feminists had mobilized politically around religion, both to mount a searching critique of patriarchal society and to envisage more egalitarian forms of social organization. Barbara Taylor has shown how women within the Owenite socialist movement in the 1830s and 1840s had struggled to advance a feminist politics through the language of radical religion.[78]

In a related way, the religious morality of repealers was not merely a passive vehicle for feminist politics; it actively empowered women and gave them the confidence to develop critical concepts. As Butler herself pointed out in language resonant with evangelical fervour, men:

> had had the opportunity for many years of looking at the question in its material phases, of appreciating its hygienic results. . . . *Now*, for the first time . . . they are asked to look upon it as a question of human nature, of equal interest to men and women, as a question of the heart, the soul, the affections, the whole moral being. As a simple assertion of one woman speaking for tens of thousands of women, those two words *we rebel* are very necessary. . . . The cry of women crushed under the yoke of legalized vice is not the cry of a statistician or a medical expert; it is simply a cry of pain, a cry for justice and for a return to God's laws in place of these brutally impure laws invented and imposed by men. . . . The slave now speaks. The enslaved women have found a voice in one of themselves. . . . It is the voice of a woman who has suffered, a voice calling to holy rebellion and to war.[79]

Here biblical images of 'rebellion' and 'holy war' were fused with recent experiences of anti-slavery and republican struggle to forge a discourse of political representation for women – the enslaved women who had found a voice, a point of identification in one of themselves. In passages such as this it is not only the content which is important (the attack on organized vice and male expertise) but the language through which the ideas are expressed. The two are inseparable; the critical concepts are very much a function of the language.

The LNA launched a dual offensive, attacking both the medical profession and the double-standard on which the acts were premised: 'the false idea that there is one code of morality for men and another for women . . . which has more or less coloured and shaped the whole of our social life.'[80] Feminists isolated male sexuality as the target for reforming intervention, in the interests of creating a higher standard of purity among men. According to the Social Purity Alliance, founded in 1873, male vice lay at the heart of the problem of immorality. The 'new and final solution' to this evil was to lay moral responsibility and obligation on men, every other method being 'fatally incomplete'.[81] Many women believed that these reforms involved transforming the whole tenor of English public life and creating an ethical and moral climate founded on the teachings of religion. Here feminists drew heavily on the evangelical stress on marriage and the family as the foundation of upright national government. They foregrounded the importance of women for national regeneration, thus forcing a connection between public and private and breaking open the separate spheres ideology. Often their attack was tempered by an anti-capitalist critique. As Mary Hume-Rothery put it in her letter to Gladstone's Liberal government in 1870, men and women had to be raised above the grovelling materialism of handsome houses, slothful ease and sensual indulgence.[82] Only by emphasizing the sanctity of domestic life and the ultimately spiritual nature of the marriage union would national morality be re-made in the image of the Maker.

It was through the use of tactics such as these that the leaders of the LNA sought to shift the representations of sexuality which had been crystallized by the medical profession and their sanitary supporters. Feminists campaigned to disrupt the gender-specific equation of active female sexuality with vice, filth and animality. The prostitute was not the source of contagion and moral corruption, but the upper-class male, backed by 'the medical lust of handling and dominating women'.[83] As a political strategy it was highly effective, successfully confronting the medical discourse which lay behind regulation. But this judicious shift of definitions carried its own problems. Middle-class women consolidated their feminism through a moral politics which implicitly reinforced the polarized representations of male and female sexuality, albeit in a reversed form. Repealers tended to view sex not merely as male-defined but *as male*, while women were promoted as the agents regulating immorality – powerful bu asexual guardians of the nation's morals. The political and social tensions thrown up by this strategy became visible in the plans for the rescue and reform of prostitutes which feminists put forward as their alternative to regulation. Such tensions had their genesis in the class and gender contradictions inherent to mid-Victorian feminism.

7   WOMEN AND SOCIAL DISCIPLINING

Repeal feminists justified their entry into the political arena on the grounds that the issues raised by the acts touched on all the great trusts of their womanhood – the questions of virtue, purity, decency and social welfare. They insisted that these issues were of paramount importance to all women because they were fundamental to marriage and the family and to its valid extension in female charity work and social reform. In arguing their case the LNA were clearly drawing on those traditions of philanthropy which emphasized the central role of women in the reform of moral conditions. Nowhere more than in the repeal movement was the link between philanthropic work and an emergent feminist discourse more clearly visible.

Many of the women repealers had a history of involvement in the type of philanthropy and social reform which we have already observed in Ellen Ranyard's bible missions. Elizabeth Kell, wife of a Unitarian minister in Southampton, and Mrs Hampson of Plymouth were both extensively concerned with work among the poor.[84] Butler had also thrown herself into similar work in Liverpool in the 1860s, setting up an industrial home for working-class girls. Her account of her first visit to the oakum sheds of the workhouse must have been typical of the experience of many women from her background. Desolate from the death of her infant daughter, with her husband immersed in his career as principal of Liverpool College, she 'became possessed with an irresistible desire to go forth and find some pain keener than my own:

It was not difficult to find misery in Liverpool. . . . I went down to the oakum sheds and begged admission. I was taken into an immense gloomy vault filled with women and girls – more than two hundred probably at that time. I sat on the floor among them and picked oakum. They laughed at me and told me my fingers were no use for that work, which was true. But while we laughed we became friends. I recalled that they should learn a few verses to say to me on my next visit. I recollect a tall, dark, handsome girl standing up in our midst, among the damp refuse and the lumps of tarred rope, and repeating without mistake in a not unmusical voice, clear and ringing, the wonderful 14th Chapter of St John's Gospel – the words of Jesus all through . . . she had seated herself and they listened in perfect silence, this audience – wretched, ignorant, criminal some, wild and defiant others. The tall, dark-haired girl had prepared the way for me, and I said 'Now let us all kneel, and cry to that same Jesus who spoke those words,' and down on their knees they fell every one of them, reverently, on that damp stone floor, some saying the words after me, others moaning and weeping. It was a strange sound, that united wail – continuous, pitiful, strong – like a great sigh or murmur of vague desire and hope issuing from the heart of despair, piercing the gloom and murky atmosphere of that vaulted room, and reaching to the heart of God.[85]

This remarkably self-conscious passage captures many of the contradictions present in middle-class women's involvement in rescue work. Here were not only class tensions and antagonisms but also the yearning – 'that united wail' – for a different form of social relations which would link all women. As always, this visionary, pre-figurative language was religious in tone and content. For Butler evangelical religion, working in the world as practical Christianity, was the means of forging a common bond with outcast women which would transcend class differences. Like Ranyard she consistently argued that the personal, cross-class, woman-to-woman dialogue espoused by philanthropy promoted reform where state-centred initiatives had failed.[86] The feminist repeal movement was highly successful in challenging the gendered power relations inscribed within medical interventionism. Its success checked sanitary dominance and set the tone of moral regulation for at least a generation. Many women used the campaign as a means of deepening feminist consciousness and as a platform for launching a wider programme of demands. Mary Hume-Rothery, for example, stressed that the sexual oppression of poor women brought to light by the acts was all the more reason to give women the vote and extend their educational provision, so that they could exercise formal political power.[87]

Nevertheless, much repeal work still displayed the ambiguities which had always marked middle-class women's participation in the domain of social reform. Temperance-style mass meetings, schemes for moral reclamation and placing prostitutes in domestic service, the setting up of rescue homes – these were all part of the feminist alternative to medical regulation. Elizabeth Kell made it clear in her evidence to the 1871 Royal Commission that she believed only 'moral measures', carried out by 'voluntary effort' rather than the state, could achieve lasting reform.[88] She countered medical arguments that repealers were not concerned with remedial measures by outlining her own moralizing schemes for reclaiming prostitutes in Southampton. The point was reiterated by F.C. Banks, secretary of the National Association, amid efforts to revive the flagging campaign in Plymouth in 1876. It was a deliberate lie on the part of regulationists to accuse repealers of having no desire to rescue women from prostitution. Since 1870, Banks insisted, the association had had an office in the town devoted exclusively to the rescue of women and children.[89] The following year, Plymouth and Devonport branches produced an enthusiastic review of their reclamation work in the association's national journal, *The Shield*. The glowing survey read like a standard report from a charity organization:

> Out of the eighty cases, thirty three have been dealt with in the following manner – 23 sent to Homes in Plymouth and London; 1 sent to service in London, where she is doing well, 5 married and doing well; 2 returned to their parents; 1 provided with employment as a machinist and doing well; 1 with children sent to the workhouse.[90]

Male repealers in Plymouth, like Banks, heartily warmed to

the growing focus on reclamation within the movement. In the hands of many such men, 'rescue' meant a punitive and puritanical regime which reinforced the status of prostitutes as fallen women, though the ostensible aim was rehabilitation. This traditionalist stress also received strong support at a rank and file level within the feminist LNA. Alice Berwicke, visiting Plymouth for the association in 1881, found reclamation and educational work in full swing in the local branch. Berwicke like many leading women repealers, found the work disturbing and felt that what was needed was a revival of the repealers' message of anti-statism and personal liberty.[91] Nevertheless, she joined enthusiastically in traditional debates on the moral effects of overcrowding, and the relation between lack of cleanliness and the growing local trade in child prostitution among the poor.[92]

Feminists' commitment to moral improvement and environmental reform had a direct influence on their image of the prostitute. They tended to stress that these women were the hapless, passive victims of debauched aristocrats and manipulative medics, who were eager to be reformed given the necessary moral intervention from without. Rescue and reclamation could restore the prostitute to her 'pre-fallen' state of virtuous morality and asexual purity. Repealers were particularly intolerant of unreformed and unrepentant women, adopting a punitive attitude towards them and explaining their resistance as a product of the demoralizing effects of forced medical inspection. Kell testified that prostitutes in inspected towns were 'vain girls' under no restraint and lacking any sense of innate morality. They were indolent and addicted to a life of pleasure: 'They get up at any hour they choose, and go out and amuse themselves.'[93] Feminist debates over prostitution contained no positive representations of active female sexuality, either for prostitutes or for women in general. Members of the LNA were themselves caught in the powerful polarizations of female behaviour embodied in official discourse and lacked a language to articulate alternative representations. It was felt that married women like Butler should lead the movement, because her status as wife and mother gave her more authority to speak about the delicate issue of sexuality. Single women – and there were many among the repealers – occupied a more ambiguous position.

II The sanitary principle in dominance 1860–80

Feminists were not opposed to reforming intervention per se. What they contested was the presumption that moral reform could be achieved through a centralized programme of sanitary intervention which reinforced the sexual oppression of women. Their struggle was over precisely how sexuality was to be regulated and who was to co-ordinate regulation; sanitary surveillance of prostitution through state medicine *or* moral reform through private philanthropy and rescue work. The campaign over the contagious diseases legislation aggravated and made explicit the tensions between male and female hierarchies of expertise which had been present in the alliance between medics and lady philanthropists from the 1850s.

Butler took up precisely this issue in her introduction to *Women's Work and Women's Culture*, 1869. She argued that contemporary social reform was becoming too institutionalized and bureaucratic; the present tendency was towards 'centralization of rule, to vast combinations, large institutions and uniformity of system'.[94] What this harsh and regimented scheme urgently needed was the integration of feminine and domestic influences, setting free 'feminine powers into Workhouses, Hospitals, Schools, Orphanages, Lunatic Asylums, Reformatories and even Prisons'.[95] Her insistence on the importance of middle-class women's participation in social disciplining was clearly an attempt to guard against their displacement by the growing authority of state sanctioned professionals in the mid-Victorian period. The struggles over the Contagious Diseases Acts need to be read both as a feminist challenge to male power *and* as a battle within the power bloc over the disciplining of the working-class. It is only by locating repeal feminism in the broader history of moral environmentalism that we can begin to understand the more obvious class and gender contradictions which surfaced in the politics of the social purity movements in the 1880s and 1890s. It is to these struggles that we now turn.

PART THREE

FROM STATE MEDICINE TO CRIMINAL LAW. PURITY, FEMINISM AND THE STATE 1880–1914

1   PROLOGUE

In July 1885 the Salvation Army launched a nationwide purity campaign.[1] In less than three weeks the army gathered nearly four thousand signatures for a petition demanding a new criminal law amendment act, raising the age of consent to eighteen and giving the police increased powers to search and arrest brothel-keepers. The monster document, nearly two-and-a-half miles long, was drawn in a waggon to the House of Commons by cadets from the Clapham training home. Over the cart was a white canopy bearing the inscription: 'In the name of the people and the Queen, mother of the country, the Salvation Army demand that iniquity shall cease.' Behind the cadets marched three hundred uniformed women soldiers of the army. The whole line of the route, through the working-class districts of Hackney, Shoreditch and Bishopsgate, was filled with crowds. At Whitehall the petition was unloaded and carried on the shoulders of eight officers into the Commons.

This dramatic demonstration was part of a series of campaigns and rallies which took place in the summer of 1885, as an immediate response to the revelations by the *Pall Mall Gazette* of the horrors of juvenile prostitution. The new popular press played a crucial role in orchestrating public opinion over the affair. In early June W.T. Stead, the paper's editor, had published 'The Maiden Tribute of Modern Babylon'.[2] Drawing on polarized representations of the passive, innocent child-victim and the debauched male client (the stock-in-trade of much popular literature), Stead's articles exposed the underlying depravity in aristocratic and fashionable London society. His sexual script employed the language of moral outrage both to fuel growing demands for law reform and to present a lurid, titillating account of the prostitution trade.

This exposé and the Salvation Army spectacle were symptomatic of a carefully organized campaign by purity workers and feminists to press the Liberal government to pass the Criminal Law Amendment Bill, which had been before Parliament since 1883. After the Maiden Tribute scandal Josephine Butler convened a special meeting with Mrs Bramwell Booth of the Salvation Army and Ellice Hopkins, a prominent member of the new purity movement, to discuss tactics. Protests culminated in a mass rally in St James Hall on 21 August, followed by an open-air meeting next day which drew over a quarter of a million people. Support came from a broad coalition of clergymen, prominent liberals, purists, feminists, trade-union leaders and some socialists. Stead waxed lyrical, envisaging a new moral order of the 'forces of Democracy and Socialism', which would abolish the 'immolation of the daughters of the people as a sacrifice to the vices of the rich'.[3] The outcome was the formation of the National Vigilance Association (NVA), whose membership included leaders of women's organizations and prominent feminists. The constitution of the association contained a strong commitment to feminist demands for the reform of male sexuality, together with a coercive policy of sexual regulation. The traditional stress on preventive and rescue work was now twinned with an emphasis on *legislation* to outlaw obscenity, indecency and the foreign traffic in young girls. Intent on winning working-class support, in October the NVA launched a nationwide crusade throughout the industrial centres of England and Scotland.[4]

The purity movement's stress on the criminal law to promote morality marked an important shift away from traditional strategies of environmental reform and private philanthropy. The NVA saw the criminal law as an instrument for improving public morals – positively educative rather than simply repressive, to be used in conjunction with preventive work. William Coote, the association's secretary, believed that the law was 'schoolmaster to the whole community'. Legislation was the best reflex of public opinion, the real moral themometer of the country.[5] This was a quite new perception of the state's capacity for transforming sexual and moral behaviour. In the thirty years before the First War purists and feminists consistently argued that criminal law legislation was the key to improving the nation's morals. As Coote himself never tired of pointing out:

III From state medicine to criminal law 1880–1914

> There is a very popular cant phrase that you cannot make
> men good by Act of Parliament. It is false to say so. . . .
> You can, and do, keep men sober simply by an Act of
> Parliament; you can, and do, chain the devil of impurity in
> a large number of men and women by the fear of the law.[6]

The 1885 Criminal Law Amendment Act signalled a new, more
coercive system of state intervention into the domain of sexuality. Subsequent legislation followed the same pattern, extending legal control over familiar areas such as indecency, prostitution and brothel-keeping and creating new offences around
male homosexuality and incest.[7]

In an immediate sense, purity campaigns for more stringent
legislation coincided with the renewed official panic over the
urban poor in the 1880s. Worsening economic conditions, the
growth of the new socialist and trade-union movements,
together with the perceived failure of traditional programmes of
philanthropy, all contributed to widespread alarm in official
circles about the immorality of the unrespectable poor, or 'the
residuum'.[8] As in the 1830s and 1840s the discourse of social
investigation, circulated by novelists and journalists, social
scientists and government commissioners, represented
working-class immorality as a major source of anxiety.[9] Lurid
semi-fictional accounts by James Greenwood, George Sim and
Jack London alluded darkly to acts of debauchery not fit even
for the pages of *The Lancet*. *The Bitter Cry of Outcast London*,
written in 1883 by Andrew Mearns, Congregationalist minister
in Chelsea, exposed a vast mass of moral corruption and
absolute godlessness at the centre of the greatest metropolis in
the world.[10]

The most extensive moral survey was contained in the *Report
of the Royal Commission on the Housing of the Working Classes*,
1884. Incest, as the rector of Christchurch, Spitalfields, be-
moaned, was the direct result of overcrowding. The one-room
system encouraged children to be sexually precocious, so that
they found out everything about physical matters from their
home experience.[11] In the familiar language of environmentalism, Mearns demonstrated that overcrowding spread the infection of immorality from the dissolute to honest and upright
working-class families.[12] Purity demands for legislation against

prostitution, brothel-keeping and other acts of immorality often explicitly addressed problems posed by the culture of the urban poor and the difficulties of keeping public order on the streets. Agitation may have been couched in a vocabulary which spoke of *national* morality, but it was clear who were being singled out as the recipients of purity action.

Yet one grouping was conspicuously absent from these campaigns. The medical profession did not contribute to the new crusades nor was there any resurrection of the medico-moral alliance. The balance of forces around sexuality had definitely shifted. Sanitary science and state medicine were now in partial eclipse.

2   THE ECLIPSE OF STATE MEDICINE

The repeal of the Contagious Diseases Acts marked a severe defeat for the medical profession. It was a defeat which was to have profound and far-reaching consequences for state medical regulation of sexuality. Though *The Lancet* and the *BMJ* fought a rearguard action right up to the moment of final repeal, it was obvious that the sanitary principle had been successfully challenged by moralists.[13] By their action, the women and men of the repeal movement had effectively re-defined the terms of the debate over sex. This defeat was itself part of the wider eclipse of state medicine in the 1870s and 1880s, which opened the space for purity groups to push for their own conception of sexual reform through the criminal law.

The initial setbacks came as part of the local government reforms of the early 1870s. As Simon himself acknowledged, English public health administration had developed in a piecemeal and ad hoc fashion for much of the early nineteenth century, with national supervision divided between his own Privy Council Medical Office and the Poor Law Board. Under the Local Government Act, 1871 the two departments were amalgamated to form the new Local Government Board.[14]

But the new act created more political problems than it solved. The old Poor Law Board and the Medical Office had developed highly distinctive forms of administration which were fundamentally conflictual in terms of aims and professional practice. Both departments were heir to the Chadwickian and Benthamite politics of the 1830s but each had crystallized a specific mode of social intervention. The Medical Department pushed for reform and regulation through the hegemony of state medicine. The Poor Law Office, on the other hand, inheriting the most utilitarian forms of social disciplining, was fundamentally opposed both to medical expertise and to any further large-scale financial outlay in aid of poor relief.

After 1871 the policy of the new Local Government Board was shaped by the poor law tradition, with the ministerial backing of its first president, James Stansfield. Stansfield's own personal antipathy to medical involvement in the contagious diseases acts, together with his ignorance of scientific matters – he knew as much of science as a cow does of conic sections, according to one contemporary – may have exacerbated Simon's problems at the board.[15] What was clear was that the new department was intent on circumscribing medical influence within the state. The battle was fought out as an intense personal rivalry between Simon and the new permanent secretary to the Local Government Board, John Lambert. Lambert was himself a skilled administrator, with a working knowledge of sanitary reform. A member of the 1868 Royal Sanitary Commission and a vigorous promoter of public health as Mayor of Salisbury, he was not fundamentally opposed to state medicine. But he typified a new breed of civil servant. Methodical, precise and administratively cautious, he carried over from his earlier experience as a member of the Poor Law Board a determination to subordinate medical experts to the lay adminsitration. He succeeded in winning Stansfield's confidence and in stamping his personal authority on all areas of the new department, including Simon's, by intercepting correspondence and seizing responsibility for the smallest details of policy.[16] The result was that though Simon and his staff were retained the poor law secretariat began to create an inner circle of administration, relegating medics to the peripheries. After a protracted battle, which raised *The Times* and the whole of the medical establishment against Stansfield and Lambert, Simon resigned as a civil servant in 1876, but the overall situation remained unchanged.

Like the contagious diseases defeat, Simon's resignation was received as a serious blow by the medical profession.[17] Going beyond the clash of personalities, *The Lancet* probed the underlying causes of this medical decline. It concluded that the Simonian concept of state medicine was far in advance of public opinion and was likely to remain so for some time to come.[18] Such explanations were comforting, if only because they pointed forward to the ultimate vindication of medical science. Yet they obviously failed to grasp the political and administrative realities within which state medicine was increasingly caught in the 1870s and 1880s. The key here lies not with personal rivalries, as administrative historians would have us believe. Much more significant were the conflicting claims of medical expert and lay civil servant over control of social policy, and the shifting relation between politician and bureaucrat in the nineteenth-century state.[19]

Simon outplayed the politicians and Treasury staff with his expansionist policy in the 1860s. However, his action provoked significant comment from Treasury permanent secretaries, committed as they were to a Gladstonian ideology of 'cheap government' and to the subordination of the extravagant missionary zeal of medical reformers. When Simon pressed and won his claim for an assistant inspector to supervise the national vaccination scheme in 1871, the current permanent secretary, Ralph Lingen, issued a general warning in the accompanying minute: 'I do not know who is to check the assertion of experts when the government has once undertaken a class of duties which none but such persons understand.'[20] Lingen typified the new breed of generalist civil servant. Arts-based and classically trained, he was convinced that professional experts of Simon's calibre did not conform to the new conception of the broad-based administrator. For Lingen, state medics represented a clear political force in their right, rather than the steady, methodical cadre of intellectuals envisaged by the Northcote-Trevelyan reforms of the 1850s. With the growing crystallization of powers within the state from the 1860s, the reform of the civil service and the abandonment of political appointments, Simon's cunning politicking now seemed out of place. Further, the growth of a discourse of formal political representation and its implementation in the 1867 Reform Act, made politicians uneasy about the political power wielded by civil servants, especially when they operated as statesmen in disguise.

The rise of the purity movement in the 1880s needs to be seen in relation to these medical defeats, for state medicine had lost the initiative not only in the field of sexual regulation but in many other areas of social intervention. Under Simon's successors the medical officership was a much more limited project than previously. Certainly there was no attempt to resurrect the grandiose principles of sexual and sanitary hygiene. On the issue of central health policy the annual medical reports from the Local Government Board were muted in the extreme.[21] Apart from the important field of theoretical research into the causes and treatment of epidemic disease, the influence of the department was severely curtailed. According to Sir George Buchanan, Medical Officer between 1879 and 1892, the current conception of state medicine was but a pale shadow of what it once was.[22]

In the closing decades of the nineteenth century it was moralists and feminists who set the pace in the field of sexual politics. Their campaigns for legal enforcement were backed by a powerful language which identified whole new technologies of sex and forged them into a popular crusade for reform. This broad coalition of forces was central to the enactment of criminal law legislation; organizing, investigating, petitioning the state to act. Government itself was rarely the active initiator in the move to criminalize immorality. Hence we now move substantially away from the state and its experts to examine these voluntary movements and popular struggles.

3   PURITY AND SCIENCE

The language of purity demonstrates how popular scientific concepts were re-worked to advance a new moralized discourse on sex. It also shows how far state medicine had been checked over sexual regulation. Purity campaigners were not adverse to drawing on science but for them it was a tool to validate morality. True scientific investigation always revealed the workings of divine law, and the medical profession needed to be kept under constant surveillance, because their narrow commitment to materialistic principles overlooked moral considerations. With the experience of the Contagious Diseases Acts in mind, Ellice Hopkins tartly remarked there were 'one or two things which the medical profession has yet to grow out of under the influence of an enlightened public opinion'.[23]

Elizabeth Blackwell's career both as a purist and a medic displayed the new approach to 'Christian physiology'. Blackwell was the first woman doctor, graduating in New York in 1849 and later opening a dispensary on New York's lower east-side. Her origins were similar to those of many leading figures in the repeal movement. She came from a prominent Bristol family of nonconformists and industrialists, where her father had long been active in the abolitionist movement. Broadly committed to Kingsley's brand of Christian socialism, she established the National Health Society in London in 1871, aimed at improving the health of the working classes. In her writings and lectures Blackwell demonstrated a firm belief in the intimate connection between physical and moral health, addressing women on domestic hygiene and on the relation between health and religion.[24] Her book *The Human Element in Sex*, 1884 was adamant that medicine could not become an end in itself but needed to discover the workings of moral law. Sex morality was the area par excellence where medics had to be governed by religious responsibility.[25]

This moral appropriation of scientific discourse was common in the 1870s and 1880s. Darwinism had initially shaken the deistic foundations of contemporary science, fuelling the avowed agnosticism and sense of spiritual crisis experienced by a generation of mid-Victorian intellectuals.[26] Many moralists responded to the challenge less by denying evolutionism than by arguing that the new biological theories could be integrated with older moral concerns. In 1872 the Catholic Archbishop Cardinal Manning announced that the majority of clerics now believed that there was nothing incompatible between evolutionary science and their own theological system.[27] Darwin's own *Descent of Man*, published the previous year, also marshalled evidence to show how the growth of moral faculties like self-control, love and altruism were key elements in progressing towards a higher moral culture.[28]

Purity workers developed their own re-reading of the Darwinist debate, though they placed less stress on integrating the two systems and more on the subordination of science to the dictates of morality. Mothers were to use stories drawn from plant and animal life to instruct children both about the reproductive cycle and the evolutionary progress from lower organisms up to man. All this was presided over by an all-seeing God. For though evolution taught that the human race was linked to plants and animals, it also demonstrated that man was separate from other species: 'a spiritual being, incarnate in an animal body'.[29] According to Blackwell, morality involved the evolution of self-consciousness which had developed only in the human species. The moral faculty needed to govern the sexual instinct, organizing it on 'broad, well-marked mental foundations'.[30] Chastity, continence and self-control were the highest forms of sexual development because they were regulated by reason and a knowledge of the providential laws of human nature.

Yet evolutionary science also pointed to the precariousness of moral progress – how it could so easily slip back into animal chaos. This was the human dilemma. In their efforts to curb immorality purists carefully distanced themselves from a world view totally determined by heredity. They were at pains to prove that moral or immoral development was not fixed or inevitable, for all the evolutionary stress on inherited characteristics. The link between sex and morality needed to be *cultivated* and *worked at*, using every resource of civilization. Animal passion could be refined to become part of the higher stages of evolution, or it could deteriorate into moral evil:

> Sex is capable of great devotion towards good or towards
> evil. . . . It may grow into a noble sympathy, self-sacrifice
> . . . and joy. . . . It also allows that perversion and extreme
> degradation of sex observable in the human race.[31]

Religion coupled with morality could 'alter the evil conditions' and 'cut into the chain which is otherwise endless and circular'.[32] Such insistences provided one important rationale for the criminal law approach to sexual reform. Criminalizing legislation was not simply respressive, it was in Coote's phrase 'positively educative and improving'.

4   PURITY AND POPULISM

Purity was a self-consciously popular movement in a way that even the repeal campaign had not been. This was evident not only in its mass organization, but also in the efforts to address working-class audiences and write them into the discourse of moral reform. In that sense purity marks a distinctive break with the earlier sanitary approach to sexual regulation which had been dominated by the élite voice of professional experts. It needs to be seen as part of the renewed offensive launched by militant evangelicalism in the 1880s, which influenced a whole range of single issue campaigns and brought pressure to bear on the Liberal Party hierarchy.

A loose network of campaigning groups formed the base of the new purity movement, with large-scale meetings and the mass publication of tracts and pamphlets. Speeches were often followed by the distribution of membership or pledge cards, when audiences were encouraged to declare their personal adherence to the rules of the movement. Dramatic cases of moral conversion and last-minute rescues from the brink of hell-fire were a particular favourite.[33] In practice, teaching the working-class to understand moral law usually meant an Old Testament affirmation of the preordained retribution which followed in the wake of sinfulness. Masturbation was most often used to demonstrate how the transgression of divine law inevitably brought down the wrath of God: 'For he that soweth his flesh, shall of the flesh reap corruption.'[34]

While the working-class was the principal target for purists' interventionary zeal they also provided rank-and-file recruits for the new movement. Some organizations laid primary stress on preventive work and moral re-education, especially among working-class girls: for example the Anglican-run Girls' Friendly Society, founded in 1874, Ellice Hopkins' Ladies' Association for the Care of Friendless Girls, 1876, and the Band of Hope Mission, 1879.[35] Other groups, like the Boys'

League of Honour and the Church Lads' Brigade, addressed the leisure activities of working-class boys, setting up night schools and organizing sport and mutual improvement societies to counter the idleness which was the first step towards dissipation and self-abuse. Lady visitors were also co-opted in campaigns designed to instruct working-class mothers on practical morality in the home, supervising children's play and paying careful attention to the bathing and sleeping arrangements of sons and daughters.[36]

The populism of the movement foregrounded a specific ideology of nationalism and national culture. Demands for the purification of national life were matters of importance which stood above class differences and the petty divisions of party politics. Practically, purity usually worked by forging alliances between sections of the evangelical middle-class, the petty-bourgeoisie and the respectable working-class against the aristocracy. Attacks on the immorality and decadence of aristocratic culture were the staple diet of purity tracts and speeches. They focused popular discontent over the double-standard and the complicity of aristocratic men in child prostitution.[37]

The movement also played off representations of *English* morality against the decadence of foreign habits. The French were a favourite target, and the new popular press was instrumental in crystallizing xenophobic imagery. When Henry Vizetelly was prosecuted in 1888 under the obscenity laws for publishing an English translation of Zola's novel *La Terre*, purists seized the opportunity to mount a sustained assault on the morally pernicious influence of French culture. Complaints in *The Standard* pointed to the rising tide of juvenile depravity caused by the availability of cheap editions of continental literature.[38] The Oscar Wilde trials of 1895 condensed representations both of aristocratic debauchery and the corrupting effects of foreign morals. Wilde, depicted as the leader of the aesthetic movement, with its unnatural taste for the sensual and the erotic, was pilloried in court as a foreign parasite. He was seen to be attacking the moral, manly roots of English public life with the aid of effeminate, aristocratic tastes.[39] *The Evening News* summed up the affair by calling for greater public vigilance to root out the canker of immorality: 'England has tolerated the man Wilde for too long . . . he was a social pest, a centre of intellectual corruption . . . who attacked all whole-some, manly, simple ideals of English life.'[40]

These new codes of popular journalism, investigative exposé combined with sensationalist melodrama, were part of the repertoire of purity campaigns. Stead's crusade against child harlotry or the press onslaught on Wilde were designed to fuel outrage and orchestrate the demand for moral action. But their injunctions did not simply denounce immorality. Purity language was transformed through these journalistic codes to produce highly wrought sexual imagery. Rituals of transgression, sensationalist violation and titillating naughtiness became the stock-in-trade of popular news reporting in the late nineteenth century. The success of this language itself needs to be read in the context of purity's growing hegemony.

5   SPEAKING OUT

In all areas of intervention the first step for purists was to speak out about sex. The aim was to confront the conspiracy of silence and shame which surrounded the subject and create a climate where immorality could be tackled seriously. Caution and silence were contrary to God's law. They were dangerous and hypocritical, providing a fertile breeding-ground for evil. Here purists were deliberately challenging official arguments which opposed fresh legislation or greater public discussion on the grounds that this would only draw attention to sex and incite immorality. In the debates over proposed changes to the criminal law, politicians continued to argue that to speak about sex was to corrupt. In 1903 the Earl of Halsbury, Lord Chancellor, wrecked legislation criminalizing incest with such arguments.[41] In contrast, social purists argued that to speak out was vital. Ignorance was to play into the hands of the enemy; knowledge through education was power:

> It is argued that to speak out on this subject is only to suggest the very evil you want to cure, and to do more harm than good. . . . Let us recognize once and for all that the modest silence . . . has landed England in child harlotry.[42]

III From state medicine to criminal law 1880–1914

Enforced silence was no guarantee of innocence or security. To classify and measure the extent of immorality – to quite literally put it into discourse – was central to getting the problem under control.

The quest for greater knowledge was underpinned by a highly gender-specific discourse on sexuality. Politically this was informed by the demands coming from women's organizations and intellectually by the moralized language of evolutionary science. Images of male sexuality twinned evangelical concepts of the struggle between flesh and spirit with an evolutionary stress on the lower and higher impulses of human nature. Campaigners launched a direct offensive against contemporary medical theories which talked of the inevitability of the male sexual urge, arguing that they failed to take proper account of Darwinist insights. Man's nature was two-sided, only half of it led to wrong-doing, the other half prohibited sin. Purists conceived of masculinity as a never-ending battle, requiring constant watchfulness and careful supervision. The dramatic conflict between good and evil either brought out heroic qualities in boys, or it exposed those who were cowardly and unmanly. In an end-of-term address at Clifton College, Bristol, the Rev. J.M. Wilson presented his students with a dramatic choice: 'It has to be settled whether you are to be your own master or slave; whether your body shall be kept under, and you will be strong enough to rule it; or whether your body shall be the target.'[43]

Muscular Christianity was the hoped-for goal, with self-control to be attained through strict mental and physical discipline. The Purity Alliances's rules for daily life advocated cold baths, regular vigorous exercise, moderation in eating and drinking, as well as prayer to guard against moral evil. Those men leading the movement, like Alfred Dyer and Wilson, projected a chivalric vision of masculinity which championed the ideal of asexual, dependent womanhood. Boys were to be taught their knightly duty to serve their mothers and sisters.[44] Many purity leagues drew on emblems from the legends of Christian chivalry, appealing to men and boys by a play on protective and gallant manhood. In the emblem of The White Cross League, founded in 1883, white stood for purity, the league for disciplined strength and the cross for the underlying truth of the fight for Christ.[45]

The language of purity opened a space for women to define their own images of female sexual identity. Speaking out enabled female purity workers to project a vision of moral femininity, which, though problematic, did address the hopes and aspirations of many women. They pressed for a particular re-reading of Darwin to add weight to the older evangelical claim that women had a rightful place in regulating sex.[46] For Hopkins, as for Blackwell, women's moral power lay in their capacity to harness and control male sexual energy by drawing out the spiritual impulses of human nature. This was guaranteed by women's reproductive role, which put them in contact with the great physical and mental powers of the race. Blackwell glossed reproduction in a highly original way, fusing it with claims for an active female sexuality. Countering medical assertions that sex passion was absent from most normal women, she pointed out that because of reproduction the physical aspect of sex weighed more heavily on them than on men:

> Physical sex is a larger factor in the life of the woman,
> married or unmarried, than in the life of the man. . . .
> Those who deny sexual feeling to women . . . quite lose
> sight of . . . (the) immense spiritual force of attraction
> which exists in so very large a proportion in their nature.[47]

Blackwell insisted that biological reproduction actively contributed to women's higher spiritual self, in contrast to many medics and evolutionary biologists who saw women as closer to nature because of their 'animal' function. In her view, it was bourgeois women who were most oppressed by social definitions of female purity. Taught to believe that sex was shameful, they were denied the spiritual experience of sex passion which involved the transfiguration of the lower by the higher elements.[48] Blackwell's radical ideas point to the tentative beginnings of a discourse on active female sexuality.

As recent research is beginning to uncover, the 1880s witnessed the beginnings of a questioning of current forms of sexual morality from feminist intellectuals – a move which was stimulated by the various public sexual scandals of the decade.

Blackwell herself discussed her ideas at the Men and Women's Club, a progressive middle-class coterie whose membership included Olive Schreiner and the social purist Maria Sharpe.[49] For these women, speaking out often led to a wider debate on sexuality and gender. But for the majority it was *purity* which provided the language both to challenge men's immorality and to stake out their own claim to speak about sex.

6   FEMINISM AND SOCIAL PURITY

In the years from the repeal campaign to the suffrage movement women's struggles were a major force in sexual politics. Women's organizations and feminist leaders emerged as a powerful pressure group whose influence was felt by male politicians and professionals at the level of the state and in public debate. By no means all purists identified with feminism, but the rapid growth of the women's movement in the late nineteenth and early twentieth century cannot be understood without reference to the purity crusades, which drew thousands of women into the political arena for the first time. All this marked a significant break with the earlier history of medico-moral politics. Women were empowered to speak about sex, challenging the authority of the experts and drawing attention to their gendered power relations. Yet as the tensions inherent in the repeal movement have already shown, this feminist discourse was itself caught in hierarchies of power around sex, retaining strong links with the environmentalist regime of social disciplining. Such contradictions were highlighted in women's growing demands for more coercive criminal law legislation.

In the 1880s and 1890s women like Blackwell, Hopkins, Laura Ormiston-Chant, Millicent Fawcett and Mrs Bramwell Booth argued that the law was central to implementing feminist demands. Their protests gained renewed impetus in the suffrage struggles immediately before the First War. They were focused on a massive campaign against the double-standard and its enshrinement in law. The immediate contrast with earlier feminist sexual politics could not have been sharper. For behind the new purity feminism lay the legacy of anti-statist struggle against the Contagious Diseases Acts. As we have seen, repeal feminists had not been opposed to moral disciplining but they had promoted it through the more 'feminine' domain of voluntary agencies, attacking the statist solutions of male professionals. Despite this a number of prominent women repealers, among them Butler herself, sat on the first executive council of the NVA and gave support to coercive state legislation. Admittedly, after the initial euphoria following the passing of the 1885 act, some like Butler began to distance themselves from the purity movement.[50] Nevertheless, many feminists did throw themselves wholeheartedly into the purity campaigns. The political and historical problem is how to understand that involvement.

Recent social and feminist historians who have considered the question have bid for explanation on the back of contemporary allegiances. This moment in the history of sexual politics is fast becoming a battleground for voicing current debates and disagreements. Edward Bristow and Jeffrey Weeks fail to see anything specifically feminist in the purity crusades. For Weeks, the purity movement was only significant as a moment of moral panic over sex, condensing wider social and political anxieties.[51] Judith Walkowitz, on the other hand, acknowledges that the latter stages of the repeal struggle were marked by dramatic contradictions within feminist sexual politics. Tensions submerged in the earlier campaign now came to the fore and led more and more to a coercive policy of sexual regulation, especially of working-class prostitutes.[52] By contrast Sheila Jeffreys' recent account, informed by the politics of revolutionary feminism, stresses that social purity *was* a landmark in the offensive against male sexuality and downplays the contradictions intrinsic to the movement.[53]

What needs re-affirming, and re-examining, is the complex inter-relation between moral languages and the history of nineteenth-century feminism. As we now know, the discourses of practical religion and philanthropy provided women with a means of representation into the male-defined world of public political debate. They also enabled women to challenge male professional power while at the same time implicating them in coercive class regualtion. To write the history of late nineteenth-century feminist sexual politics as a 'seduction' by the conservative purity movement, is to ignore this much longer, contradictory history of women's participation in social reform. These tensions were graphically illustrated in the career of Ellice Hopkins.

7   ELLICE HOPKINS

In February 1883 Ellice Hopkins addressed a mass meeting of working men at the mining village of Bishop Auckland, on the invitation of the Bishop of Durham. After prayers and a stirring speech, purity pledge cards were distributed among the men, listing rules for personal conduct:

1   To treat all women with respect, and endeavour to protect them from wrong and degradation.
2   To use every possible means to fulfil the command, 'keep THYSELF pure.'
3   To endeavour to put down all indecent language and coarse jests.
4   To maintain the law of purity as equally binding upon men and women.
5   To endeavour to spread these principles among my companions, and to try and help my younger brothers.[54]

The meeting was an enormous success. Out of an audience of some three hundred miners and clerks, one hundred and thirty came forward to pledge themselves for purity.

Ellice Hopkins was a central figure in the feminist agitation for criminal law regulation in the 1880s. She was an 'organic intellectual' of the new purity movement. Her rise to prominence was the culmination of a career which combined a feminist commitment to challenging male sexual behaviour, with traditional beliefs in moralizing philanthropy directed at the poor. The daughter of a distinguished Cambridge mathematics tutor, she began work as a Sunday school teacher in the 1850s. In 1860 she turned her attention to the condition of male agricultural workers in the village of Barnwell, near Cambridge. Through her efforts a mission hall was built, where she started to lecture on moral purity. Hopkins always maintained that work with men was her favourite form of campaigning. It posed

119

a challenge both to her religious motivation and her feminist principles. In *An Englishwoman's Work among Workingmen*, 1875 she recounted how the dramatic language of evangelical religion enabled her to press her case:

> But how did I try to get this influence over working men? I will try and reply in some detail. In the first place, it was quite useless to preach ready made doctrine to them. My first effort, therefore, was to get them to believe in moral law. . . . And little by little they came to see the great Christian doctrine that eternal sin must be, in the very nature of things, eternal punishment or eternal misery.[55]

As a populist Hopkins was well aware of the problems facing middle-class reformers in the dialogue with working-class audiences. She warned fellow women workers that it was useless to address workingmen with 'plain commonplaces'; what was needed was vivid and dramatic language: 'the men want strong meat, thoughts as racy as their own expressions; they reject sweet pap fit for children.'[56]

Evangelical religion furnished Hopkins with a powerful rhetoric to arouse mass meetings and personally motivated her to embark on a public career exposing immorality. She represented it quite literally as a call to God's service. On the death of her father in 1866 she suffered physical and mental breakdown, confiding in a letter that it was her religion that held her up. While recuperating in Brighton she plunged into work at the Albion Hill Rescue Home. The job was not easy, and the girls themselves were resistant to her crusading philanthropy. Hopkins saw the need for a revival of the personalized approach to rescue work. Rather than organizing mass midnight meetings to confront the evil in working-class areas she judged it more effective for women to go into the 'dens of infamy' in the morning as friends and advisers. Her efforts sometimes backfired, when she was confronted by a robust culture from the prostitutes themselves.[57]

Her own power and presence as a speaker was perhaps her greatest asset in converting audiences. Many had testified to Josephine Butler's impact on the rostrum. Hopkins had an equally clear awareness of the importance of personal presentation and she worked hard to perfect an appropriate style of public speaking. 'If anyone supposes', she wrote, 'that my power of speaking was a gift that came naturally to me, without any effort on my part, let them once and for all dispossess themselves of any such ideas.'[58] Throughout her career she was subject to a range of nervous disorders. In common with Butler and Florence Nightingale, illness related to the strain experienced by middle-class women who moved into the public sphere. But these women also employed medical definitions of physical and mental weakness as an effective tactical weapon in the battle with men. Hopkins used her frailty, her diminutive size and a 'beautiful speaking voice' as symbols of the power of female purity. She counselled other women to do the same: 'You can make your womanhood a sort of external conscience to them. You can appeal to them never to say or do things which they would be ashamed for you to know.'[59]

All this was done in the face of considerable hostility from her male audiences. On one occasion in the early 1880s she was persuaded to address male students at Edinburgh University medical school. It seems that medics have not changed much over a hundred years. She recalled that many eminent men had declined to give the address because of the expected barracking. Hopkins tamed the students with a characteristic blend of religious fervour and moral conviction:

Spirit and flesh both quailed before so difficult and rowdy an audience on so difficult and perilous a subject . . . as I sat in the committee room while the order of the meeting was being arranged, and heard my audience shouting, singing, crowing like cocks . . . and keeping up a continuous uproar, I thought to myself, 'I have got to go into that and control it somehow so as to be heard'. . . . The only thing was to push me at once to the front; and almost immediately, after a very few brief words from the distinguished chairman, I found myself face to face with an audience that evidently meant mischief. By some instinct I told them . . . about the lost and degraded womanhood of England, the hosts of young girls slain in body and soul . . . met with at night in our terrible streets. This seemed to strike and sober them . . . a thing which to all of them was

121

so familiar, and to many had been only the subject of coarse jest. They listened to me with profound attention, and I could see that my words went home.[60]

It was not only the antagonism of male audiences that Hopkins was up against. The opposition her public career provoked – as a single woman speaking about sexuality – showed that despite the gains made by repeal feminism, women still risked censure and social ostracization when they crossed the boundaries from the private to the public sphere.

Hopkins was clear about the dual strategy of the new purity movement. It needed to focus on the reform of male sexuality *and* the improvement of working-class morals. On both issues she acknowledged the importance of the 'women's movement' in promoting reform, 'the ever increasing activity in all agencies for the elevation of women . . . above all that new sense of a common *esprit de corps* . . . which is now beginning to bind all our efforts together.'[61] For Hopkins as for Blackwell, feminism centrally meant bringing the private sphere of bourgeois womanhood to bear on the public world of social and moral problems. Here again is the connection between feminism and the philanthropic tradition. Women were the 'conscience of the world', social reform concerned women because it touched on 'all the great trusts of womanhood, the sanctity of the family, the purity of marriage, the sacredness of marriage, the sweet innocence of children'.[62] Both argued that women needed to play a decisive role in public debate over the nation's morals, precisely because it was *women* who were centrally concerned with sexuality. Hopkins was militant and uncompromising about the source of moral evil. *Male sexuality* was the fundamental problem. Prostitution was the direct result of men's immorality, creating an outcast class of women tacitly sanctioned by church and state.[63]

Along with many women in the purity movement Hopkins increasingly looked to the criminal law to enact feminist demands. This is the key to understanding purity feminists' commitment to coercive legislation in the 1880s. The law could be used to 'protect' women and children, to educate men into self-control and chastity, and to reform working-class morals. Looking back on these campaigns at the end of her life, she defined the law as the chief agency for enacting God's work and for abolishing the double-standard, which menaced the young and ultimately contributed to the disintegration of the state. Men's immorality not only threatened the stability of the family but in the end posed a danger to the foundations of good government. It was imperative that the state should intervene to preserve the higher life of the nation:

> When shall we learn that whoever touches the higher life
> and well-being of the family still more vitally affects the
> wider family of the State, and threatens its disintegration
> . . . the State as an organized polity, capable of embodying,
> preserving and promoting the higher life of the nation.[64]

In forging this connection between familial morality and the strength of the nation state, Hopkins was drawing on a long-established tradition of moral philosophy dating at least as far back as the late eighteenth century. But the idea that the ethical state had an obligation to protect the weak, to promote actively moral conduct and encourage human evolution was specific to the late nineteenth century. Purity ideas here resembled philosophic conceptions of the ethical and organic state outlined by T.H. Green, and slightly later by theorists like J.A. Hobson and L.T. Hobhouse.[65] For these new liberal thinkers, society was viewed as a biological organism, with state intervention designed to promote healthy functioning of the body politic as an integrated totality.

However, in Hopkins' case the aim of reforming intervention remained the overt regulation of working-class behaviour, especially of working-class women. She stressed that middle-class ladies needed to unite with their poorer sisters if men's immorality was to be effectively challenged. 'Feminism' had to be a movement which cut across class barriers.[66] But the dialogue purists envisaged between women of different classes was still the traditional bond of philanthropy, which linked the middle-class 'donor' to her working-class recipient through notions of moral and material charity. Hopkins appealed to working women in the name of 'the common dignity . . . of our womanhood', but moral responsibility was often seen to be precisely what these women lacked and what middle-class women could give. Contradictions such as these were glaringly apparent in her pleas to working women:

> be sure of this . . . no one class can fight this evil alone. We must all combine together. And if I speak a bit plain . . . just think of me as the woman who gave up everything to save you girls from their worst dangers. . . . Dear sisters there is not one of us ladies . . . who won't tell you that we have learnt our most precious lessons of faith . . . and patience, and self-sacrifice and contentedness under trials from you. But on the other hand, our large houses, our separate bedrooms, our greater education, make us . . . more particular in our ways than you – make us feel the importance of little things, little decent ways, little safeguards, and the little constant watchfulnesses in bringing up our children, which the terrible struggle for existence and the pressure of space but too often make you forget and grow careless about.[67]

Many of the women's purity associations were shot through with similar class divisions. Purists could be utterly ruthless about the menace working-class immorality posed to the middle-class home. Hopkins advised against sending reclaimed prostitutes into domestic service because of the danger to middle-class sons: 'better a thousand times that this fearful social evil should be localized in certain spots, which we call dens, than by our hasty and injudicious benevolence it should be struck into the very bosom of our families.'[68] Middle-class ladies needed to vet prospective female servants; they could so easily be morally defective. Purity workers believed they had an obligation to reclaim their 'fallen' sisters, but the problem of prostitution was always tackled by a mixture of benevolent charity and coercive threat.

These disciplinary aspects of Hopkins' work had already become apparent in the later stages of the repeal struggle. They were particularly visible in the campaigns over the Industrial Schools Amendment Bill. In 1879 she visited repealers in Plymouth to canvass support for the new bill, which proposed that the courts should remove children living in the society of depraved and disorderly persons and place them in industrial schools. The measures became law the following year. They were explicitly aimed at the unrespectable poor, subjecting their children to the full disciplinary regime of the new training schools. The Vigilance Association for the Defence of Personal Rights, a radical anti-statist grouping whose members included some repealers, launched a counter-attack against the new act, complaining that: 'Miss Hopkins . . . is at present . . . crying for the wholesale kidnapping of little girls who may not have perfect domestic surroundings and their consignment to large prison schools.'[69] But Ellice went a stage further; she began to construct alliances with regulationists – especially with the local police chief, Inspector Aniss, *bête noir* of the repealers – who warmed to her clear message of rescue backed by greater control of the streets. Declaring that the local rescue home was far too laxly run, she demanded a stricter system of surveillance. The repeal movement's national leadership, alarmed about Hopkins' activities, wrote warning her against any collusion with the enemy.[70]

At other moments Hopkins, along with many purity feminists, displayed a real awareness of the class contradictions embedded in the new movement. A *Special Report of the Girls' Friendly Society* in 1879 pointed out that middle-class women tended 'to over regulate those women whom we would serve', because they were ignorant of working-class life.[71] Hopkins understood that purity workers needed greater self-awareness of the class power they wielded. Sometimes this consciousness developed into a critique of middle-class morality and economic exploitation. The home happiness, refinement and sheltered grace of middle-class women, she insisted, was bought at the price of other women's toil and suffering. Girls from the upper classes were brought up to believe 'that they were born with a prescriptive right to their social advantages, their graceful culture'.[72]

Hopkins stands very much as representative of the new-style purity feminist. Her biography displays many of the class and gender contradictions which bedevilled women's participation in the purity campaigns of the 1880s. These ambiguities were not merely the result of unfortunate political alliances but of the much longer history of middle-class women's involvement in the field of social regulation. Once again it points to the power of particular historical languages in constructing individuals and shaping their political demands. The moral discourses of purity feminism were neither a reactionary barrier to feminist progress nor were they the simple expression of militant feminist consciousness. They were the battleground on which conflicting aims and intentions struggled for space.

8 PURITY, FEMINISM AND THE RELUCTANT STATE

The tensions in the purity feminist position, and the government's own difficulties in coming to terms with the new movement, surfaced in the debates surrounding the 1885 Criminal Law Amendment Bill. The proposed legislation appeared to mark a stronger move towards direct state regulation of sexuality. But the struggles over the bill bring to the fore much more general questions about how we understand state intervention. They point to the dangers of seeing official action in a unified or monolithic way. The state's approach here fragmented into a number of competing positions: parliamentary and cabinet debate, ministerial and administrative directives, government inquiries and reports. Further, the decision to implement criminal law legislation did not originate with the state in the narrow sense at all, but with purity and feminist groups who were increasingly taking the lead in sexual politics.

The call for fresh legislation was stimulated by the perceived growth in child prostitution and the traffic in girls to the continent – the so-called 'white slave trade' of Stead's *Pall Mall Gazette* revelations. During 1879 and 1880 Alfred Dyer and George Gillet paid several visits to Brussels as representatives of the Society of Friends.[73] Their investigations exposed a well established trade in English girls, who, Dyer maintained, were being held in tolerated houses in the city. Great publicity was given to their allegations in the British press, with demands for government action. Josephine Butler, together with Stead and Henry Wilson, set up the London Committee for Suppressing the Traffic in British Girls. Butler herself presented a memorial to the Foreign Secretary, signed by a thousand women and calling for changes in the law, so that 'it should be impossible for any young girl to be deprived of her liberty by fraud or force'.[74] The government found itself in a difficult diplomatic position, given the fierce denial of the allegations by the Belgian authorities. Rather than intervening directly, the Home Office appointed an independent commissioner, whose report vindicated Dyer's accusations. A series of prosecutions took place and a number of Belgian officials were dismissed or resigned.

In the face of mounting pressure the British government at last sensed it was incumbent on them to act. Instead of introducing immediate legislation, the Home Office responded with time-honoured delaying tactics. It set up a House of Lords Select Committee in 1881 to examine the extent of juvenile prostitution. The recommendations advocated widespread changes in the criminal law. They proposed raising the age of consent from thirteen to sixteen and extending the provisions of the Industrial Schools Amendment Act. Most controversially, they recommended stronger police powers to search and arrest brothel-keepers and make soliciting on the streets illegal.[75] Political pressure for these latter proposals came from the police themselves, who now formed a strong lobby for increased state regulation. Superintendant Dunlap of the Metropolitan Police and Inspector Arnold of Whitechapel Division argued a convincing case before the Lords' Committee on the advantages of greater state powers. More stringent legislation, they claimed, would lead to improved morality and decency on the streets and bring benefits to public order. They also stressed that prosecutions should be taken up by a state prosecutor, rather than left to the ineffective parish vestry committees.[76]

At the same time women's purity organizations made their move, petitioning the Home Office for a new bill. In February 1884 Sir Vernon Harcourt, Liberal Home Secretary, received petitions from Bath Preventive Mission and Ladies' Association for the Care of Friendless Girls, calling for immediate legislation raising the age of consent to eighteen and giving the police greater powers.[77] In April the London Women's Christian Association appealed directly to Gladstone for better laws to protect children and young girls.[78]

The Home Office response was cautious. It made public declarations supporting the work done by purity groups, insisting that child prostitution was one of the burning issues of the day. But in private the department held deep reservations about the benefits of fresh legislation and about its purity protagonists. In January 1883 Henry Thring, the Attorney-General, drew up a draft bill which incorporated the main recommendations of the Lords' Committee. The bill was introduced by Lord Rosebery, Under-Secretary of State at the Home Office. But despite apparent government support a number of ministers objected and the proposals made little headway.

Ministers' main worry was the issue of greater police powers, and with it the question of increased state involvement in regulating sexuality. Lord Hartington, the War Secretary, initially welcomed the proposals as filling the gap created by the recent suspension of the contagious diseases legislation. He was sure that the clauses extending police action would have a beneficial effect on national morality.[79] But Hartington soon became alarmed at the plans to give increased powers to what he termed 'fanatical local authorities', and he wrote to Rosebery asking him to withdraw support for the measures. Like a number of other senior ministers he was ambiguous about purity campaigners. The discourse of feminists and evangelicals cut against official Home Office ideology, with its deeply embedded male attitudes towards immorality and its implicit stance of toleration. Hartington confided that he did not really believe that prostitution could ever be eliminated. Fresh legislation would only drive it into some more objectionable form. Similarly, the Town Clerk of Hereford, in a letter to the Home Office, claimed that the bill actively discriminated against men by ignoring the innate immorality of many women and girls.[80]

Outside the state apparatuses public opinion was becoming increasingly polarized over the contentious issue of greater state powers. Opposition from the Vigilance Association for the Defence of Personal Rights and from parliamentary Liberals and trade-union leaders focused on the growing threat to personal liberty. They saw the bill as part of the renewed offensive against the poor, following in the wake of the Contagious Diseases Acts.[81] The repealer James Stuart wrote to Samuel Smith the purity MP complaining that the bill had 'far too much of the police in it'.[82] Opponents alleged that police powers had dangerously expanded in recent years while police accountability had diminished. As ever, their remedy for im-morality was not a centralized state system of surveillance but a co-ordinated network of voluntary efforts directed towards moral education and rescue work.

The purity movement was itself divided over the new pro-posals. There were those like Hopkins who saw legislation as a growing sign of the improved moral climate in the country and its changing attitude towards women. Others, including Stead, attacked the bill for increasing the arbitrary power of the police on the streets. He believed that public outrage about the prostitution trade could be far more usefully channelled into forming local vigilante groups, as residents in the St Jude's Parish of King's Cross had done.[83] The sticking point for purists was over the balance to be struck between state power and voluntary efforts. Many of them supported the move to recruit the law into their plans for moral reform, but they did not wish to see their own efforts displaced by police powers. Anna Wilkes, who ran a rescue home in Poplar, outlined a form of regulation in which purity workers shared responsibility with the police and the courts, preserving the delicate balance between voluntary bodies and state institutions.[84] It was this solution which was incorporated into the working of the 1885 act in its final form, when the new Conservative government dropped the contentious clauses extending police powers of search and arrest.

What became enshrined in the new legislation were more stringent penalties for brothel-keepers and the raising of the age of consent to sixteen. Along with these measures went the catch-all clause, introduced at the last moment by the Liberal MP Henry Labouchère outlawing all forms of male homosexual contact.[85] General responses were mixed. *The Times*, which had hitherto kept a dignified silence on such a distasteful subject, pronounced itself well-pleased with the modified outcome. But successive editorials warned against 'trusting in showy mecha-nical remedies' to the exclusion of examining the deeper causes of juvenile misery and vice.[86] Jubilant reaction from the purity camp showed just how central legislation had now become to their programme. When the Salvation Army met on 18 August to hold a thanksgiving service for the passing of the act, William Booth emphasized that the connection between legislation and morality was the keynote of victory.[87] Mrs Booth closed the meeting by announcing that as soon as sufficient numbers of rescue homes had been opened, female 'soldiers' in the army would make a series of daring raids on London's streets to rescue as many fallen women as they could.

9   THE COMPROMISE SOLUTION

In the early years after 1885 purity groups received little or no help from the state in implementing the new act. It soon became disappointingly clear to the NVA that what had been conceived as a two-way process between voluntary bodies and the state, in practice placed the burden of day-to-day regulation on private initiatives. A number of factors influenced this highly cautious approach by central government, local councils, the police and the courts. Some arose from the difficulties of practical implementation, others had to do with the longer term history of state involvement in sexuality. In an immediate sense it was clear that local authorities were ill-equipped to begin the type of prosecutions purity groups were pressing for. In the months after legislation was passed, the Home Office was inundated with letters from local police chiefs and magistrates demanding clarification on the extent of the new police powers of prosecution. Police evidence to the Lords' Committee had already shown that parish vestry councils were generally incompetent, badly run and lacked the funds to embark on private prosecutions. The police themselves did not possess the necessary internal organization to root out specific forms of vice, which often necessitated painstaking investigative work.

It was only late in the 1890s, under pressure from the NVA, that New Scotland Yard established a special department to deal with indecent books and pictures. Until then, police practice involved turning a blind eye to minor breaches of public decency rather than embarking on lengthy prosecutions. Moreover, as Coote acknowledged, magistrates themselves were initially hostile to the aims and methods of purity groups. They were loath to convict, especially in cases which seemed to contradict common law.[88]

The difficulties in the working of the new act quickly came to

a head. In December 1886 the Home Office received a memorial from the Clapham Vigilance Association, complaining
that Clapham Common was 'infested' with prostitutes of the
lowest type and that actual fornication was shamelessly committed on benches close to the public roadway.[89] Ratepayers
who formed this local group grumbled that the police were
conspicuous by their absence. Records show the local constabulary to have been remarkably tolerant towards prostitutes
and apparently sensitive to the sexual practices of the poor. One
suspects that police constables had more in common with local
popular culture than with evangelical vigilantes. The superintendent's report asserted that though prostitutes did ply their
calling on the common they conducted themselves in an orderly
manner, as did large numbers of respectable, well-dressed
courting couples who 'roamed about the place after dark cares-
sing each other'.[90] As the metropolitan police complained three
years later, the whole question of dealing with prostitutes was
fraught with problems. While many citizens clamoured for the
removal of public women from the streets, any attempt to
introduce a continental system of tolerated areas would be
rejected immediately as implicating the state in the immoral
recognition of vice.[91] Under these circumstances it was hardly
surprising that the police adopted a laissez-faire policy.

But nervousness and vacillation over direct state intervention
was more than just a problem of administration. The doubts
expressed by ministers and Home Office officials in the 1880s
were symptomatic of much deeper structural problems. Central here was the political and ideological legacy of the Contagious Diseases Acts.

Successive Liberal and Conservative governments had lost
the battle for the state medical regulation of women, largely as a
result of sustained feminist opposition. Politicians did not
relish a repeat performance of the humiliating defeat they had
suffered over the suspension and repeal of the acts. Added to
this was the deep suspicion felt by senior ministers, influential
judges and lawyers about purists themselves. As an aristocrat
Hartington was not untypical in regarding them as evangelical
fanatics who needed restraining. For Sir Vernon Harcourt the
issue was even more clear-cut. All the great middle-class moral
reforms of the age had been achieved at the expense of pleasure

and enjoyment. The English were in danger of becoming a nation dominated by dullness and decorous solemnity.[92] Many senior politicians regarded the purity movement as beyond the pale; an unwelcome intrusion of issues and personnel which had no rightful place in the discourse of parliamentary politics. A number of the purity leaders, like Coote and Alfred Dyer, came from respectable working-class or petty-bourgeois backgrounds. Their strident moralism jarred with both the measured middle-class radicalism of the repealers and the dominant patrician language of high politics. The suspicions of establishment politicians were fuelled by the renewed nonconformist assault on the Liberal Party in the 1880s. Purity MPs like Smith and Wilson mounted a direct challenge to the political and cultural assumptions of men like Hartington and Harcourt. Wilson himself noted enthusiastically that 'the backbone of the Party is more and more teetotal in its sympathies'.[93] When the prominent Liberal Sir Charles Dilke and the Irish nationalist Charles Parnell became involved in divorce scandals, it was Stead and the Methodist leader, Hugh Price-Jones, who were instrumental in politically destroying them.

It was also clear that feminist involvement had much to do with the opposition purity provoked – especially from men within the state apparatuses. Administrators and politicians had been keen to circumscribe the power of scientific experts like Simon. But they were alarmed to discover that sanitarians had been displaced by a new force in sexual politics: the militant voice of articulate middle-class women who pointed to men as the root cause of immorality. For many men within the power bloc this was a direct challenge to their own masculinist culture, rupturing the ideology of separate spheres and the double-standard. As the women's movement became increasingly central to purity campaigns before the First War, Home Office officials developed a range of tactics to stifle feminist pressure, from diplomatic stone-walling to outright misogyny.

At a different level a key factor affecting the uneasy dialogue between purists and the state was the partial transformation of political discourse itself. We have already noted the crystallization of parliamentary language working to exclude sexuality in the repeal struggles. The late nineteenth century witnessed a heightening of this process. Focus on the two-party system, the growing strength of the organized working-class and the gradual decline of the big single-issue movements which had been such a central feature of the mid-Victorian political scene were visible signs of this transformation. The political itself was redefined. Successive governments from the 1880s hesitated to introduce fresh legislation on immorality partly because the area was seen to lie outside formal politics. Home Secretaries like Reginald McKenna and Herbert Gladstone consistently refused to pledge their government to support a new criminal law amendment bill in Parliament. As Coote himself protested, both men were privately committed to legislation but believed they could not involve the government on the issue.[94]

The highly cautious approach to purity demands undercuts any simple notion of more active state intervention over sexuality in the late nineteenth and early twentieth century. In the fields of economic management, labour relations, political ideologies and educational and welfare programmes the state began to exercise a new and constitutive function in this period. It redefined the nature of social and political problems and their solutions. It altered the relation between dominant and dominated groups by creating new apparatuses with different modes of administrative rationality, and drew in key intellectuals and professional experts. The state was not the originator of all these transformations but it was implicated in them in quite new ways. Compared with these other fields of intervention, the state itself rarely took the lead in the area of sexuality. There was no expansion of government departments here; no recruitment of intellectuals into the state apparatuses; no equivalent of H. Llewellyn Smith at the Board of Trade or Sidney and Beatrice Webb on social policy. The criminal law emerged as more and more significant for sexual regulation before 1914 but the impetus did not come from the state. Government was a relatively junior and often passive partner in the dialogue with purists and feminists. Purity groups remained absolutely central to the enactment of legislation. There was no shift away from these private voluntary initiatives.

Between 1890 and 1910 the dominant strategy of regulation involved a pragmatic compromise between the state and private organizations. In the early years the executive committee of the NVA, angry at the tentative approach of the Home Office, police and the courts, decided to initiate prosecutions themselves. In a test case of 1887 the Home Office ruled that vigilance associations could not recover their costs for prosecutions from government funds.[95] Out of the NVA's annual income of two thousand pounds, half was spent on legal work. Prosecutions concentrated on indecent advertising, the music halls, prostitution and pornography. Occasionally the NVA's enthusiasm brought members into direct conflict with state agencies, as for example in its campaign against the Rabelais Picture Gallery in the early 1890s. An exhibition of paintings by the French artist Jules Garnier, illustrating the work of Rabelais, was launched amid a blaze of hot publicity. The association complained of obscenity and Coote brought his case to the House of Commons in an effort to persuade Sir Richard Webster, the Attorney-General, to take up the prosecution. Webster's reply demonstrated the government's extreme caution: 'It is utterly impossible. . . . We cannot help you. I am in hearty agreement with you, and privately I am quite prepared to subscribe towards it. But officially the Government cannot be identified with it.'[96] The NVA faced similar problems in their efforts to press successive governments to introduce fresh legislation. As early as 1886 its legal sub-committee had drawn up a whole series of amendments to the criminal law which it wanted to see on the statute book. These included raising the age of consent to eighteen, abolishing the notorious 'escape clause' (allowing male defendants in assault cases to claim they believed the girl to be over sixteen), extending the time limit for prosecutions and criminalizing incest and male importuning. It took until 1922 before all these measures had been passed, under continuing pressure from feminist and purity groups.

In the 1890s purists began to make headway at a local level by persuading the police and the courts to support their programme. A number of local police chiefs became members of the association, like the Chief Constable of Birmingham and the notorious Inspector Burroughs in Manchester.[97] A two-way system of regulation began to be established, whereby purity groups either presented information to the police or the police referred cases to purists themselves. Co-operation of this kind was most effective in cities with strong nonconformist councils. In Manchester, Sheffield, Leeds, Liverpool and Cardiff the police and the NVA worked in close contact, closing brothels, prosecuting for obscenity and investigating cases of abduction. In Liverpool purity became a hot politcal issue, when purists succeeded in overturning the lax Tory council sympathetic to publicans and brewers.

Incest was another area which pointed up the growing convergence of opinion between purists, women's groups, the police and the Home Office. The offence was still not covered by any effective punishment under law. By the early 1890s the NVA had begun to pass on evidence of cases to the Home Office, complaining of the difficulties of prosecuting under existing legislation. In 1894 the Ladies' National Association, veterans of the repeal movement, mounted a campaign to amend the 1885 act to criminalize incest. Though no progress was made when Henry Wilson introduced a bill in 1896, there was growing police backing for legislation. A letter from the NVA to chief constables in 1899 revealed that almost all police chiefs were in favour of a law prohibiting incest.[98] Opposition came mainly from lawyers and magistrates, protesting that prosecutions would increase the number of offences on account of the publicity. Pressure for reform was also mounting from women's organizations. The National Union of Women Workers, NUWW (a philanthropic offshoot of Hopkins' Ladies' Association for the Care of Friendless Girls formed in 1895), launched a fresh assault on the conspiracy of silence over incest at their annual conference in 1906.[99] When the Incest Act was finally carried in 1908, purity feminists claimed it as a personal triumph.

But it was prostitution which continued to be the major preoccupation for purity workers at a local level. In 1901 many of the newly organized London borough councils appointed their own officials to monitor the trade and liaise with purists.[100] The increased closure of brothels as a result of this drive forced poorer women to solicit in the open, where they were subjected to police harassment. In 1905 the number of women charged with public indecency rose dramatically.[101] This problem was examined in the 1908 Royal Commission on the Metropolitan Police. Allegations by prostitutes of police bribery and unjust and arbitrary exercise of powers of arrest were discounted in favour of evidence from purity workers. Coote, along with other campaigners, backed the new aggressive police action, testifying to the special relationship which now existed between purists and the police. The Rev. F.B. Meyer, minister of Christ Church Westminister, felt that it had been encouraged by the fact that 'Christian men' were backing their efforts.[102] Coote, to his credit, did object to the double-standard enshrined in police practice, and recommended that the existing law should also be used to prosecute male clients.[103] The royal commission's report countered this by reasserting the fundamental difference between occasional soliciting by a man ('addressed to a woman who does not resent it') and the prostitute's immoral business, which was offensive to public decency. Besides, it was argued, prosecutions against male clients would not be acceptable to the community at large.[104] Despite this setback Coote pronounced himself well pleased with the state of the streets in the metropolis. London was now 'an open-air cathedral', whereas forty years earlier 'it was vicious in every particular'.[105] Coote bothered little about the effects of his work on the prostitutes themselves. He was much more intent on maintaining public order. What was needed was more of the same – intensified police action backed by the ever-watchful vigilance of the purity movement.

10   SUFFRAGE AND SEXUALITY: 1908–1914

Sexuality was a major political issue in the suffrage movement. During the years before the First War the history of sexual politics became intimately bound up with the progress of feminism. Alongside the battle for the vote, women launched a major campaign to transform male sexual behaviour and to protect themselves and their children. Legislation was seen as the key to securing reforms that were in women's interests. It was the language of purity which mobilized many women to develop a trenchant critique of male sexuality. Purity became hegemonic in the early women's movement, though it did not go entirely unchallenged. Other feminists, often from libertarian or utopian socialist backgrounds, rejected purity and worked to forge a new discourse, stressing women's right to active sexual pleasure. The first decade of the twentieth century witnessed the polarization of these positions under the impact of growing political activism.

The purity language of outrage, like the militant tactics of suffragette politics with which it was linked, continued to provide women with a powerful weapon to challenge men. Feminists perceived that in a world where men and masculinist attitudes had monopolized notions of physical sexual pleasure, purity stress on chastity and the importance of human love provided a positive alternative. Coupled with this language went a growing stress on the state to enact feminist demands, in the moral as well as the political arena. Many women saw a clear convergence of interests between their own struggle for the vote and purity pressure for legislation.

There was in fact no clear-cut division beween purity asociations, suffrage groups and women's oganizations – membership often overlapped. Millicent Fawcett, a moderate suffragist and President of the National Union of Women's Suffrage Societies (NUWSS), was also prominent in the NVA as head of its preventive and rescue sub-committee. Many women in the NUWW also belonged to purity groups. In the period immediately before the First War, the growing political militancy of the Women's Social and Political Union (WSPU), along with the publication of feminist books and pamphlets on sexuality, radicalized the older, more traditional women's organizations. Groups like the British Women's Temperance Association and the NUWW began to define their long standing crusade for purity and the reform of male sexuality as part of the contemporary feminist struggle. Though the NUWW continued to foreground traditional philanthropy, its annual conferences displayed a growing concern with the problems of male sexual behaviour, informed by current feminist demands.[106] The LNA also became repoliticized under the impact of suffrage politics. Conference delegates at the 1903 Congress of the International Abolitionist Federation insisted that prostitution needed to be opposed because it isolated women as an outcast class. It sanctioned the sexualization of women by men, making them ' a thing, an instrument devoted to appeasing the sexual passion of the man'.[107] Here was a new wave of feminist militancy, proclaiming that women had the right to a life of their own and should not be the sexual property of men. Throughout, the memory of Josephine Butler's early struggles acted as a powerful motivating force. Following her death in 1906, *The Shield* produced extracts from Butler's speeches and writings, and in 1912 the NUWSS republished a de-luxe edition of her *Personal Reminiscences of a Great Crusade*. *The Suffragette* proclaimed: 'the work of this dedicated woman has sown the seeds of a mighty harvest which others are about to reap.'[108]

11   MOBILIZING A LANGUAGE

Feminists combined practical demands for criminal law legislation with an effective propaganda campaign. In books, pamphlets and speeches women drew on and re-worked the languages of purity, religion, medicine and even mysticism to develop a critical feminist discourse. Representations of female sexuality here were not merely negative, they now offered women positive images of their own autonomy through a stress on celibacy, evolutionary superiority and the power of human love. The vocabulary of social purity was employed to demonstrate that male immorality was the problem to be addessed, not the norm against which women should be defined. Religious and biological concepts of moral and natural law were used to argue that chastity and self-control were essential to personal health and to the future progress of the nation. Feminists were effectively articulating what had been implicit in much of moral purity – an opposition to the idea that the male sexual urge was uncontrollable, and that frequent intercourse was necessary for men's health.

Many feminists insisted that celibacy was a positive step in women's self-advancement. Evidence exists from the period before the First War to show that some women were choosing not to have sexual relations with men as a political act.[109] Anti-feminist articles in the press noted with alarm the growing trend towards celibacy in women, attributing 'spinsterhood' to degeneracy or an aversion to motherhood.[110] But as Lucy

138

Re-Bartlett asserted, chastity was part of women's revolt against false social conditions.[111] Cicely Hamilton's *Marriage as a Trade*, 1909 was a superb polemic in favour of celibacy, which reasoned that marriage represented a narrowing of women's hopes and ambitions. Through the sex act, men secured women's continuing subordination, by cutting off every avenue of escape from the gratification of their desire, and by denying female sexuality any outlet other than compulsory heterosexuality. Men hated and despised spinsters, Hamilton claimed, because the 'perpetual virgin' proved that the sex act was not 'an absolute necessity for women'.[112]

In polemicizing for celibacy and spinsterhood feminists were challenging the growing sexualization of all women in medicine, psychology and in the work of male sexual radicals like Havelock Ellis and Edward Carpenter.[113] Both Christabel Pankhurst and Hamilton argued that such recent theories were deeply linked to male attitudes, which saw women as 'primarily created for the sexual gratification of men'.[114] In the future evolution of society under women's guidance, sex would be raised to a higher plane, where physical passion would be transmuted by the power of human love. Quasi-religious languages derived from theosophy or mysticism were used to formulate a new spiritualized conception of sex relations, freed from male control.

Frances Swiney, who began writing in the 1880s, published a large number of books and pamphlets on female sexuality. As president of the Cheltenham branch of the NUWW, she was a prominent lecturer and speaker in the suffrage movement, where her ideas on sexuality were influential. Her own career was remarkable. She was brought up in the colonial culture of India and married to a senior military figure. In her fifties she began developing an elaborate theory – part religious, part mystical – on the natural supremacy of women and the need to return to a matriarchal society. Her cosmic vision prophesied that as the race evolved intercourse would only be practised for the purpose of reproduction, and then only at carefully spaced intervals under women's direction.[115] Swiney orchestrated a mass of medical, anthropological and religious material to back her arguments. The bible was reinterpreted; even Christ, she argued, had spoken of the eventual disappearance of the male

139

species. For as women delivered them from the sex obsession, men would become more and more like women. This was what Christ really meant when he spoke about the unity of the male with the female in one flesh.[116] These ideas were circulated in her theosophical society, The League of Isis, which listed rules on chastity and continence, aimed at promoting women's higher self.

Many women were interpellated by this religious and mystical imagery, because potentially it projected a spiritualized fusion of sex and love. Traditions of feminine religious experience, expressing a mystical, quasi-sexual communion with God, had always been a current within Catholicism and in many Protestant sects, and some women drew on its potential. But religion was now twinned with other languages to define pleasure more positively. Evolutionary theory, theosophy, even platonic idealism, all played their part. Bartlett talked extensively of the great evolutionary movement to spirituality through passion: 'Spirituality is, of course, the great counteracting force and ultimate conqueror. But spirituality has to be aroused, and passion is often the medium – the conducting channel.'[117]

12   PETITIONING THE STATE

As the suffrage struggle intensified many feminists began to insist that their campaign for citizenship and demands for legislation to curb men's immorality were interlinked. The vote was perceived as bringing political and *moral* benefits to women. Christabel Pankhurst argued that 'when women are citizens they will have the power to secure the enactment of laws for their protection'.[118] Militant feminists pointed out that sexual antagonism lay at the heart of the suffrage struggle and could never be resolved within the discourse of political liberalism. Bartlett, herself closely associated with the WSPU, claimed that sexuality was the underlying issue in the feminist movement:

The public roughly seems divided between people who deny the struggle any sexual significance at all, and those who, seeing the significance, attribute it to sexual morbidity and hysteria. The situation with which we are face to face represents indeed a sex war. . . . It is a war which signifies vitality, not decadence.[119]

Purity feminists viewed the state as the tool to circumscribe male power in the moral as well as in the political sphere. Hamilton asserted that in ordinary life it was the strong arm of the law and not the strong arm of the husband which protected women from hurt or molestation.[120] The state-orientated approach adopted by many feminists clearly related to their affiliations with social purity. Yet it also had much to do with the overwhelmingly middle-class and aristocratic composition of the suffrage campaigns. Many came to the women's movement from backgrounds where the state was viewed as an instrument for enacting their own class specific demands. In as much as feminism represented a split within the dominant classes, creating multiple fractures within liberalism, there were many women who carried with them their class perceptions of the ethical and beneficent state.

But feminists rapidly became aware that the state itself was patriarchal and needed profound transformation if they were to be fully represented in the nation's political and moral life. Christabel Pankhurst reasoned that the state was composed of men who not only denied women the vote but also tacitly condoned male immorality and sexual violence. Men had all the power in the state and therefore made both its laws and its morality.[121] As women escalated their campaign of militant action in 1912 and 1913 they were acutely conscious that male attitudes – deeply embedded in the legal profession, the police and the courts – sustained not just men's political power but also women's sexual oppression. Suffrage papers began to carry reports of cases of sexual harassment and male sexual violence, in an effort to raise consciousness and sustain pressure for law reform. *The Vote* reported one incident of child assault in Surrey, where a man was sentenced to only four months hard labour. Feminists organized a local protest over the issue at election time, returning a woman to the local council on the specific platform of curbing male immorality.[122] *The Common Cause*, reporting a case of the wrongful arrest of a woman for alleged prostitution, commented that the suspect was 'taken to a man's court, tried and sentenced by men under men's laws for a fault she cannot commit alone'.[123] One suffragette, Rosa Lamartine Yates, recounted that she had witnessed the double-standard in action while standing bail for two women at the west London police court. The preceding case had involved prostitution:

> After, two women filed into the dock, and with a whisper of mock modesty an official suggested that I should leave the court as the case concerned prostitution. 'Are you a respectable woman?' quickly interpolated the magistrate when I said I wished to remain.[124]

As Yates argued, the women's movement was dedicated to abolishing the distinction between 'respectable' and 'fallen' women which was reproduced by the state, upheld in official attitudes and predicated on 'fallen men'.

The NUWW and the LNA had long been campaigning for legislation to raise the age of consent to eighteen and to enforce more stringent penalties against procurers and brothel-keepers. The government's attitude, and its relation to feminists and purists, displayed all the hesitations and ambiguities which had characterized similar debates in the 1880s. Male sexual attitudes were deeply entrenched among senior politicians and civil servants, revealing themselves in suspicion of feminist demands and often in outbursts of anti-feminism and misogyny. Behind the doors of the Home Office, feminist pressure for moral reform, combined with the escalation of the suffrage campaign, was confronting the 'gentlemanly' conventions of state administration. Home Office records for the period show how politicians and administrators negotiated feminist pressure by a mixture of amused contempt and double-dealing. While pledging themselves publicly to legislation, they worked privately to block many of the attempts to secure new acts and statutes.

A new criminal law amendment bill had been drawn up in 1909. This was a result of pressure brought to bear on the Home Secretary by the Jewish Association for the Protection of Girls and Women and the NVA, concerned about fresh revelations in the press over the white slave traffic. When an influential purity deputation petitioned the Home Office, Herbert Samuel, then Under-Secretary of State, expressed himself personally committed to legislation in the interests of national honour, but he refused to pledge the government to introduce proposals in the house, or even to support them publicly. Here were familiar ambiguities over state support for purity demands first experienced by Coote twenty years before.

The government kept aloof, if not quite deliberately obstructive. It was true, as successive home secretaries explained to pressure groups, that the government was committed to a mountain of fresh legislation in the new Parliament. What was looming was the protracted constitutional wrangle over Lloyd-George's budget and the House of Lords. However, the usual suspicions over purity aims and intentions were now intensified by the militant stance of suffrage feminists, especially the WSPU. Civil servants were keen to discern how widespread public support was for the new measures, though they were aware, as they euphemistically put it, that there would be 'cause for complaint' with the government if the bill were blocked.[125] And official hesitation as to whether legislation on immorality was a proper area for state intervention continued. In response to parliamentary questions, demanding that the government introduce their own bill rather than relying on private members' initiatives, the Home Office made its familiar position clear: 'We strongly support the proposed Bill . . . but do not see how it is possible for the Government to undertake legislation.'[126]

Meanwhile, purity groups and feminist organizations stepped up their pressure with a nationwide campaign. In April 1911 the NUWW had convened an emergency meeting in the face of continuing delays, 'expressing the desire that the government will give immediate facilities for the passing of the Criminal Law Amendment Bill'.[127] The LNA acted as the focus for protests, organizing a mass rally in June 1912 at Caxton Hall, with deputations from leading feminist and purity groups. A special Pass the Bill Committee was formed and the Home Office was inundated with letters and memorials from suffrage societies. The LNA forwarded to Asquith nearly three hundred resolutions in favour of the bill, with over seventy coming from feminist organizations.[128] McKenna, the new Home Secretary, again pledged his personal support but insisted that he could not guarantee the bill government time. By this stage even Asquith was worried about government inactivity. He wrote to McKenna, concerned about the continued obstruction and urging that the Home Office should speed up the bill's progress. In the face of mounting political and industrial unrest, Asquith may have been anxious to head-off further confrontation with feminists.

The bill became law in December 1912 as the Criminal Law Amendment Act. But in its final committee stages the clauses giving the police greater powers to search and arrest brothel-keepers were revised, rendering them almost useless. Though the original clauses were eventually restored, feminists and women's organizations were deeply split on the issue of increased police powers. Just as thirty years before, here again were feminist divisions over using the repressive state to enforce women's demands. There were those in the LNA, the NUWW and the NVA who argued that a more coercive police approach was essential to protect innocent women and children. In a telling exchange at the NUWW annual conference in 1912, one delegate asked if the new police measures would infringe the liberty of prostitutes on the streets. Lady Laura Riding, speaking in support of the proposals, declared that if prostitutes were at times 'liable to be harried', that was the consequence of their own actions. Purity feminist support for these clauses of the bill accepted the traditional polarities of 'pure' and 'impure' women. Lady Laura was insistent: 'though we may feel deep pity for them, their trade is not one of blessing to the nation, to our fathers, sons, husbands; you have to think of that. It is not a trade that should be specially protected.'[129]

The NUWSS on the other hand warned that though the bill deserved general support, the clauses extending police powers needed careful monitoring, 'lest they should lead to further harrying of the unfortunate women'.[130] *The Common Cause* argued that coercive legislation was no substitute for tackling the more fundamental problems of poverty and men's immorality which stimulated the prostitution trade. These feminist differences surfaced in a more extreme form in the months after the passing of the act. The LNA saw the new measures as only a

144

beginning. *The Shield* insisted that there was enough conviction and enthusiasm among women to carry further legislation,
despite the blatant obstructionism from men at the Home
Office and in Parliament.[131] The Pankhurst-led WSPU made
the twin issues of male immorality and white slavery central to
their whole campaign in 1913, as part of a new militant offensive. When Emmeline Pankhurst was tried at the Old Bailey in
April she drew attention to the white slavery issue in her speech
from the dock. Women, she claimed, believed that the horrible
evils now ravaging British civilization would never be removed
until women got the vote.[132]

Not all feminists were so enamoured with such tactics.
Teresa Billington-Grieg of the Women's Freedom League
condemned the strategy of coercion and the sexual ideology
implicit in the new act. In an article in *The English Review* in
1913 she argued that the legislation had been carried by hyster-
ical stories circulated by 'neuropaths and prudes' about the
entrapment of white women.[133] The government had yielded to
sensationalist claims by the three chief agents of irrational
emotion – Parliament, the pulpit and the press. Grieg's was a
rationalist and intellectual critique. She reasoned that the law
and the police had long been shown to have little or no educative
or preventive power, and that the only way forward was a
changed moral outlook and a gradual reorganization of economic and political conditions. And she went even further.
Pointing her finger at the misplaced moral fervour of the
WSPU and the LNA, she claimed that these 'dabblers in
debauchery' had set middle-class women on the rampage
against an evil they knew nothing about. They were 'feeding
and flattering' misconceptions which pitted the moral perfec-
tion of women against 'the bestiality of men'.[134] Nothing had
been done for the women who were exploited by prostitution.
All that had been achieved was a more punitive regime, while
the cause of sex reform had been set back by the whitewashing
of women and the doctrine of the uncleanness of men. Grieg's
attack was reinforced by Sylvia Pankhurst's *Women's Dreadnought*, paper of the East-End Suffrage Federation. Reports
pointed out that though the act had been passed for women's
protection, it seemed it was being used almost exclusively to
punish poor women.[135]

Other critics developed similar lines of argument. *The Free-woman* (an individualist feminist weekly pledged to a 'new morality' of free sexual unions) strongly criticized the purity lobby and the coercive consequences of its campaigning.[136] In 1912 the pages of the journal featured a heated debate between self-styled 'new moralists' and purity feminists over the implications of the new act. Purists were quick to counter-attack accusations that the legislation threatened individual liberty and encouraged prudish self-satisfaction. Contributors emphasized that purity was a positive advance for women and that the paper's editors should declare themselves on the side of reverence and self-control. Others insisted that the so-called toleration of new moralists would merely lead to licentiousness and hinder women's real sexual freedom.[137] Nevertheless, it appeared that the legislation was dividing the movement, bringing to the surface awkward questions which had remained invisible in earlier purity campaigns.

13   THE LIBERTARIAN CHALLENGE

Feminist differences which erupted around the 1912 amendment act were symptomatic of growing divisions within the women's movement over sexuality. Though purity remained hegemonic in the years before the First War, there was another feminist strategy for speaking about sex. This was the libertarian and utopian discourse of new moralists and sex reformers. The fierce debate between these two tendencies pointed to the difficulties – and personal anguish – women often experienced when they tried to develop positive representations of their own sexuality. Here again, questions of discourse and power surfaced in women's attempts to develop a feminist sexual politics. New moralists, as much as purity feminists, were confronted by the power relations embedded in existing languages and the difficulties of transforming them.

Broadly influenced by new continental theories of sexology and psychology, including Freudian psychoanalysis, new moralists projected 'sexual liberation' as part of a wider utopian socialist vision, or as a radical liberal ideal of individual self-realization. The Legitimation League was a characteristic example. Founded in 1893 with the American feminist Lillian Harman as president, it worked to liberalize the law and educate public opinion towards freedom in sexual relationships. Those associated with the League included utopian socialists such as Edward Carpenter and George Bedborough and radical individualists like Orford Northcote. They placed great emphasis on the individual's freedom to enter into personal relationships independent of church or state. All were careful to insist that 'free love' was not to be confused with 'libertine sexual intercourse', but that it involved a combination of the aesthetic and spiritual sides of the human personality, with a frank and open attitude towards sex.[138]

A major part of this enterprise stressed the importance of female sexuality and women's valid right to sexual pleasure – that is, in relationships with men. New moralists argued that contemporary society denied women 'those varied love-makings from the other sex', which would arouse in them a desire to fill life 'with a space of joy and delight'.[139] Sexology and psychology had proved that men and women had the same instinctive need for pleasure and fulfilment. The problem was that through centuries of doctrinaire education and repression women had become ignorant of their own sexuality. They needed to be initiated into sexual pleasure by men!

Men tended to dominate these movements, both personally and intellectually. It is often hard to gauge the exact nature of feminist involvement. We do know that responses by women members of the Legitimation League were cautious and ambiguous, highlighting the tensions felt by feminists in committing themselves to a libertarian politics. Harman herself warned that men's libertarianism only meant that women became the common property of the herd, instead of the property of one man. An anonymous correspondent to the league's journal complained that there was no recognition that woman could be 'the property of herself'.[140] Men and women members had quite different understandings of the political implications of free love. For many men it implied that women would be introduced to freedoms and pleasures previously enjoyed only by themselves, and conceived in exactly the same terms. In the words of one man: 'Women have a right to all they can get.'[141] Feminists like Harman glossed free love quite differently. It meant that women could work towards defining their own autonomous sexuality, independent of the social institutions of marriage and the family which had fixed them in oppressive relationships with men.[142]

New moralists caricatured purity feminism as a repressive moral code based on ignorance and punitive condemnation. Stella Browne, the Canadian socialist feminist, argued that female desire was a powerful natural force and that women had a valid right to sexual enjoyment.[143] Browne's radicalism owed much to Havelock Ellis' writings on sex psychology. But her use of the language of sexology carried its own problems. Calls for positive definitions of female sexuality were inevitably projected as compulsory heterosexuality for women, organized around penetration. Such a vision was heavily normalizing. Though Browne did see masturbation as a valid outlet for women, it was only permissible when 'normal sexual relations are difficult or impossible'.[144] 'Artificial lesbianism', as opposed to 'true' homosexuality of the 'congenital invert', was condemned as the product of a culture which segregated the sexes and manufactured perverts out of women who instinctively preferred the love of a man.

The exchange of letters in *The Freewoman* gave this debate a public airing. Purists argued that celibacy and spinsterhood were positive acts of self-determination, in contrast to the illusory freedom of libertarianism.[145] The alternative put forward by new moralists celebrated the power and joy women could discover within active heterosexuality. Sex passion was conceived in almost messianic terms, as a form of psychic union with the consciousness of another.[146] Their emphasis on the absolute centrality of heterosexual experience made it impossible for them to see that purity feminism had anything to offer, with its emphasis on celibacy, and its view of sex as male-defined, vicious and depraved. In reality, these increasingly polarized discourses offered women a 'choice' only between celibacy and heterosexual dependence on men. While purity was silent on questions of pleasure and desire, libertarianism sat uneasily with feminist demands and priorities. The problem was quite literally the lack of alternative languages developed by women themselves.

In the inter-war period the growing sexualization of women and the concerted attack on celibacy in sexology and marriage manuals effectively challenged the credibility of purity feminism. But if purists lost out, so too did those who envisaged greater freedom and equality in sexual relations with men. The optimism and confidence invested in heterosexuality proved to be greatly misplaced.

14   CONCLUSION

The campaigns of the purity movement marked a distinctive moment in the history of medico-moral politics. The growing centrality of the criminal law in the years between 1885 and 1912 represented a sharp break with the earlier sanitary principle governing sexuality. State medicine's defeat over the Contagious Diseases Acts effectively heralded the displacement of the medical profession by a new force in sexual politics, with a different conception of the state's responsibilities in the moral sphere. There was no continuous, uninterrupted growth of scientific expertise or medical control over sex throughout the nineteenth century. What we have encountered is a much more unstable hegemony, which was successfully challenged by competing groups.

This history of purity forces us to reassess accounts of 'modern sexuality', such as Foucault's, which stress the subordination of legal controls to the growth of more dispersed techniques of discursive power. In legislative terms the reverse occurred in this period. The law dominated the field, but it did not operate through the simple mechanisms of censorship and repression. The law was itself productive: seeking out and redefining forms of dangerous or 'deviant' sexuality, organizing the cultural experience of dominated groups and stimulating their political demands. There was no neat distinction between juridical and discursive forms of power.[147]

This transformation in sexual regulation was not the product of some internal dynamic in the technologies of power. The move to a more strongly state-oriented approach was not the result of initiatives taken within government at all. It was the outcome of protracted political struggles taking place 'outside' the state in the narrow sense on the terrain of civil society.

III   From state medicine to criminal law 1880–1914

Purity campaigns not only registered a shift in modalities of control, but a change in the personnel responsible for sexual regulation and in the sites from which power was exercised. As a significant movement of popular protest over sex purity marked a successful assault on the authority of male professionals, thereby drawing into the political arena groups hitherto denied access or without a voice.

At the same time the stance of the purity movement was deeply contradictory. For it provided a continuing source of private regulation – and the political will for further coercive measures – in an area where government remained cautious about direct involvement. Feminist purity campaigns were built on this contradiction. Purity provided women with a language which challenged men's sexual power and projected images of their own autonomy. Feminist campaigns around the state effectively unmasked the unofficial masculine culture of politicians, experts and administrators. They exposed the deeply misogynist attitudes which formed the hidden element in policy making. But these positive achievements were enmeshed with the longer history of middle-class women's involvement in social regulation and class disciplining. To reiterate, the purity movement was neither a conservative barrier to women's sexual freedom, nor was it the passive vehicle for an emergent feminist consciousness. It was the battleground on which conflicting aims and intentions struggled for space.

PART FOUR

FROM PURITY TO SOCIAL HYGIENE: EARLY TWENTIETH CENTURY CAMPAIGNS FOR SEX EDUCATION

1   THE DRONFIELD CASE: THE TEACHER AND THE GIRLS SHE TOLD

In the autumn of 1913 scripture lessons for the pupils of Dronfield Elementary School, Derbyshire, took a radical turn.[1] The girls from standard six were reading the bible with their class teacher and headmistress, Miss Outram. One of the set texts for Advent dealt with the birth of John the Baptist. The verses prompted questions from the children about pregnancy and childbirth. At first Miss Outram told them to ask their mothers, but feeling she might lose the girls' confidence if she blocked their curiosity she took a more direct approach. Telling them to close their bibles, she read them two stories; one about the beginnings of life, the other a warning on the dangers of immorality. Part of the accounts went as follows:

The First Story

Shall I tell you a story of how God made things in the beginning, a true story? Well, once upon a time there was no world at all. Doesn't it seem strange to think about it? And everything was dark. But away back in the beginning God was there just the same. And God said, 'Let there be light,' and there was light.
Then God made the wonderful world that we live in. . . . Now, how do you suppose God planned always to have plants on the earth? God said, 'Let them have seed, each after its kind.' He knew that by-and-by, when they were ripe, they would drop down into the ground; there they would keep soft and warm for a while, then they would grow into more plants, with seeds, so there would always be plants on the earth. . . . Then God wanted to have fish in the waters, so He made a mother fish to lay eggs in the water

153

and a father fish to swim about over the eggs and take care of them. . . . 'And God saw that it was good.'

. . . Now how do you suppose God planned always to have animals on the earth? Every living thing was to come from a seed or an egg. We saw how it was with the plants and the seeds, and the birds and their eggs but the animals God made could not make nests and lay eggs, because they were so much larger. Such large nests and so many of them would be in the way on the earth. The eggs would get broken if the mother animal tried to keep them warm, as the mother bird does, because she is so heavy. So God did not make the mother animal to lay her eggs. Instead, the eggs stayed safe inside the mother animal's body until they grew into little animals right there. Then, when they were large enough, God brought them out and the mother took care of them until they grew big enough to take care of themselves. 'And God saw that it was good.'

Perhaps some of us knew before of God's plan for the animals. I know of a lovely teacher who told her boys and girls in school about God's plan for the animals and they had a mother bunny in her cage right in the schoolroom. The children knew that the little bunnies were coming and they were so careful of the mother when they fed her with lettuce and cabbage. One morning when they went to school the little bunnies were there in the cage and they were all very happy.

But I must tell you of God's plan for the people. 'In the beginning' there were no people on earth and God said, 'Let us make man in our image,' that is, like ourselves. So he made a man, tall and strong like father, to take care of the plants and animals. And when God saw that the man was lonely He made a beautiful woman like mother to be his wife and to help him. 'And God saw that it was good'. The people were the best of all that God had made, so God planned always to have people on the earth.

Shall I tell you about the very first little baby? Just think, there had never been a little baby on the earth. God knew it would be the most precious of all. He wanted it kept very safe from all harm. So He made a tiny egg, so small that it could not even be seen, and a little room, on purpose for it to grow

in, right inside the mother's body. It stayed there and grew
for a long time, until it was a real baby. Then when it had
grown enough God brought the baby out and the mother
took him in her arms. There he was, the very first baby boy.
Nobody had ever seen a baby before, and when the mother
saw his little body and his little feet and hands, and his little
cunning face, she thought 'why he just looks like a little
man.' She was very thankful and happy and she said 'I have
gotten a man from the Lord.' This is part of God's
wonderful plan always to have people on the earth. Once
each of you was a tiny egg inside of mother's body. And
when father came and took mother for his wife, to live with
her and to take care of her, the little egg began to grow and
grow into a real little baby. Mother knew you were there
and she loved you. She carried you there near her heart a
long, long time while you were growing. The food she ate
made you grow too, so she was very careful to eat only good
food and to take nothing that might harm her little baby.
You were really a part of her. The fresh air she breathed
made pure blood for you, and often during the day she
wondered what you would be like, whether your eyes would
be blue or brown, and prayed God to make you a good
child. Then when you had grown enough and mother had
carried you there nearly a year, God opened a door for you
and brought you out into this world.

The Second Story

'Where is Jack?' asked Mr Rogers, as he came in at six
o'clock. 'He was late last night for dinner and he's going to
be late again to-night.' 'I saw him with that Jones girl,'
answered his sister Dorothy. 'She is a new girl in town, very
pretty, but terribly bold. I'm sure she's not nice. I do wish
Jack wouldn't go with her'.

Presently the door opened and Jack came in. 'Jack,' said
his father, 'I want to show you something.' Relief and
interest showed instantly in the boy's face. The dread
question was not to be asked after all.

Mr Rogers led the way to his workroom in the attic.

There were his carpenter's bench and his tools and his lathe, and in the corner was the dynamo that worked it. Jack had seen them all many times.

'What is it, father?' he asked. Mr Rogers laid his hand upon the dynamo. 'Jack, by means of this, a mysterious power becomes mine. We call it electricity, but no one knows what it is. We only know that if *we treat it in the right way* it will enable us to do wonderful things. It will work our mills, and light our houses and streets, and run our cars. It will enable man to do more than any other power that has been discovered. But at the same time, if you treat it in the wrong way, it will strike you dead.'

'Yes, father, I know that,' said Jack. His father turned toward him with an earnestness that Jack had never before seen in his face. 'There is another power, very like this in its results. There is the mysterious feeling that men have for women and women have for men. Treat that right, and it will bless your life and ennoble it, and make you ten times, yes, a hundred times, the man you could ever be without it. . . . But, treat that feeling wrong, and it will curse you, and blast your life, and *kill your immortal soul*.'

For a moment they looked at each other square in the eye. Then together they went downstairs in silence. In the hall below, Jack put his hand on his father's arm. 'I know what you mean, father, and I'll follow the right,' he whispered.[2]

Miss Outram claimed to have obtained her stories from an American publisher, yet they were typical of early twentieth-century British sex education teaching. Emotive and negative purity style moral warnings pointed to the twin dangers of promiscuous women and the threat of VD. These were combined with more positive guidance, where the language of evolutionary biology was used to represent sex as responsible parenthood. The natural world, presided over by the image of the benevolent patriarch, was moralized to carry the significations of goodness, health and social harmony integrated through sound procreation. On the other hand, modern science was used to list a new vocabulary of transgression. This was distanced from the earlier stress on Old Testament religious morality by its rationalism; as in the story's metaphor of electricity, wondrous yet calculable, which demonstrated the inexorable consequences of wrong-doing – disease, death and social degeneracy. The juxtaposition of these polarized accounts of sexuality in the headmistress's teaching was intentional. The girls of standard six, like so many of their contemporaries, were offered the 'choice' between radiant motherhood and unlawful promiscuity.

Outram was not naive in introducing sex education into her teaching. She may also have anticipated trouble with her school managers. Earlier in the year she had discussed circumcision, infertility and basic ante-natal care with her twelve-year-old girls, as part of classes on domestic economy and home-management. She was a committed eugenist (involved in a local campaign to get 'race hygiene' onto the syllabus of elementary schools) and an equally strong feminist, having read the children extracts from *The Suffragette*. These two discourses of eugenics and feminism, seemingly distinct yet so often linked in the political language of many early twentieth-century feminists, had clearly influenced Outram's educational thinking. According to the extracted deposition of one pupil, Doris Harrison, Miss Outram had told the older girls about the forced feeding of suffragettes in prison. How: 'One woman went to prison and she would not eat anything so, to open her mouth, they broke her teeth and put something down her throat.'[3] There had already been one heated exchange between herself and the school managers, when Outram had pointedly refused to apologize for introducing controversial subjects. The managers, all men, had been incensed. They were clearly on the lookout for a second opening to pillory their headmistress.

Inevitably, news of Miss Outram's exploits travelled fast in Dronfield. This tightly-knit community, lying six miles south of Sheffield on the Derby coalfield, had a population of less than four thousand. Most of the men were employed in local iron and steel foundries and in metal manufacturing. It was the intellectuals of the skilled, respectable working-class, in alliance with the local petty-bourgeoisie and small professional men (the grocer, publican, magistrate, two doctors and the Anglican vicar), who set the tone in the village and orchestrated public opinion. A number of children told their parents about the new-style scripture teaching. The publican's daughter told her elder sister, who told her aunt, and so it got back to the girl's parents. One pupil told her grandmother, who was so shocked she had to be calmed down by her son and daughter-in-law. All the children said that Miss Outram had impressed on them not to 'go home and tell your mothers and make a bother about it'.[4] The parents were outraged; the managers had got the opportunity they had been waiting for.

  The contest which followed involved parents, the school managers and their headmistress, and eventually implicated the local and central state. The case typified the competing forces and class and gender conflicts which surfaced in early sex education campaigns. The first clash occurred at a school managers' meeting the following January. The headmistress was summoned to account for her actions, following a formal complaint by Mr Bradwell of the Victoria Inn. Bradwell was clearly a force to be reckoned with in the village. He used his pub to orchestrate his case as a 'non-conformist conscientious objector'. He condemned Outram's teaching in the language of purity outrage as: 'most disgraceful and disgusting and abominable and I won't have my child taught like what she is teaching'.[5] Bradwell also claimed that the issue highlighted conflicting rights of parents and school over the moral education of the children. The publican's aggressive stance towards the headmistress touched on deeper currents which were becoming condensed in the affair. Outram, the feminist and progressive, was clearly the target of an unrelenting campaign of bigotry and misogyny organized by the local working-class and petty-bourgeoisie. Parents identified the headmistress as an agent of professional control, setting her knowledge against theirs and condemning their own cultural and moral values. Their anger and frustration may also have been fuelled by Outram's highhanded dismissal of their protests, evident in her exchanges with Bradwell. She consistently refused even to acknowledge his right to protest, let alone answer his questions. As she put it: 'That man is not here to ask me questions. I refuse to answer his questions.' She insisted she would only address herself to the managers.[6] How far Outram's hostility to Bradwell stemmed from a feminist critique of his chauvinist behaviour, how far from the conflicting claims of expert and parent is impossible to say. The two elements were probably interlinked.

IV From purity to social hygiene

For the managers the issue was clear-cut. Their headmistress
had wilfully departed from the scripture syllabus and her
stories had stimulated a prurient interest in sex, thereby corrupting childhood innocence. In her defence, Outram explained that the teaching had led quite naturally out of the
children's questions. Right knowledge was a necessary safeguard against the immorality and perversion which stemmed
from ignorance. Their exchange illustrated a major bone of
contention in early debates over sex teaching:

Miss Outram	. . . I should not have discussed it at all if I had not been asked the questions.
Managers	Do you mean to tell me that the girls ask you for such stuff as you have been reading? I shall never believe it.
Miss Outram	Well. I was asked questions, and this led out of it.
Managers	. . . The very effect of reading was knowledge to the girls.
Miss Outram	But this was the outcome of their questions.
Managers	That story you have read is not in the syllabus. You have no authority to read stories like that.
Miss Outram	I acknowledge it was a mistake. I shall be careful in the future. It is a lovely little story all the same and there is no harm in it. We all make mistakes. I was not wilfully doing anything wrong. I do not acknowledge that I have done wrong . . .[7]

Moreover, the managers saw a clear link between Outram's
feminist politics and her interest in sex education. As one of
them sneered, 'I have heard of several ladies in Dronfield
having these books and recommending them. There seems to
be a movement of that sort amongst a certain class of the
people.'[8] They decided to ask the County Education Committee to dismiss Outram at once, though there were disagreements among them over the rights and wrongs of sex education.
The local doctors believed that when undertaken by the child's
mother it could have positive effects but fundamentalists like
the magistrate insisted that any such teaching was morally
wrong.

IV   From purity to social hygiene

Unfortunately for the managers their plan misfired. The county council committee refused to comply with the request to remove Outram, pronouncing themselves well-pleased with their head-teacher. Almost inevitably the issue had become caught up in a tangled web of local education politics. It is unclear whether Derbyshire Education Committee actively endorsed Outram's sex education lessons. But there had been a long-standing dispute between managers, parents and the county over school premises. The county authority claimed that this was the real reason for local hostility to the headmistress. Parents were merely using it as a front to hit back at them over the premises issue.[9]

Dronfield responded with an open public meeting, where the residents mounted a strong defence of their parental rights – systematically vilifying Outram into the bargain. This time local mothers were to the fore. They protested that the teacher's disgusting and abominable information had undermined the sacredness of the home and the mothers' authority. Many perceived the affair as a struggle between the competing claims of parents and teachers over the education of the child. The fundamental question was: who had the right to initiate children into the laws of sex and with what precise forms of knowledge? Did authority reside in the parents, with their popular language of purity (and one suspects a commonsense discourse about the naturalness and inevitability of procreation and parenthood), or with the power of professionals? Mrs Milnes was clear in her own mind that parental authority was being unsurped:

> It is too disgusting for the children to know; they have not the same respect for their parents when they know that. (Weeping) There is a proper time and place to tell children. They are old enough when they leave school. . . . I think it is time the thing was put a stop to.[10]

Other parents complained that Outram's action was tantamount to an assault on the moral innocence of childhood. The girls who had been 'initiated' were corrupting their brothers and sisters and there had been marked signs of mental deterioration in these children. The parents' defence of their own

160

interests was complicated by a vicious attack on Outram as the archetypal spinster. One mother claimed: 'She would not have said such a thing if she had been married. That is what is the matter with her.' Another had told her daughter that *Miss* Outram knew nothing about babies.[11] The managers carefully channelled resentment towards the county council, who, they suggested, were in league with their headmistress. A unanimous resolution, backed by a petition with twelve hundred signatures, demanded Outram's prompt dismissal. This was accompanied by a thinly veiled threat that her retention would cause a serious impediment to the educational efficiency of the school.

By February the local press had got wind of the affair. If the doctor, the vicar and the local publican represented one major force constructing public opinion in this small community, then the popular press was the other. Articles in *The Weekly Dispatch* and *The Derbyshire Times* presented the case through a familiar blend of factual reportage and lurid sensationalism designed to titillate local audiences. *The Dispatch* led with the headline: 'Teacher and the Girls She Told', and carried a picture of the wicked Miss Outram surrounded by her innocent young charges, while *The Derbyshire Times* called for the Board of Education to step in to arbitrate.[12]

The board was in fact already informed; its response was superbly bureaucratic. Fearing there might well be public outcry and an appeal to its authority, the central secretariat had asked one of the inspectors, W.J. Hands, to report on the affair. Hands was thorough. He saw his own role as something between a scientific investigator and a secret agent, and he sent a verbatim report of the managers' meeting back to the board, together with a sheaf of press cuttings. The inspector counselled caution. It seems likely that his real mission was to find an escape route for the board, so that it could steer clear of the incident and avoid involving the central state in any direct decision over sex education. As with contemporary campaigns around the criminal law, the state opted for a neutral course of non-intervention. It was unwillingly propelled into action by the competing forces within civil society.

Hands kept well away from Dronfield, staying at a hotel in Derby, on the grounds that the appearance of an HMI would only implicate the board in Outram's dismissal. His enquiries revealed that the sex teaching had been given in scripture time. Here was the escape clause the board was looking for. The secretariat minuted that under the 1870 Education Act and the existing code the board had no control over the content of religious education. On receiving the petition demanding Outram's resignation they stuck to the principle of laissez-faire. Joseph Pease, the board's president, approved a tactfully worded reply to the Dronfield parents. He explained that the appointment and dismissal of teachers was a matter for the local authority alone and that the board had no authority other than to help supervise the 'educational efficiency' of the school.[13]

But educational efficiency had already been impaired. *The Derbyshire Times* noted that defiant parents were voting with their feet by keeping children away from school. Towards the end of April matters came to a head when parents were threatened with prosecution. They remained firm; if anything their opposition had hardened, particularly against the Education Committee who they saw as pushing them around. According to one parent:

> The Committee had simply patted them on the back like spoilt children and told them, 'Now just send your children back to school.' Were the parents of Dronfield to be treated as naughty boys and girls, or were they to be treated as intelligent working people? Miss Outram was still at school, and the parents' wishes had been ignored in London and Derby.[14]

The protagonists looked to be heading for an all-out clash, but the outbreak of war in August put an abrupt end to the contest. The local papers turned their attention to the German invasion of Belgium and the problems of recruiting while the Board of Education closed its file on the case without any apparent resolution.

The Dronfield affair was not an isolated incident. In the first decades of the twentieth century sex education took on great importance within public debate. A broad and often uneasy coalition – of medics, clerics, social purists, eugenists and some feminists – campaigned to raise the question as a matter of vital national and even imperial concern. Books and pamphlets directed at children and parents, conferences and public meetings, together with the formation of influential pressure groups, all testified to the seriousness with which the issue was being treated. The sexual instinct, now re-defined as the racial instinct, was to be channelled into healthy and responsible parenthood. In the words of the 1911 *Manifesto* of the National Council of Public Morals, an influential campaigning force, the solution to national immorality lay in educating young men and women into the physiological knowledge and lofty ideals of marriage.[15] Increasingly, sex education was advanced as the alternative to criminal law regulation. There was a growing consensus that sex hygiene teaching held out the best assurance for eliminating vice. Behind this gradual shift of emphasis lay the re-emergence of a broad and powerful alliance around the issue of national health. It was backed by the renewed prominence of the medical profession and medical discourse as a voice within public debate.

2   IN CORPORE SANO

Though state medicine suffered a period of retrenchment in the closing decades of the nineteenth century, *medical research* enlarged its scope and sphere of influence. Despite the restrictions placed on the Medical Department of the Local Government Board, investigations carried out by its research team into the aetiology of the major infectious diseases greatly enhanced its reputation.[16] Medics might bemoan the lack of any broad initiative in public health policy but they could point to this expanding area of research as a mark of contemporary achievements. When the *BMJ*, in its special commemorative number for the Queen's Diamond Jubilee in 1897, reviewed the development of the profession over the previous sixty years it was this aspect that it chose to trumpet. Discovery of the microorganic causes of disease and the mode of their transmission had opened up a domain which 'to the minds of our immediate ancestors seemed almost outside of the knowable'.[17]

Major transformations within medical discourse provided the theoretical conditions for this perceived advance. The gradual acceptance of the germ theory of infection, following the research of Louis Pasteur and Robert Koch into viruses and vaccines in the 1870s and 1880s, had resulted in the rapid isolation of the bacilli of all the major infectious diseases.[18] Medical staff at the Local Government Board impressed the importance of these discoveries on their local health authorities through a constant barrage of memoranda, visitations and staff consultations. Integral to this research was an understanding of how the healthy body provided its own defences against invading bacteria by developing anti-toxins. This 'medical semiotic' produced a new conception of the body as the site of health and disease. It was more and more focused on the internal biochemistry of the individual, as against the older and simpler individual/environment equation. Parallel investigations into cellular pathology worked with the notion that disease had its origins at the level of the cell.[19]

This medicalized scrutiny of the individual, and his/her role as an agent in the maintenance of health or the transmission of disease, formed a central tenet of medical discourse in the early twentieth century. It was premised on a qualitative shift in the intellectual organization of medical concepts. As a programme of state medicine it was quite as significant as that which had shaped the environmental reforms seventy years before. For Sir George Newman, first Medical Officer to the newly created Ministry of Health in 1919, contemporary medicine was now entering its 'biological setting'. The concept of the environment possessed a new meaning, more personal, intimate and integrated, concerned with the 'life history, heredity, family and domestic life, personal habits and customs' of individuals.[20]

In practice the administrative shift away from environmentalism was much less dramatic than ideologues like Newman were insisting. There was of course no sudden abandoning of the principles of nineteenth-century public health policy. The broad programme of environmental medicine remained intact. Health measures enacted at the Local Government Board between 1871 and 1918 extended and deepened state intervention in familiar areas: sanitation, working-class housing, the industrial environment, nuisances, water-supply, etc.[21] Where the new principles of bodily health posed a direct challenge to environmentalism, as in the eugenics movement, they were opposed by the majority of medics. *In corpore sano* was given its

most expansive expression in the broad general pronouncements from the profession. It was put forward in the reports of
medical officers such as Newman and his colleague Arthur
Newsholme and in growing public debate over national health
in Parliament and the press. At the level of policy implementation, impact centred on carefully demarcated areas. Especially
important was the growing state medical scrutiny of key individuals within the population – soldiers, mothers and children.
In isolating such groups for surveillance and regulation, the
profession was drawing on changes within medical discourse.
These were themselves deeply implicated in the political and
intellectual struggles of the conjuncture before the First War.

State medicine's involvement in campaigns for improved
military efficiency and health regeneration has usually been
loosely ascribed to the growing move towards 'collectivism' in
the early twentieth century. Medics have been cited as a key
example of a modern breed of technical expert, instrumental in
extending and deepening state intervention into new and familiar areas.[22] What is absent from these accounts is a structural
analysis of the political and administrative conditions which
enabled the profession to reassert its position, and to insist on
increased representation within the state. This involves grasping the dynamic inter-relation between new scientific knowledges and the much broader public debates over national
efficiency and imperial survival.

From the late 1860s there had been repeated attempts to
obtain greater state aid and recognition for science, in the wake
of increased technical competition from Germany. Such efforts
had met with little success from Liberal and Tory politicians
alike. The *Report of the Royal Commission on Scientific Instruction and the Advancement of Science*, 1875 had polemicized for
the importance of a Ministry of Science and Education. But its
recommendations were dismissed as utopian. In the same way,
attempts by a small but highly articulate pressure group around
the journal *Nature*, founded in 1869 to argue for the social
utility of scientific research, gained only limited success. Within the state itself, as we have seen, scientific and technical
experts were increasingly confronted by a hostile cadre of lay
civil servants.

The immediate origins of a greater alliance between the state and science lay in military anxieties over the Boer War débâcle. Britain's poor military performance sharpened the perceived economic, political and cultural threat to the predominance of the Empire from other burgeoning nations, especially Germany and to a lesser extent the USA and Japan. Science now occupied a central place in the ensuing debate over national efficiency. For diverse and often disparate groupings, the language of scientificity stood as a metaphor and a referent, which condensed specific anxieties and signified different solutions to different people. Science in this sense came to stand as a meta-discourse, framed by the broader contours of the conjuncture.

In the late nineteenth and early twentieth century the fabric of mid-Victorian hegemony was shattered by a series of structural contradictions, from economic retardation and industrial unrest, to growing socialist and feminist political militancy and intensification of anxiety over a whole range of social issues. Each had their own particular history and political trajectory. However, their multiple condensation at the level of the state makes it possible to speak, not just of a set of regional problems but of a general crisis of hegemony. The swing back to scientific explanations and solutions and the re-entry of the expert into the state apparatuses, needs to be understood both in terms of the internal transformations within scientific knowledge and in the light of these broader economic and political developments. The new cadre of experts were not mere effects of the wider crises and destabilizations. But their professional debates were continually being penetrated by these extra-discursive conditions. At the same time, politicians were increasingly pressed for answers to problems against which the measured, patrician tones of the lay administrator seemed amateur and outdated. Medics in particular capitalized on this state of affairs, mobilizing the results of scientific research as part of their broader push for increased representation with the state.

Campaigns to improve the health of the armed forces represented a classic instance of the inter-relation between science and politics. Recruitment was a major source of anxiety following Boer War revelations about the high rate of recruits rejected on grounds of ill-health.[23] More disturbingly, military statistics seemed to confirm the findings on poverty by Charles Booth

166

and Llewellyn-Smith. Both sets of inquiries pointed to the existence of a degenerate underclass of the population which formed a residual pool of infection. In 1903 the Director General of the Army Medical Services and the Royal College of Physicians and Surgeons responded to these revelations by medically verifying the distinction between the healthy and respectable working-class and the diseased residuum. Militarily, the demand was for major reforms in army training which took note of new developments in nutrition, hygiene and physiology.[24] Capitalizing on the alarm in official circles, the *BMJ* complained that military chiefs had still not learnt the terrible lessons of the South African war. Bacilli were far more deadly than bullets in the battle for imperial survival.[25]

Behind this medical pressure lay the thinly veiled threat that if the government refused to acknowledge its responsibilities towards the armies of the Empire, then the result would be destruction. During the Russo-Japanese War of 1904–5, the *BMJ* noted ominously that the Japanese were capable of great feats of endurance on account of their strict attention to the laws of hygiene.[26] Moments of panic in the national efficiency debate – often orchestrated by the new popular press – enabled medics to dramatically represent their new scientific concepts in ways that gained them intellectual hegemony and popular credibility.

The model most frequently projected by medics was of a militarized conception of health, which could be extended to key groups within civil society. Though scientists were highly critical of the aristocratic amateurishness of many senior army administrators, they were keenly attracted to the image of a militarily organized society. Their vision was of functionally integrated systems and ordered hierarchies, transcending the atomized, petty divisions of party politics. This sort of militarism made professional sense to many medics because of its connection with their own reformulated medical discourse. Here representations of organicism and physiological integration were pre-eminent, and biology frequently carried an overtly political message. Moreover, as specialized professionals, medics warmed to an ideology of national efficiency precisely because it privileged rational experts over those generalist administrators who had earlier curbed the power of the Simoneon specialist.

IV   From purity to social hygiene

Pressure for health regeneration was not confined to the army. The medical model of militarized efficiency was carried over into key areas of civil society. Politically sensitive groups, notably the schoolchild and the mother, were specific targets for intervention. The school system of physical training put forward by the Board of Education in 1902 in close consultation with the War Office, took its impetus directly from military methods. Groups of exercises were designed to strengthen target areas of the body (limbs, trunk, bone structure, the nervous system) in order to promote greater physical efficiency in later life, at work or on the battlefield.[27] This military model of the disciplined body, responding instantly to word of command, remained paramount in the years before the First War. Though it was aimed most directly at boys, girls were also addressed. The board's medical department insisted that PT was a more effective way of improving national physique than compulsory military service, because army training began too late and excluded women and girls.[28] As always such a system was seen to deliver distinctive *moral* benefits. For the working-class child correct physical development could help eliminate the immoral effects of a dissolute culture or unhealthy environment, contributing to a gradual improvement of national physique. Medics and educationalists were keenly aware that the best way of inculcating the laws of health was through a stress on the *pleasures* to be gained from PT. Pleasure was to be produced by the body's obedient and systematic conformity to certain physical norms. As Sir Robert Morant directed in his introduction to the 1909 syllabus:

> The Board desires that all lessons in physical exercise . . . should be *thoroughly enjoyed* by the children. Indeed, freedom of movement and a certain degree of exhilaration are essentials of all true physical education.[29]

The broadly conceived programme of health education not only demonstrated the ideal of militarized efficiency, it also embodied the new scientific concepts derived from physiology and biochemistry. In the panics over the declining birth-rate and the continuing high levels of infant mortality, medics campaigned around these new knowledges to shift emphasis away from environmentalism towards close scrutiny of the health of the mother.[30] Scientists like Dr John Ballantyre, Assistant Physician to the Edinburgh Royal Maternity Hospital, together with progressive local medical officers like Newman and Newsholme, insisted that recent research into pregnancy and embryonic pathology pointed to new methods of tackling the high infant death-rate.[31] The demand was for a state-backed campaign to educate women and girls. They were to be prepared for their maternal duties and given material assistance to maintain a higher standard of motherhood. More often than not the driving force behind this movement was a concern with population politics, a belief that a qualitative as well as quantitative increase in the birth-rate was the key to imperial progress and power. Even Newsholme, who usually avoided the emotive rhetoric of the social imperialists, felt that the choices facing the Empire were stark and dramatic:

> It cannot be regarded as a matter of indifference whether the unfilled portions of the world shall be peopled by Eastern races, by negroes, by Slavonic or other Eastern European peoples, by the Latin races, or by the races of Northern Europe.[32]

3   RACIAL HEALTH

An emphasis on the *racial* component in health maintenance marked a significant development within contemporary medical knowledge. From the 1870s Darwinist theories of racial progress and evolution had worked to transform the way in which physical and moral processes were understood. For social Darwinists like Herbert Spencer, evolutionary theory demonstrated scientifically what earlier social scientists had only grasped in moral terms. The individual and the nation needed to be seen as part of the evolutionary development of the race, through processes which obeyed observable and scientifically predictable laws. The rise of the eugenics movement in the early twentieth century crystallized the intellectual and political imperatives of evolutionary biology. The concept of eugenics was defined by its founder, Francis Galton, in the early 1880s as

169

the 'study of those agencies under social control, which may improve or impair the racial qualities of future generations.'[33] But eugenics only gained theoretical legitimacy and an institutional base in the political and international conjuncture before the First War. The Eugenics Laboratory, founded in 1907 under the psychologist and social imperialist, Karl Pearson, and the rival Eugenics Education Society, begun in the same year with its journal *The Eugenics Review*, brought together a broad coalition of biologists, medics, clerics and prominent intellectuals and politicians.

At the heart of the eugenist strategy lay a sustained attack on nineteenth-century environmentalism in all its forms – medical, charitable and philanthropic. Environmentalism was unscientific. It was at best a mere palliative and at worst it actively sustained the unfit and degenerate elements of the population in their reckless overbreeding. Medical science mitigated suffering, but by preserving the diseased and degenerate it flew in the face of natural selection and the iron laws of heredity.[34] Eugenists insisted that it was crucial to redefine the terrain of social intervention. The site needed to be shifted back to the regulation of life itself; to the study of sound offspring and to the elimination of all those racial poisons (alcoholism, venereal disease, feeble-mindedness) which were leading to national degeneration. Havelock Ellis emphasized that the new aim of social reform was to purify conditions at their source.[35] For C.W. Saleeby, concern with race culture stood above politics, cutting across petty divisions of class and self-interest and pointing the way towards national regeneration.[36]

Concern about the relation between national power and the strength of the population was not of course new. There were distinct continuities here between eugenics and the population politics developed in the statistical societies and the General Register Office from the 1830s. We have seen that this strategy had addressed the relation between certain population habits (what Farr had defined as the vital statistics of marriage and divorce, fertility and fecundity) and the nation's economic prosperity, health and happiness. What distinguished eugenists from Farr and his colleagues were the laws and theoretical concepts used to assess the population. Earlier statisticians had based population predictions on arithmetical averages, derived from bills of mortality and other statistical tables, and had been primarily concerned with legal and moral intervention into the family. Eugenists argued for a quite different understanding of how norms and averages were to be calculated. Pearson's new science of biometry used calculus rather than arithmetic to conceptualize the population as a bounded space, with individual variation following predictable laws. Increased mathematical precision was deemed to give a new scientificity to biological and evolutionary phenomena. It pointed to man's ability to master his organic environment.[37]

Allied with this theoretical shift went a reconceptualization of the role played by heredity in individual development. For earlier social reformers, human progress or decline had been seen to depend on the constant interplay of the individual's moral faculties and the state of the environment. This scheme had been modified with the introduction of Darwinist concepts of heredity. But the theories of urban degeneracy put forward by Charles Booth and Llewellyn-Smith in the 1880s still followed the principle set by Lamarck – that acquired characteristics could be inherited. Eugenists drew on recent research by the German biologist August Weismann to claim that the germ cells which controlled reproduction were distinct and independent of body or somatic cells.[38] Hence inherited characteristics could not be modified by environmental factors. The way lay open for a sustained attack on environmentalism.

The medical profession was deeply divided over eugenics. Pearson acknowledged that the new racial science could do little without the hearty co-operation of medics. Yet his persistent efforts to woo the profession in 1912 only emphasized the distance between the two discourses on the heredity/ environment issue. In fact, Pearson's *entente cordiale* involved a scathing outburst against the type of social inquiries undertaken by local medical offices of health. Statistics, he claimed, were incompetently used, while sanitary science still perpetuated the pernicious myth that questions of back-to-back housing, privies and breast-feeding were more important than the hereditary character of the parents.[39]

Proposals by Dr Robert Rentoul for the compulsory sterilization of the unfit had already been given short shrift by the BMA in 1904, on the grounds that they were contrary to medical ethics.[40] Nevertheless, a number of prominent medics continued to push the eugenic case. At the BMA's annual meeting in 1913, eugenists denounced medics' long-standing but misguided dependence on environmentalism, arguing for amendments to the marriage laws in the interests of eugenically fit unions.[41] The *BMJ* intervened swiftly with a lengthy editorial, bringing the profession out strongly against eugenics. While acknowledging the supreme importance of physical and moral regeneration for national survival, the journal displayed the liberal assumptions of the medical establishment.[42] The BMA could not countenance the challenge eugenics posed to its specific brand of social and physiological individualism, with its stress on the importance of individual initiative and on the value of each and every human life.

Eugenics never achieved the overall hegemonic position that its advocates hoped for. Eugenists gave evidence to the Inter-Departmental Committee on Physical Deterioration, 1904, as well as to other government inquiries into feeble-mindedness, alcoholism, marriage and divorce and venereal disease.[43] But their explanations of the deterioration of national physique in terms of the reckless breeding of the unfit, and their policies of forced segregation of degenerates and the issuing of marriage certificates, were not implemented.

It was hardly surprising that preventive medicine, and state medicine in particular, refused to give unconditional support to eugenics. The ideology of environmentalism was cautiously optimistic about social amelioration and human progress. Such optimism was too firmly embedded in the culture of the profession, and too deeply bound up with medical authority and status, for it to be in any way seriously threatened. Environmentalism remained paramount. What occurred was the expansion and deepening of its concepts to include racial and hereditary factors. At the level of the meta-discourse of the profession, few statements on the future of the nation's health failed to reference the new dimensions of race and evolution. Human biology was now to be studied as a series of stages in the process of evolution. The life history of each and every individual needed to be grasped not merely in the context of his/her immediate environment, but as part of a broader racial history.[44] Newman was aware that when eugenics was deployed in this way – shorn of its critique of environmentalism – it made a valuable contribution to the philosophical underpinnings of the profession. It was useful in raising broad questions about human progress or decline and projecting a grandiose vision of health.

Such a vision was of course racist, patriarchal and anti-democratic. In practice, the philosophy of racial health involved laying down expert injunctions to the working-class and to women on the importance of preserving imperial stamina and physique. This was posed both against other competing 'civilized' nations and against those black and brown races who threatened to swamp the globe with their animal savagery. Britain would advance to a higher stage of civilization via favourable environment *and* sound heredity. In other words, by the harmonious integration of nature and nurture. Racial theories fared best in policy areas already sensitized to the new conceptions of bodily health – motherhood, insanity and poverty, as well as birth-control and venereal disease. Eugenics owes its specific place in our history to its influence on the emergent pedagogy of sex education.

4   SOCIAL AND MORAL HYGIENE

In 1917 the eugenist and social purist, the Rev. James Marchant confidently pronounced: 'It is now being fully recognized that all moral reforms for the regeneration of mankind must be brought about by the combination of religion and science.'[45] Under the banner of social hygiene, moralists, clerics, eugenists and some feminists joined forces with medics to resurrect a dialogue between medicine and morality. The new movement condensed a wide range of competing aims and strategies, but two linked concerns remained paramount in the early twentieth century. On the one hand there were the claims of morality and religion, stressing the importance of self-control and discipline for racial progress, and on the other the new medical discourse with its reconceptualization of the rules of health and hygiene. The resulting interchange of ideas and expertise redefined the terrain of moral problems. It simultaneously produced a renewed moral emphasis within preventive medicine.

173

The holistic strategy for health forged by the social hygiene campaigns fixed on particular sites of intervention. Along with the problems of adolescence and insanity, sex was singled out by hygienists. The new movement worked vigorously to redefine the domain of sexuality – developing concepts of identity and sexual difference, even a vocabulary of satisfaction and pleasure, which was differentiated from social purity. Training the sexual instinct cut against purity's criminalizing strategy, at the moment when purists were achieving their maximum effect in legislation.

Social hygiene took off in the years immediately before the First War as part of the growing debate over national health and efficiency. Almost immediately the new coalition began to question the criminal law approach to moral problems. In 1911 the inaugural conference of the National Council of Public Morals (NCPM) announced that prevention rather than punishment was to be the keynote in the regeneration of the nation's moral life.[46] According to their rhetoric, public morals were now not merely a job for the criminal law, but for a wide spectrum of social agencies. Repression through fear, combined with rescue work for the fallen, was no longer enough. Positive education, channelling the sexual instinct towards socially approved goals, needed to counter older, negative moralisms.

It would be wrong to over-emphasize the distance between purists and social hygienists; concepts and personnel often overlapped. Those moralists who joined the new coalition were usually motivated by the same structural factors which brought together other groupings: the economic and military threat to Empire, alarm over the falling birth-rate and the residuum. But as in the 1830s their participation involved a reworking of moral discourse. Morality itself now began to be redefined. Its significations were shifted away from the evangelical, nonconformist emphasis of the purity movement. Nowhere was this clearer than in moralists' take-up of scientific logic and a language of rationality.

We have already noted the obstacles preventing any renewed dialogue between medicine and morality in the last decades of the nineteenth century. The eclipse of state medicine, combined with the renewed political clout of nonconformist religion and the stern voice of the purity movement, militated against a revival of the medico-moral alliance. Purists had of course drawn on medical and evolutionary concepts, but always with the proviso that they were subordinate to the dictates of a higher morality.

It was the changed set of political and social conditions in the years before the First War which paved the way for the re-emergence of an alliance between medics, natural scientists and the established church. Along with this rapprochement went a corresponding attack on the fundamentalist tenets of nonconformist morality. The metaphor of scientific rationality and the figure of the state-sponsored expert were used to attack older voluntary and 'amateur' approaches to social reform. National efficiency campaigners were particularly scathing in their critique of the 'provincial chapel-going radical', who was seen to promote sectional and petty self-interest at a time when national survival was in question.[47] Many historians have commented on the decline of nonconformism as a political force in the early twentieth century. What is less often recognized is the emergence of a new type of moral discourse. Here evolutionary science was fully integrated with moral pronouncements about society's future progress or decline. This religion was more rationalist and ethical, much stronger in defence of the established social order and much less populist in tone and organization. Old Testament morality, wreaking vengeance on the political establishment, was displaced by imagery of 'the perfect man', as Dean Inge of St Pauls called him, whose overriding concern was with 'his' duties to the state.[48] This 'gentleman' was to be the product not of a 'fallacious biologism', but of true evolutionary progress which preserved the physical and spiritual unity of the organism.

Anglicanism provided the largest number of clerical recruits to national efficiency and social hygiene. Marchant, Dean Inge, Mandel Creighton Bishop of London and Canon Lyttleton were all prominent hygienists, equally committed to eugenics. The Church of England may have found it easier to accommodate the cult of hygienics and efficiency. It had a long-standing concern with the problems of authority and discipline, and its stronger philsophical tradition made it more compatible with the intellectual rigour of hygiene theories. Dean Inge was typical of the new type of moralist. From the clerical aristocracy, he had been a leading Anglican theologian as Lady Mary Professor of Divinity at Cambridge before his appointment to the prominent public position of Dean of St Pauls in 1911. Inge was a strong Tory, vigorous in denouncing 'bolshevism'. But he insisted that organized religion needed to meet the challenge of social unrest and moral decay.[49] A member of the Eugenics Education Society, the Clerical and Medical Committee of the BMA – where he campaigned for a stronger moral lead from the profession – and the National Council for Combating Venereal Disease, he moved freely between religious, political and scientific spheres. Inge was important as the type of agent who linked the disparate cultures and intellectual milieus which formed the backbone of the social hygiene movement.

The reverse side of the coin was the renewed visibility of moral concerns within the medical profession. Physiological theories provided the point of entry for a sustained moral logic. Dramatic, popular depictions of cellular processes and biochemical reactions generated a language which was itself implicitly moral in its narrative stress on dynamic causalities, portrayed as inevitable and irreversible. Eugenically-based metaphors lent themselves particularly well to this type of moralizing treatment. Hygienists spoke of the need to grasp the actual moment when the nerve centres of life were poisoned through hereditary influence or degenerate living. Newman was a master of populist medical rhetoric. In his grandiose overview of the history of medical science published in 1919, he made a powerful case for a totalizing conception of preventive medicine. Although disease was now increasingly defined as an internal malfunction of the body, its causes included the whole of the social and moral history of the nation:

> The essentials of disease are thus . . . habit and the powers of resistance of man's body; the seeds or germs or cause of abnormal action . . . lastly, the whole process is profoundly modified by a vast concatenation of variable social, personal, external and even economic factors . . .[50]

The creation of the Ministry of Health in 1919 registered a self-conscious application of this moralized medical ideology.

IV   From purity to social hygiene

Under the banner of health education, the Ministry's aim was for the creation of an enlightened public opinion. Sanitary legislation could only go so far in monitoring personal health; what was vital was a popular campaign stressing the individual's own responsibility to observe the rules of health.[51] Equally, voluntary initiatives like the People's League of Health, founded in 1917 under royal patronage, with a membership which included medics, moralists and eugenists, pronounced: 'A Nation's Health is a Nation's Wealth.'[52] Popular pamphlets stressed heredity and environment as 'the two determining factors in our lives', and pointed to the inevitable moral consequences for those who broke the laws of health: 'nature knows nothing about "Forgive us our trespasses" . . . she demands payment for every one of her laws which is broken.'[53] Commercial advertising, for Pear's soap, bleach and disinfectant, addressing women as consumers and domestic labourers, intensified the focus on home health and cleanliness in keeping the moral and physical threat of disease at bay.

Like Dean Inge, the careers and culture of leading medical intellectuals displayed distinctive connections between science and morality. As so often in our account, an engagement with official agents pinpoints the way discursive structures were negotiated at the level of personal experience. Both George Newman and Arthur Newsholme combined a commitment to the scientific principles of preventive hygiene with a muscular Christianity. Newman began his career in the 1890s at Edinburgh University and King's College, London, where he was senior demonstrator in bacteriology and lecturer on infectious diseases. He went on to become medical officer of health for Bedfordshire and then for Finsbury, during which time he published research on the bacteriology of milk and on infant mortality. He later became Medical Officer at the Board of Education and then at the Ministry of Health, pioneering school medical inspection and education for motherhood. An active Quaker throughout his life, editing the journal *The Friend's Quarterly Examiner* for many years, Newman integrated his duties as medical administrator with more traditional forms of philanthropy and self-help. He worked in the adult school movement in girls' clubs run from the Friend's Meeting House in St Martin's Lane. His interpretation of preventive medicine was founded on an unswerving faith in the evangelical principles of his own religion and a fervent belief in the duties owed by the citizen to the nation state. It also encompassed a eugenist and imperialist gloss on the importance of domesticity and motherhood. For Newman, homes were the 'vitals of the nation', and the British Empire depended 'not upon dominions and territory alone, but upon men, not upon markets, but upon homes'.[54]

Arthur Newsholme, Newman's older colleague, had his origins in a similar nonconformist background. Medical Officer for Brighton and later to the Local Government Board, where he championed statistical inquiries into infant mortality, Newsholme felt the evangelical revival of the late nineteenth century to have been a potent factor in the social hygiene movement. His participation in the NCPM and the National Council for Combating Venereal Disease (NCCVD) stimulated him to write tracts and pamphlets on sex education and the perils of promiscuity. Like Newman, he frequently used his official status to polemicize for a holistic conception of medicine, which took in moral and social factors as part of the new scientific advances.

The institutional and intellectual alliances illustrated by the careers of leading protagonists formed the backbone of the social hygiene movement in the early years of the twentieth century. As in the 1830s and 1840s, this medico-moral domain specified key concepts of sexuality as part of its concerns. But there was no simple continuity between the two movements, no simple development of knowledge about sex. The hygienics of Newman and his colleagues was highly differentiated from the early social medicine of Kay and Southwood Smith – in the organization of their discourse, their forms of social regulation and in the political and institutional conditions through which they were produced. The field of sexuality was now much more clearly specified and theorized, in comparison with its relatively undifferentiated treatment in the moral repertoire of earlier environmentalists. Newman and Newsholme displayed a high degree of self-consciousness about the place of sex within social relations, which was absent from the work of Kay and Chadwick. A further structural difference was the impact of feminism. As we know, the history of medical politics from the mid-nineteenth century witnessed a growing feminist presence in official debates over sex. It is important to turn again to feminist involvement here. For the hygienist alliance was forced to operate through a series of negotiations with the women's movement.

5   FEMINIST RESPONSES

How did feminists orientate themselves towards the cult of social hygiene? In the early years of this century many women still retained a deep suspicion of medical intervention in the moral arena. The sticking-point was the continuing legacy of the Contagious Diseases Acts, and the wider fear that the profession was still sunk in 'blind materialism'.[55] Yet some, particularly purists, believed that the growing rapprochement between medics and moralists necessitated a serious re-think of attitudes towards state medicine. How did this come about?

On the repeal of the acts in 1886 *The Shield* had ended its campaign. But it quickly re-formed in 1897 to challenge fresh regulationism introduced into India, keeping up a constant barrage of propaganda against any return to compulsory medical inspection and detention of prostitutes at home.[56] By the first decade of the twentieth century the majority of medics saw return to enforced regulation of VD as out of the question. Recent knowledge concerning the disease's diagnosis and treatment, and its redefinition as a primarily civilian rather than a military problem, made the regulationist strategy impracticable.[57] The changed stance on VD paved the way for a partial reconciliation between purity feminists and medics over the twin issues of morality and health. Tentative articles in *The Shield* from as early as 1905 began to reconsider the role of science in promoting moral reform. Provided medics stressed the absolute necessity for sexual responsibility and self-control then 'the microscope need not be despised'.[58] As one delegate to the International Abolitionist Conference of 1906 argued, science with her austere voice ought to tell man that a higher stage of civilization depended on the mastery of his instincts.[59] Over the next ten years, the journal recorded an ongoing debate between old-style moralists and younger, often newly professionalized women, who held a more rationalist approach to moral reform. The growing dialogue with medics heightened the moral input into medical discourse. Helen Wilson, daughter of the repeal campaigner and editor of *The Shield*, was herself a trained doctor, as was the purist and eugenist, Mary Scharlieb. When in 1913 Alison Neilans of the Ladies' National Association announced that 'we and our former antagonists can work cordially together', Wilson explained that the olive branch was a result of the change of heart among medics and their new expansive definition of health.[60]

Organizational shifts, alongside changes in the language of purity, reflected this new feminist position. In 1915 the LNA merged with the British Abolitionist Association to form the Association for Moral and Social Hygiene, with Wilson and Neilans effectively in control. The new name, with its medical inflection, still had the power to evoke old hostilities and suspicions among some purity feminists. *The Shield* tactfully explained the shift. In the past the association had been dedicated to the supreme claims of morality and to the exposure of the error of 'so-called hygiene', which sought to subordinate justice and personal liberty to alleged physical necessities. However, abolitionists who began as moralists had been 'constrained by the necessities of their struggle' to become hygienists. Purists had recently found that the name 'abolitionist' hindered further progess, implying a problem of 'long ago and far away' and alienating potential allies.[61] Henceforward, members of the new body would be proud to call themselves hygienists, because they had rescued the concept from the degradation into which it had sunk during a 'materialistic age'. They had shown that science must take account of the whole man and not only of his body. To lend weight to the claim, members were reminded of Sir John Simon's own expansive definition of the moral responsibilities of preventive medicine. The readership was offered a vision of the new city of 'Hygeia' – a recurrent image projected by both medics and moralists. The irresistible force of the city was attracting pilgrims from 'widely-sundered starting points'. Like the New Jerusalem it was planned by God on the foundations of equal justice and morality, but this modern vision of a sanitized cosmopolis was governed by health-giving purity and the sanctity of family life.[62]

180

IV From purity to social hygiene

Feminist responses to hygienism were rarely unambiguous, partly because physiological medicine and evolutionary biology were so powerful a mainstay of anti-feminist campaigns. But these concepts did provide some women with categories of self-definition around which to mobilize, negotiate and occasionally disrupt and claim as their own. For many, the issue of national health, like social purity, was used to advance women's influence in the social sphere. It enabled them to hold their own in the face of calls from male experts for a greater professionalization of the field. *The Shield* alerted its readers to the great possibilities opened up to women by the growing focus on hygiene. The woman of the future would be far more than a nurse or consoler, she would have a positive religion to realize as a high-priestess of health.[63] Eugenists like Scharlieb and Alice Ravenhill insisted that biology now conclusively proved that responsibility for safeguarding the nation's morals lay with women. For Scharlieb, it was women's unique position as reproducers which made them so central to the physical and moral training of future generations.[64] Ravenhill saw the revelations of medicine and eugenics pointing to a greater role for women, not only as mothers but as guardians of those aesthetic qualities which made for physical, intellectual and moral progress.[65]

This alliance of some purists and moderate feminists with the medical profession needs to be contrasted with the ongoing hostility displayed by many. The militant wing of the movement did consciously draw on medical and evolutionary concepts, but to extend and deepen their attacks on men. Both Christabel Pankhurst and Swiney used medical authorities and statistics instrumentally to win specific arguments, while distancing themselves from what they saw as the corrupt power of male professionals. *The Great Scourge* was not only a vigorous purity polemic, it mobilized the evidence of countless medics to insist that up to eighty per cent of the male population was infected with gonorrhea – the race poison of the eugenists.[66] Speaking the language of race and nation, Pankhurst demonstrated that innocent wives were being continually infected by their adulterous husbands, resulting in degeneracy on a scale which heralded race suicide. Her book concluded that continence was both physiologically and morally essential for the fit reproduction of the race.

As always, Frances Swiney's medical polemic was even more extensive, claiming women's innate biological and mental superiority over the rest of creation. In a dazzling subversion of medical and eugenic theories she insisted that women, as the reproducers of life, were not merely central to perpetuation of the race but were the dominant motivating force behind the human species. They were 'the centre of gravity of the whole biological system', while men were becoming more and more superfluous.[67] Swiney proposed that women's racial superiority was evidenced both by their physical and mental capabilities and in their internal cellular composition. Darwin and Spencer had been wrong to argue that women were in a state of arrested development. Man was the intermediate form. The shape of woman's face was far in advance of that of man; in the number of teeth they were leading evolution; they had more grace and more perfect physical beauty. Challenging the biologists Patrick Geddes and J.A. Thomson, Swiney pointed out that 'femaleness' was due to the presence of a chromosome *absent* in the male. Hence women displayed a more complex cellular composition, which was the positive force behind reproduction, whereas the katabolic male cells led to racial disintegration.[68] Current panics by eugenists and social reformers over national decline were misplaced in blaming the mother. It was *men* who were the cause of racial decay. In language which coupled purity outrage with a conceptual grasp of eugenics and the new biology, Swiney drew together the major social problems – disease, feeble-mindedness, degeneracy and insanity – to expose male vice as the root cause of national decline:

Well may Dr Rentoul claim that the health of the woman is our greatest natural asset, that the physically and mentally healthy woman has been so ruthlessly, so brutally, so generally mercilessly exploited by the male as women . . . She stands as the martyr of organized and systematic sexual wrong-doing on the part of the man who should be her mate, and whom alone she has evolved to the human plane. Church and state, religion, law, prejudice, custom, tradition, greed, lust, hatred, injustice, selfishness, ignorance, and arrogance have all conspired against her under the sexual rule of the human male. Vices, however, like curses, come back to roost. In his own enfeebled frame, in his diseased tissue, in his weak will, his gibbering idiocy, his raving insanity and hideous criminality, he reaps the fruits of a dishonoured motherhood, an outraged womanhood, an unnatural, abnormal stimulated childbirth and starved poison-fed infancy.[69]

Swiney's feminist hygienics and Pankhurst's medical polemic were part of their broader criminal law strategy to halt male vice. But the fact that these arch-opponents of male professionalism now referenced the concepts of social hygiene – albeit in subverted form – was a measure of the changing language of purity feminism. The feminist take-up of hygienics was in part a skilful form of campaigning, involving an imaginative reworking dominant knowledges. Yet it also testified to the increasing power of the new medical strategy and its ability to force a dialogue with competing political forces. The decline of purity feminism in the 1920s and 1930s needs to be seen in relation to the overall decline of feminism, and especially to the unmitigated hostility of male sex reformers. But it was also the result of the growing hegemony of the social hygiene movement. In the period during and immediately after the war feminists were confronted by this changing situation across a whole range of sexual issues: venereal disease, birth-control and, crucially for our argument, sex education.

6   SEX EDUCATION

Our detour has taken us far from Dronfield school and Miss Outram's sex education teaching. But now we can begin to unravel the complex tangle of ideologies and political forces which were condensed in the affair. Outram was very much a bearer of the new social hygiene alliance. She began from a position of speaking out about sex, in the face of silence and hostility from managers and parents. But her conception of right knowledge was distanced from the traditional purity approach. It certainly involved negative proscriptions – especially on the terrible dangers of active female sexuality – but these were now combined with positive representations. Sex was defined as procreation, benefiting racial evolution and ultimately contributing to the divine plan for human progress. Outram's political commitment to the women's movement and to eugenics gave her the power to speak this new language. Yet as a professional as well as a feminist she was caught in contradictions which beset many women members of the purity movement and the social hygiene alliance. While these discourses gave her a lever of political representation, they brought her into conflict not just with male patriarchs on the local school management committee, but also with the mothers and fathers of her pupils, who saw their headmistress as hell-bent on depriving them of their own parental rights. Outram's high-handed dismissal of her parents' protests – her refusal even to acknowledge that they had a right to speak – reveals how her position as expert and educator enmeshed her in some of the power relations of professionalism.

And what of the opposition? The local doctors, vicar, shop-keeper and publican, the parents, together with Mr Hands, the HMI sleuth, and the faceless men at the Board of Education counselling administrative caution – that time honoured code-word for keeping your hands clean. The headmistress's tactics were a direct challenge to the local clique of male experts, who must have sewn-up so many pacts of patriarchal power in the vicarage and the surgery. Their deeply misogynistic response to Outram as a woman provides evidence enough of the way these men perceived her as a threat. As for the parents, their own defiance and outrage at the situation took a largely conservative form. They pilloried Outram, mounting a whispering campaign to remove her and asserting traditional, proprietorial rights over their children. But they did grasp defensively what too many middle-class women failed to understand. The displacement of one form of expertise by another is no substitute for a real shift in the balance of power/knowledge relations. How could they fail to grasp this essential fact? they felt themselves to be on the receiving end of it! Dronfield parents also had a radical, if again conservative, critique of the growing move to professionalize each and every particle of knowledge about sex. They countered this with a commonsense discourse on the naturalness and inevitability of human sexual relations –

what 'every man and woman knows' and does! The board's role in all this, its deliberate and self-conscious fence-sitting, was to set the pattern for the state's response to sex education for the next thirty years.

Many of the issues depicted in the Dronfield affair can be transposed onto the broader canvas of national hygienist politics. The importance awarded to sex education within official debates in the early twentieth century provides a major instance of the way social hygiene transformed the meanings and politics of sexuality. Like Outram, the vast majority of the medico-moral alliance believed that the purity-derived stress on speaking out needed to be maintained. The conspiracy of silence was still perceived as the major obstacle. Right knowledge was the surest protection against polluting influences. Yet as *The Lancet* insisted in 1913, the question of *how* to dissipate ignorance and with what precise forms of knowledge remained contentious.[70] Most groups agreed that prohibition and moral warnings were not enough. Negative moralizing against dirty and indecent practices was an insufficient safeguard because it offered no *positive* images of sexuality for adolescents and young adults. What was vitally needed was a programme of teaching which acknowledged the importance of sex as a positive force in human life.[71]

This approach signalled a clear departure from the purity strategy and a partial critique of it. Apart from Blackwell's writings, positive images had figured only marginally in purity thinking. With the new knowledge derived from physiology, conceptions of sexuality and sexual difference now became firmly rooted in the biological functions of the human organism. The sexual instinct was potentially a component of every normal citizen. The way lay open for a more affirmatory approach to sex.

What were the features of this sexual model, and how did it differ from earlier conceptions of instinctual behaviour? Mid-nineteenth-century medics like Acton had theorized the sexual instinct as a mechanical process of evacuation, dependent on environmental stimuli. It was a model which served as an apology for the inevitability of the male urge. Post-Darwinian scientists re-classified the instincts, seeing them located deep in the physical consitution of the organism and operating relatively independent of social influences. Havelock Ellis' *Analysis of the Sexual Impulse*, 1903 concluded that research into sexual behaviour was becoming more and more a question of physiological chemistry. The whole object of the social ritual of courtship, Ellis argued, was to set in motion processes of sexual tension and release which were instinctually motivated.[72]

In one sense this new understanding tended to reinforce representations of sexuality, and especially male sexuality, as extra-social – a primitive and uncivilized urge, the beast lurking in man. But the powerful voice of moralists and feminists within the social hygiene coalition insisted that men's instincts could and should be educated towards positive goals. Renewed moral stress within contemporary medicine ruled out any return to Acton's notion of uncontrollable male sexuality. As Ellis himself pointed out, crude instinctual theories which remained at the level of biology, refused the whole question of the moral development of the race.[73] It was the mark of man, the only species with true intelligence, that his instincts were plastic and capable of infinite transmutation through education.

All comentators were agreed on the image of sexuality which needed to be put forward for adolescents and young adults. Healthy and responsible *parenthood* was the ultimate goal. In the years before 1914 every voluntary body concerned with social hygiene (from the NCPM to the Eugenics Education Society) placed the concern with parenthood high on its agenda.[74] A recurrent problem voiced by many social hygienists was one of language. What vocabulary and concepts should they use to represent sexuality as parenthood for the young? According to the purist and eugenist Dr Schofield the language of sex education needed to be systematically 'eugenized', shifting the significations away from 'the sexual' to 'the racial'. He counselled teachers: 'Never use the word "sexual" but say racial (propagating the race), and you get a word that is totally free of objection and cannot be resented by parents.'[75] Racial truths looked at the sex organs from the health point of view, while 'the sexual point of view' looked at the same organs selfishly, as self-indulgence and self-gratification. Helen Wilson, speaking at a conference on sex education during the war, argued that sex teaching needed to fuse concepts of sex and parenthood in the minds of the young. Parenthood had to be presented as the *raison d'être* of sex.[76] Purists had been wrong to represent the sex instinct as 'animal and low, a thing as far as possible to be ignored, repressed, treated with silent contempt'; positive sex teaching needed to sanctify and hygienize the sexual act. Science alone held out the promise of a rational approach.

In line with political alliances within the social hygiene movement, science was consistently moralized in the tracts and pamphlets on sex education. Like Miss Outram, Elizabeth Sloan Chesser (a prolific writer on sex education material and lecturer to the Institute of Hygiene and the Women's Imperial Health Asociation) was confident that elementary botany could be used to introduce young children 'in a perfectly chaste and simple manner' to the great secrets of life, even before their own sexual instincts were awakened.[77] The National Birth Rate Commission (formerly the NCPM) put out a model syllabus for use in elementary schools in the early 1920s. Simple lessons on personal hygiene (care of hair, nails and teeth, together with 'modesty and reticence in the discharge of bodily functions') could teach habits of personal self-respect. The body, especially its visible orifices and extremities, was to be trained to emblematically display a set of inner moral qualities which prepared the ground for sex hygiene teaching. From there lessons could move to the study of parenthood in the animal world:

> Simple lessons on animal life enable the teacher to inculcate
> all unconsciously to the the child ideas of parenthood, e.g.
> the life of the bird, loving care and thought in the
> preparation of the nest, the laying of the eggs, the patient
> sitting of the mother bird, the father's attention to and care
> of the mother bird; his finding food and the efforts of both
> to teach them to get their own living.[78]

Here were Outram's lessons in natural harmony and sound procreation raised to the level of policy directives.

When addressing adults, dramatic polarized imagery was to be used to inculcate moral norms. Health-giving representations of nature were contrasted with the ill-health and disease which followed from immorality. With the aid of government grants the NCCVD fielded an effective propaganda campaign of pamphlets, talks, films and slide-shows, which reached an estimated two-and-a-half million people between 1914 and 1920.[79] The council's film and lecture tours, given to troops at the front, youth groups and women's organizations, carried lurid titles like: 'The Gift of Life', 'Damaged Goods' and 'The End of the Road'. Campaigners were quick to grasp the importance of the visual media in putting across the message. With their powerful ideologies of immediacy, actuality and truth, films and still photographs could translate scientific concepts into a popular language. Sport, sunshine, nature and the animal world were most frequently used to connote health. The sinister temptations of sexual immorality on the other hand were portrayed via images of the city and the 'amateur prostitute' or 'good time girl' – superficially brilliant and attractive but fundamentally unclean and polluting.

   Images of health and evolutionary biology not only confirmed the link between sex and parenthood, they also demonstrated that the *power to love* was an important part of all human sexual development. Heterosexual monogamy, cemented by a spiritualized conception of love, was claimed as the high-point of species evolution. Such a notion of spiritual bliss was different from the chivalric imagery of purity. It fused the higher emotions with the physical experience of the sex act. Geddes and Thomson noted that zoologists had identified the appearance of 'physical fondness' and 'aesthetic appeal' in lower mammals – tendencies which had become infinitely more beautiful in human relationships.[80] This spiritualized and emotional side of human nature pointed the way forward to further racial progress. In contrast, promiscuous sex, divorced from love and procreation, was not only immoral and unhealthy but was identified as retarded or regressive. Contemporary studies of prostitutes and sexual perverts by the Italian criminologists Lombroso and Ferraro and by Havelock Ellis defined them as atavists – primitive throwbacks to an earlier stage of development. The promiscuous sexuality of primitive women studied by early anthropologists was presented as proof of such atavism in the female prostitute.[81]

   This essentially Darwinist gloss on the evolution of spiritual and emotional life was also backed up by the work of early social psychologists. It was their approach to mental and instinctual life which tended to be privileged above that of Freudian psychoanalysis in Britain before the war. Professor William McDougall, in his influential *An Introduction to Social Psychology*, 1908 understood all mental life as 'the affective aspect of instinctual processes'.[82] Lower forms of social behaviour, in animals and in primitive races, were the direct product of 'the prompting of the instinct', but the higher stages of social and sexual conduct were always marked by 'voluntary control and regulation of the instinctual impulses'.[83] An uncompromising stress on self-control and a clear and direct relation between mind and body, these concepts fitted more comfortably with the hygienist plan for the evolution of 'the perfect man' than did Freud's dream theory of repressed sexual wishes and fantasies. The minimal impact of psychoanalysis in Britain in these years needs to be understood in relation to the intellectual and political dominance of social hygiene. Though reviewers in the medical press gave Freud's early work a favourable reception, they were concerned that psychoanalysis gave unconscious life too much autonomy from basic physiological processes. While for moralists like Scharlieb, Freud's challenge to the sexual innocence of childhood was intolerable.[84] When Freudian concepts did begin to enter mainstream British psychology in the inter-war period, it was the biologistic and evolutionary strands, pointing the way forward to correct patterns of psycho-sexual development, which were appropriated by the mental hygiene movement.[85]

7 THE CONSTRUCTION OF SEXUAL DIFFERENCE: ADVICE TO GIRLS

Hygienists always spoke of the 'human' sexual instinct, but their discourse was highly gender specific. Early sex education was not only dependent on gendered knowledges and assumptions, it actively constructed a new ideology of sexual difference by emphasizing the absolute polarization of male and female sexuality. What was taking place was the transformation of older moral categories of gender difference under the impact of evolutionary biology.

Physiologists and psychologists were agreed that adolescence was the crisis point – a product of linked physical and mental changes within the body, which were highly unstable and bordered on the pathological. It was especially dangerous for girls. Dr Scharlieb argued that puberty was delicately balanced between the normal and the abnormal, when any sudden excitement was 'likely to lead to disaster'.[86] A modicum of knowledge was necessary to guide minds and bodies towards maternity; keeping the love instinct pure in the early years of womanhood by guarding against any form of promiscuous activity. Carefully prepared talks could monitor dangerous tendencies towards 'unruly behaviour', or to the type of 'unhealthy attachments' to older women which were so prevalent at this unstable period. Teachers and youth leaders were told to be on the lookout for a particular type of 'flighty girl' – not always from the poorest home – who dressed over-smartly and was allowed far too much freedom in the evenings. One headmistress, in her evidence to the London County Council inquiry on sex hygiene teaching, 1914, confirmed that London girls were far from ignorant, and that many 'bold girls' had a tendency towards 'sexualism' and were in need of vigorous restraint.[87] Boys were 'at risk' not from the ordinary class of girl but from the type who had a great deal of knowledge from the wrong source.[88]

This scrutiny of active and 'dangerous' female sexuality paralleled similar anxieties voiced earlier by the purity movement. But what distinguished hygienists' concern was the focus of their disquiet. It was no longer the 'professional prostitute' who was isolated as the source of danger but a new form of threat – the promiscuous girl who gave sex for free. As Lucy Bland has shown, the 'amateur prostitute', as she was christened, was the source of a series of moral panics during the First War, condensing fears about the rising tide of immorality, illegitimate births and the spread of VD.[89] Though sex teaching was designed to give girls some knowledge for their own protection, there was ambiguity over precisely *how much* information should be supplied. Educationalists hoped to preserve a delicate balance between innocence (cum-ignorance) and self-knowledge among girls. Such ambiguity reflected continuing confusion over manifestations of female sexuality) It also registered the commonsense assumption that ultimate responsibility for their own moral behaviour – and that of their menfolk – lay with girls themselves. Social hygiene perpetuated the double-standard by insisting that male self-control, though possible, was problematic and that girls should help men to act responsibly by watching their own behaviour:

> you can help the men; they are very largely what women
> make them, what women expect them to be. It is very
> specially in the relation of men and women, that women and
> girls have a great responsibility. . . . A girl cannot be too
> particular. . . . If a man's friendship is worth having she
> will not lose it by refusing familiarity, but will make it a
> better sort of friendship. . . . She will also set a high
> standard of womanhood and for what women expect of
> men.[90]

Girls were not told why they needed to be so 'particular', yet the imputed blame for any subsequent wrong-doing was usually laid on them. When girls had already become 'bold and flighty', teachers were advised to isolate them from their friends in order to prevent contamination. Once a girl had 'fallen' there was little to be done other than contain the danger.[91]

The positive pole of girls' early sex education centred on preparation for motherhood. This strategy worked not merely with regulation by ideas and propaganda, but through a regime of pleasure. Girls were promised definite joys and satisfactions if they conformed to their maternal role. In the early years of the twentieth century motherhood not only became central to the construction of women's identity, it also began to be acknowledged as a valid site for their spiritual, sensual and even erotic experience. The sexualization of motherhood was usually implicit, evoked in the rhetoric of speeches and pamphlets. Though muted, it marked the beginnings of a shift away from the discourse of purity, by sanctioning a positive domain of female sexual/sensual experience.

For Elizabeth Chesser, the desires and pleasures women experienced during pregnancy, childbirth and lactation were essentially spiritual and ethereal. It was a holy and mystical experience for a young woman when she brought a new 'eternal soul' into the world.[92] Chesser further believed that most women sought happiness in the sex union, a desire which was felt as an instinctive longing. This sensualized representation – with pleasure produced through *conformity* to biological and social roles – contrasted sharply with that dominant form of male sexual experience, where satisfaction was gained through notions of transgressive and illicit behaviour.

The debate over female desire was extended by Havelock Ellis in his 'search' for the sexual impulse in women. Drawing on the theory and politics of libertarians and new moralists, Ellis magisterially pronounced that 'true' female sexuality was only expressed in relations with men. But he also noted secondary or subordinate manifestations of women's sexual instinct.[93] A woman experienced definite pleasures when suckling her child; this 'physical satisfaction' was the basis for the emotional bond between mother and offspring. Ellis, like other male experts, sexualized the female body. Women's anatomies were dissected to reveal a hierarchy of erogenous zones, moving from the nipples and clitoris to the vagina. There was, he insisted, a true 'physiological analogy' between heterosexual intercourse and the relation between mother and child during lactation:

> The complete mutual satisfaction, physical and psychic, of mother and child, in the transfer from one to another of a precise organicized fluid, is the one true physiological analogy of the relationship of a man and a woman at the climax of the sexual act.[94]

The most familiar take-up of the joys of intercourse and the cult of maternity was in the writings of the eugenist and birth-control pioneer, Marie Stopes. Stopes was emphatic in denouncing any expression of female sexuality outside marriage as unhealthy and unclean. Yet her celebration of the acceptable forms of women's erotic experience in *Married Love*, 1918 included both marital intercourse and the sensual experiences of motherhood. These two forms of pleasure, she claimed, were inseparable in the experience of most 'normal' women:

> The sensitive inter-relation between a woman's breasts and
> the rest of her sex life is not only a bodily thrill, but there is
> a world of poetic beauty in the longing of a loving woman
> for the child which melts in mists of tenderness towards her
> lover.[95]

For Stopes as a eugenist the pleasures and desires of marital sex
could be socially sanctioned because they perfected the spiritual
side of procreation and led the race onward and upward to a
higher completion of its powers.

It is tempting to read these representations of female sexuality solely as ideologies of expertise aimed at the regulation of
women's behaviour. Clearly, the 'choice' offered to women and
girls between promiscuity and maternity, together with the
aggressive stance on heterosexuality, worked as a form of sexual
policing. But the opening up of a discourse of desire around
motherhood, though highly contradictory, did provide the
space for women like Stopes and Chesser to ask questions about
female erotic pleasure which were taboo in the purity movement. The privileging of maternity, while socially normative,
gave some women the opportunity to think about their own
sexual/sensual experience. In the inter-war years the contradictions involved in these representations of femininity became
more pronounced. Popular manuals stressed that it was vital for
women to experience pleasurable, reproductive heterosexuality
within marriage, rendering all other forms of female behaviour
inadequate or deviant.

8   MASCULINITY

Sex hygienists also defined puberty as the flashpoint for boys.
Here the danger was thought to be more immediate, more the
direct product of physiological changes. The boy's organs
became sensitive to any stimuli for the pressure of the sexual
instinct was ever-present in the adolescent years. The main
approach was still deterrence, centred around moral warnings
on the crucial importance of self-control and the perils of
promiscuity. But as the Rev. Edward Lyttleton, headmaster of
Eton, made plain, his experiences had taught him that boys

needed to be offered something more than negative prohibitions – they needed positive images of sexual conduct.[96] It was through the idea of mastery and control of the sexual instinct that new militarized and scientificized representations of masculinity were produced, holding out the promise of particular satisfactions and powers.

Purists had projected the young man's fight between conscience and immorality as a fundamentally religious battle, mobilizing chivalric images of combat and contest. Hygienists drew on a similar language of conquest, but this was now depicted through biological metaphors as an essential test of masculinity. Instinctual forces needed to be fought, tamed and finally conquered in the progress towards physiological maturity. Boys' ability to 'master' them was conceived as an initiation rite. Success guaranteed lads of all classes their *rite de passage* into adult manhood, with all its privileges; failure was a sign of atavism and effeminacy.

This was the point of entry for militarized conceptions of male sexuality. Obedience to command, rational control over mind and body, technical know-how of physical laws – all this prepared the lad for combat on the battlefield. In 1909 Dr Schofield explained the facts of life to boys using army metaphors. When the embryo was first formed it was simply a mass of cells, but an 'unseen power' detached 'certain patrols' to co-ordinate the campaign.[97] Sir Robert Baden-Powell, hero of the Boer War and founder of the Boy Scouts, presented his own system of masculine hygienics in similarly military style. Boys who were in 'the human rutting season' were to be taken aside by the scoutmaster to have the facts explained.[98] Baden-Powell recommended a frank man-to-man chat, supplemented by selective renderings of popular science. The body was entering a new phase of operations which originated from perfectly natural causes – namely 'the spreading of semen'. At this crucial stage in the battle the boy needed to draw on all his reserves of energy and fighting strength. Otherwise victory would not be his; he would lose his self-respect and risk the consequences of venereal disease. Under pressure from eugenists, teachers and youth leaders also included specific instructions on fatherhood, but this was envisaged less as an introduction to duties and responsibilites than as a male romance. Life was 'a sacred torch', handed down from father to son, which had its beginnings in the first dawn of life on earth.[99] To remain unmarried was not only selfish from the racial point of view, it was also unmanly because it broke the patriarchal chain which linked countless generations: 'If you marry and hand this life onto children, it does not die out. If you die celibate without marrying then it ends with you.'[100]

At the same time the medical input into sex hygiene produced a different and competing construction of masculinity, with a stronger emphasis on the link between mastery over nature and scientific advance. In the early 1920s A.G. Tansley, University Lecturer in Botany at Cambridge, believed that the romance and intellectual appeal of science was a sure way to hold boys' attention in sex hygiene lessons. The teacher needed to present himself as a fearless questor after truth. He was to be dressed in the 'long white coat of a hospital doctor' and give instruction in a special room kept scrupulously bright and clean and fitted up like a laboratory. Medicalized imagery carried definite moral benefits:

> The hospital is everywhere associated with beneficent healing . . . and purification, based upon sound objective knowledge. . . . the clean austere atmosphere, both physical and mental . . . would probably have exactly the right psychological effect . . . on . . . boys.[101]

This was not a vision which connoted the masculine culture of the Scouts, nor the public-school ethos of the muscular Christian gentleman. These scientificized representations had most to say to the academic middle-class boy, produced through intellectual competition and a form of 'epistemophilia' – the pleasure gained through the strenuous search for knowledge.

All these pedagogies derived a large part of their strength by affirming forms of masculine culture which systematically excluded women. The all-male preserves of the Scouts and the Boys' Brigade were the clearest examples, but the images of scientificity were also male-defined. Male teachers were advised that it was better if boys were deliberately kept in the dark about the sexual development of girls. Lyttleton heartily recommended one pamphlet entitled *In Confidence to Boys* because it dealt with their difficulties frankly but reverently 'without mentioning the female side at all'.[102] Such instruction was often explicitly racist. Initiation into masculinity meant initiation into the echelons of *white* manhood. Boys were warned that only 'among primitive men' were physical pleasures experienced as animal lusts. Among the white races, control of mind over body had raised the sex act to a sacramental level.[103] Differences of age, rank and class may have separated the scout-master from the raw recruit and the science teacher from his pupil, but they were linked together by a common bond of élite masculinity which celebrated both misogyny and sexual racism.

9   SCHOOL SEX HYGIENE TEACHING: COMPETING STRATEGIES

The ideology of sex education at first sight appears so coherent and confident, so seamless in its handling of conflicting demands, that we might be tempted to tip over from the moment of ideological production to that of implementation. This error is particularly seductive when dealing with new liberal or state socialist programmes in the early twentieth century. There is a utopianism in these social and political philosophies in the very worst sense, with their projected vision of social order which assumes society to be conflict-free. Most forms of official power are wilfully covert about the tensions in their projects, but many of the initiatives around motherhood or eugenics reproduce the Benthamite mania of the 1830s. Contemporary sex education stands squarely in this totalizing tradition. Comparison between Freud's early work and social hygiene is instructive. While not wanting to privilege Freudianism as a more advanced or sophisticated explanation of sexuality – a common mistake in modernist or evolutionary histories of sex – there is an acknowledgment of complexity in Freud's approach, an awareness that individuals *resist* official discourses, which throws the buoyant optimism of social hygiene into relief.

The contradictions in sex hygiene only become visible at the point of implementation; the moment of dialogue between competing political forces over the enshrinement of policy in legislation. In the early twentieth century the issue of state-backed sex education teaching in elementary schools was a sharp focus for disagreement among members of the alliance. Most hygienists believed that under ideal conditions the parents, and especially the mother, were the proper agents of instruction. Yet given the continuing perception of working-class family life as immoral, many looked to *the state* to enact their demands.

Medics were the most vociferous group in support of a full programme of sex teaching in schools. Given the renewed importance of state medicine, the profession was keen to promote its prestige through the education system. Eugenists also provided a powerful lobby for the inclusion of hygiene as a school curriculum subject; as future citizens children had a right to know the laws of life and the state had a duty to impart them.[104] Teachers themselves were divided. Those women teachers, like Outram, who were committed eugenists tended to favour a comprehensive educational programme. Miss T.E. Bonwick, headmistress of the Girls' Department of Enfield Road School, Hackney, felt it was her responsibility to offer her girls some protection because she believed local parents were morally and intellectually bankrupt.[105] The majority of male teachers were more tentative, fearing the destruction of the child's 'natural reticence' and, more to the point, possible subversion of the master's authority in the classroom. The headmaster of Millwall Central School in London's docklands hinted ominously that if 'precocious boys' were addressed directly then 'the worst features would come out'.[106] In working-class areas fear of disruption and disorder from resistant pupils outweighed any commitment to sexual reform.

For women's organizations and for feminists the issue was clearly more problematic. Professionals like Dr Scharlieb viewed state-sponsored hygienics as a useful extension of philanthropic intervention into the working-class family. It would impart to children 'in a decent way' what they currently grasped 'in a most undesirable way'.[107] Militant feminist sex education material, on the other hand, was largely designed to raise women's consciousness and stimulate public debate about male immorality. On the whole, in the years before the First War feminists remained lukewarm over introducing sex teaching into schools. This reflected their suspicion that once institutionalized, control would be lost to the power of male experts. Significantly, Helen Wilson was more in favour of privileging sites of female culture, such as mothers' meetings and bible classes, to promote sex education.[108]

There was of course a structural block to the implementation of social hygiene deeper than mere internal political differences. This was the purity movement itself. Early sex education campaigns were mounted at precisely the moment purity was at its highpoint. There was of course no total division between the two groups. But it became increasingly clear that each projected competing forms of regulation and distinctive representations of sexuality. At its starkest, the contrast was between a commitment to criminalizing legislation, mobilized around the old moral/immoral, virtue/vice polarities, as against a broad educational pedagogy, defining sex more positively, under the rubric of national health. If the two strategies were jostling for position before 1914, how was it that hygienists were successful in their bid for hegemony, to such an extent that by the inter-war period a growing consensus held that sex education, not the criminal law, promised the best assurance of regulating sexual behaviour?

The 1920s and 1930s witnessed the increasing marginalization of purity. After the 1922 amendment act the statute book records no further additions to the criminal code. The movement which had been spawned by the repeal campaign – a mixture of popular protest, incisive feminist politics underpinned by a harsh regime of social disciplining – had finally been displaced. When the Home Office moved into this area again in the 1950s and 1960s, it was ostensibly to decriminalize many of the offences created under purity pressure in the late nineteenth and early twentieth century: homosexual practices, obscenity, censorship. What structural factors set the conditions for this shift, sustaining the educational approach to sex so that it has remained of paramount importance through to our own period? These questions take us into the concluding sections of our history. We need to return to the themes which have been central to the project – the role of the state, the entanglement of professional knowledge and voluntary pressure groups and feminist initiatives for the reform of personal relations.

10   THE STATE AND SEX
HYGIENE

First the state. The central point here is that the shift away from a criminalizing to an educational pedagogy was not initiated by the state in the narrow sense. Despite the strong move towards increased government intervention in many areas during the First War and in the inter-war years, the Home Office, the Ministry of Health and the Board of Education remained highly cautious about introducing sex education in schools. The stance taken over the Dronfield affair was part of a wider laissez-faire policy by government which continued throughout the 1920s and 1930s. At a local level the situation was much the same. Extensive discussion of the issue in London by teachers, school-managers and the London County Council led to the setting up of a special LCC inquiry in 1914. Their report came out strongly against formal school instruction, ostensibly on the grounds that the difficult mixture of social classes in London militated against direct class teaching.[109]

The specific conjuncture of the war produced no major rethink by the state. The extensive panic over venereal disease – condensing fears about the amateur prostitute as a threat to military health – did prompt repressive government control of prostitution (via the wartime Defence of the Realm Act, Regulation DORA 40d) along with state funding for medical treatment of the disease. But the interventionist approach was more fractured than it appeared. It marked out clear distinctions between the short-term demands of wartime (i.e. the control of infected prostitutes) to be enacted by the state, and long-term educational objectives, to be covered by the voluntary sector. In the *Report of the Royal Commission on Venereal Disease*, 1916, a broad educational offensive was recommended to inculcate the laws of moral hygiene in 'all types and grades of education'.[110] However, it was not in practice government agencies which spearheaded reform. While the commissioners were convinced that a solution to VD could be 'accomplished only by the action of Government directed to the solution of a great national problem', they emphasised that private voluntary efforts, notably the NCCVD, should take the lead.[111]

The 1918 coalition government adopted these proposals, thankful to shift the burden of responsibility onto other shoulders. In fact from 1917 and throughout the 1920s the NCCVD received substantial treasury grants for its educational and propaganda work. Joint liaison committees were set up between the new Ministry of Health and the National Council. Yet the state was content to be cast as the junior, passive partner in these negotiations, leading to complaints that the ministry was not pulling its weight. In 1920 Viscount Astor re-stated the government's position on the principle of delegated responsibility:

> The Government can do a certain amount in education and propaganda, but . . . there is a real sphere for voluntary effort. Voluntary bodies conducted by people who understand the subject can do a great deal which a Government Department or a local authority could not do.[112]

The position at the Board of Education was not dissimilar. As inter-war independent surveys showed, many schools and training colleges, supported by progressive local authorities, took advantage of the board's deliberately ambiguous policy to introduce their own schemes for sex hygiene, especially for girls. By 1934, for example, Pontypridd in South Wales had a co-ordinated programme, moving from the usual simple talks on plant and animal life in their infant departments, to specific class instruction on reproduction at upper school level.[113] It was not until 1943, with the publication of the Board of Education's *Sex Education in Schools and Youth Organizations*, that space was made for sex education within secondary schools. It had taken a campaign of over thirty years, and a quite different conjuncture, before government took action in response to voluntary sector pressure.

11   THE PERSONAL AND THE POLITICAL

Why did the state continue to be so deeply ambiguous about intervening in sexual regulation? What did this register about the wider parameters of state action? These questions return us to the more general issue of the relation between formal political discourse and sexual politics. We have already noted the passive role played by the Home Office in the fierce campaigns to pass fresh criminal law legislation before 1914. Government handling of birth-control in the 1920s displayed a similar timidity. The Ministry of Health initially refused even to commit itself on the question of whether maternity and infant welfare centres could be used for contraceptive counselling. As in the area of sex hygiene, individual authorities could capitalize on this ambiguity to push for birth-control facilities at a local level. It was only when councils and health authorities overstepped the mark that the state moved in negatively to delimit the permitted scope for action.[114]

It is all too tempting to ascribe such non-interventionist policy to financial stringency or administrative lethargy. But our history of state entanglement in medico-moral politics reveals that much trumpeted economic or administrative constraints were rarely just that. They were almost enmeshed with broader political and cultural imperatives. More significant than the tight fiscal surveillance of the Treasury in these years were the cultural meanings attached to sexuality within political discourse; in particular the increasing construction of the field of sex as outside politics.

At a number of different moments we have noted how the structures of formal politics excluded discourses on sex. The process of reconceptualizing and tightening the political field, begun in the late-nineteenth century, was accelerated in the face of party destabilizations and realignments of the immediate post-war years. This move was institutionalized in the Representation

201

of the People Act, 1918 and through the creation of a new representative state. The act staked out a new political language, based on the broad categories of citizenship and 'near' universal suffrage. But the discourse also marked out a tighter conception of what politics was and what it was not.[115] At its most banal it signified mere passive participation at the ballot-box, though its scope could embrace key areas of the social – notably motherhood, health and education – via the linked concerns of nation and citizenship. Sexuality was rarely included in this new political repertoire. Instead, the domain of the sexual was constituted as extra-political. Sex was now defined as an area to be administered by neutral expertise, or it was aligned with 'the personal', with private domestic life, and hence only tangentially related to formal politics.

This correlation of the sexual with the personal was a key factor in the state's non-interventionary stance. When the National Birth-Rate Commission reviewed sex hygiene teaching in 1920, Christopher Addison, Minister of Health, warned of the problems ahead:

> I think it is obvious that you touch subjects which are more nearly personal than any other class of topic, and in regard to which people as a whole resent, or are apt to resent, outside interference and direction more than any other.[116]

Here was the recognition of the personal life of mass society as outside the politician's orbit. The twinning of sex and personal life had its antecedents in earlier religious and radical liberal traditions. But these had been élite conceptions, confined to sections of the bourgeoisie and professional classes. The interwar years witnessed the reformulation of these ideologies in relation to much wider levels of popular experience. A number of economic and cultural changes provided the conditions for this: decline of family size, increased emphasis on the emotional content of family life by the churches and in popular marriage manuals together with a rise in real wages for those sections of the respectable working-class and petty-bourgeoisie in work. The growth of new consumer markets, backed by the expansion of popular journalism – especially women's magazines – were also instrumental in reconstructing domestic life.[117]

Further, the impact of parliamentary feminism had important effects on the way sexuality was handled officially. The entry of women MPs into Parliament after 1918 produced a political discourse which was now implicitly gendered. Specific areas of administration, such as welfare provision, child-care, even health to some extent, were increasingly defined as 'women's issues'. This process of delegation had contradictory effects. While it gave many political women an authoritative voice on certain areas of policy, these were ranked as inferior to masculinist preserves like foreign affairs or the economy. At those rare moments when sexuality crept into political discourse, it was frequently defined as a women's issue, and trivialized. This meant that it was viewed as unimportant for any form of state action. Moreover, the feminization of sexuality reinforced its associations with the private. For women politicians were still largely perceived as representatives of the private sphere in the public arena. The debate over birth-control was a case in point. Significantly it was Frances Stevenson, Lloyd George's mistress and private secretary, not Lloyd George himself, who handled the prime ministerial dialogue with Marie Stopes.[118] When the Tory feminist Nancy Astor raised the question again in Parliament in 1935, she still felt compelled to apologize for introducing such a 'disruptive issue' into members' 'valuable time'.[119]

These structural factors underpinned the state's nervous dialogue with the social hygiene movement over sex education. Yet the relative absence of state intervention here did not of course mean any abandonment of responsibility for sexual regulation. It was the experts and voluntary bodies who were nominated as the proper agents of control. The inter-war politics of sex points us towards the network of professionalisms and struggles within civil society.

12   PURITY POLITICS IN DECLINE

The major change in pressure-group politics in the 1920s was the demise of purity. The ongoing decline of nonconformist religion and the re-working of middle-class and popular culture left their mark. But more important for our argument, the growing marginalization of the purity movement was also the result of its own vacillation over sex education.

Characteristically, the NVA perceived sex education more as a threat to morality than as an essential part of preventive work. There was also the underlying, justifiable fear that any full-blooded sex hygiene programme would ultimately displace their own moral discourse by the power of biology and the new preventive medicine. With Coote at the helm until his death in 1919, the NVA placed its weight very firmly behind traditional struggles against vice, which now embraced the modern dangers posed by the cinema, jazz and dancing.[120]

Early in 1919 Coote had announced his resignaion from the hygienist-dominated NCCVD over what were coyly termed 'disagreements over policy'.[121] It was no accident that the bone of contention was sex teaching. Throughout the following decade the NVA continued to distance itself from the educational approach. But ten years later the issue erupted again, this time splitting the purity movement. When the 1928 Biological Education Congress passed a series of resolutions calling for a more enlightened approach to health education, this became the cue for delegates – including some members of the NVA itself – to launch a strong attack on older purity methods. There was still too much emphasis, they claimed, on legislation and prohibition, too little on building the solid foundations of morality through education.[122] Purists were failing to come to terms with the post-war world. Stimulated by the press, the cinema and literature, adolescents were determined to find out the facts of life. No amount of legal control could prohibit immorality. It was this disagreement from within which marked a watershed in purity's decline. The NVA's official response was almost a foregone conclusion. The executive committee ruled that in view of the great difficulty of arriving at any consensus on the subject, it was wiser to leave it alone![123] Although the language of purity continued to exert a powerful influence on public debate, as a campaigning force it now lacked intellectual coherence and popular support.

Shifts within the other strands of the original social hygiene alliance exacerbated the problems facing purity. For the medical profession and the progressive wing of the Anglican church, the most significant factor was the beginnings of a discourse on the importance of sexual fulfilment for *both* partners within marriage – discussion hitherto largely confined to libertarians and sex reformers. In 1918 *The Lancet* intervened in the debate on celibacy and spinsterhood. It presented research by Sir Arbuthnot Lane, Consulting Surgeon at Guy's Hospital, on the importance of glandular and hormonal secretions for the physical and mental health of women. Drawing on biochemistry, Lane asserted that the production of fluids associated with female sexual desire had a beneficial effect on women's health and vitality. Women who were deprived of these secretions tended to develop 'chronic intestinal stasis, diseases of the breast and a growing feeling of disgust for sexual intercourse'![124] Despite his scientific caution, Lane had no hesitation in recommending both the traditional importance of motherhood and women's active participation in intercourse for their general well-being.

As always, these medical prescriptions were conceived as political interventions, with an implicit attack on purity feminism. Lane claimed to show how the 'poor, thin, static virgin' could be metamorphosized into a 'plump, healthy, happy' individual through intercourse and pregnancy. Subsequent editorials and letters took up the implications of the research with gusto. Sexual fulfilment for married women was hailed as the key both to their happiness and to eliminating those female nuisances (i.e. spinsters) who interfered in all aspects of political and public life with their bizarre demands. According to *The Lancet*, Stopes' *Married Love* was a much more acceptable solution to the problem of female sexuality than the militant politics of purity feminism.[125]

It would be unwise to overstate the scope and impact of these developments. Yet the new emphases did mark a move away from the focus on chastity and marital continence, dominant in medico-moral discourse before the war. Medics further justified their new approach by appealing to contemporary events, which for them pointed to the bankruptcy of purity solutions to sex. Under the impact of the war, followed by new styles of dancing, mixed bathing and greater freedom granted to women, there was a growing desire for the relaxation of moral standards. Along with the spirit of mere licence and rebellion, such trends contained a valid demand for 'a new moral evolution'. Insights from Freudianism were also showing that 'the barriers of repression were too narrowly set'.[126]

Political and theological ruptures within Anglicanism brought similar changes to the medico-moral alliance. The modernist challenge from inside the church, coming to a head in the 1920s, pushed for reinterpretation of Christian faith in the light of the upheavals of the war and the renewed expansion of 'scientific materialism'.[127] Theologically, the movement was influenced by pragmatist philosophy. It was a belief that God was only knowable through personal religious expression in prayer and mystical experience, and that the Deity was not only transcendent but immanent in man's highest faculties and creative acts. However, the partial take-up of modernism in the recommendations of the Lambeth Conference, 1930 had as much to do with the church's response to the social and political problems of the post-war world as with the niceties of theological debate. The *Encyclical Letter*, produced at the conference, stressed that the growth of a materialistic culture and a socialist politics 'rooted in the denial of God's existence' demanded a new approach to Christian doctrine.[128] The keynote was a humanist emphasis on God working within the world and in men and women at their best.

It was this more personalized religious discourse which informed the church's revised statements on sex and marriage. The conference's recommendations re-affirmed the absolute centrality of Christian marriage and family life, condemning 'illicit intercourse' and remaining cautious on birth-control. But the sex act itself, now partly differentiated from procreation, was viewed as a 'noble and creative function', a potentially God-given factor in the life of mankind.[129] Delegates acknowledged that marriage as an equal partnership now meant emotional and sexual fulfilment for both partners. Marriages, sealed by the 'fullest development of the sex relationship', were part of God's plan for joining two personalities in life-long union.

Both medical and religious discourse fed into the expanding repertoire of popular marriage manuals and sex education writings in the 1930s. With their dual stress on physical health and spirituality, they projected a vision of sexual fulfilment, especially for women. At the same time, such writing – like

IV From purity to social hygiene

Theodore Van der Velde's *Ideal Marriage*, 1928, or M.J. Exner's *The Sexual Side of Marriage*, 1939 – continued the unremitting assault on celibacy and purity feminism. Draconian warnings were issued to women who refused to be aroused by their husbands' newly acquired sexual technique.[130]

The combined attack from medicine and religion, together with a popular language of sex reform, contributed susbtantially to the marginalization of purity politics in the inter-war years. This was as true for purity feminism as it was for Coote's NVA. In the 1920s many feminists, erstwhile supporters of criminal law legislation, began to shift their allegiance towards sex education. The sea-change had much to do with women's experience of the implementation of purity legislation, which proved a political education in itself.

After their successful conclusion of the 1912 campaign, *The Shield* had pronounced that this triumph was merely the beginning. Purity would go from strength to strength, pressing for more stringent legal sanctions to promote feminist demands.[131] The war years provided a fresh impetus for further legislation, but the results proved more contradictory than feminists had envisaged. Above all, there was a growing awareness that the administration of the law was almost invariably directed towards policing *women*. Feminist analysis of the DORA regulations, and of the clauses contained in a number of unsuccessful criminal law amendment bills between 1917 and 1922, provided practical proof of what many had long suspected. Proposals for the criminalization of VD's transmission and the coercive reform of young convicted prostitutes, demonstrated that it was women who were usually on the receiving end of punitive purity legislation.[132] Moreover, in line with basic tenets of social hygiene, many feminists now believed that the whole question of sexual promiscuity belonged to the sphere of public health policy rather than to the criminal code. At a Women's Freedom League Rally in 1917 one woman doctor made an impassioned plea for a move away from all forms of criminal legislation as the solution to sexual difficulties. Drawing on direct experience of the war, she equated the habit of punishment and coercion with all the old ideas of force and fear which had done so much damage in the world. Repressive legislation was just another example of male law, which politicians fell back on when they had no real answer to social evils.[133] It was a position echoed by many leaders of the women's movement, from the Association for Moral and Social Hygiene to the NUWSS. As *The Common Cause* put it in 1918, 'our great hope is in education.'[134]

The inter-war years witnessed growing feminist participation in sex education, both in moralizing writings addressed to children and adolescents and in books and pamphlets stressing the importance of pleasurable heterosexuality within marriage. The biting attack on male sexual behaviour was certainly lost, though the new discourse did provide some women with a language for thinking through questions suppressed within purity feminism. There was no 'glorious unfolding' as Marie Stopes envisaged, for much sex education material was centrally aimed at the regulation of female sexuality. Rather, what occurred were a series of contradictory movements which reflected the more general uncertainties of feminist politics in the inter-war period.

13   CONCLUSION

The white-coated male scientist and the plump, happy mother – these highly gendered representations of sexual responsibility and satisfaction were distinctive motifs of hygiene-based sex education in the early twentieth century. The growing hegemony of social hygiene was secured by an extensive shift in the balance of political forces and intellectual knowledge informing social policy. In the years before the First War this whole domain underwent substantial transformation, as different forms of expertise responded to a series of domestic and international crises which were seen to be interlinked.

One result of these transformations was that the criminalizing approach to sexual regulation was gradually but substantially displaced. The re-emergence of preventive medicine and an imperialist discourse of health and racial survival were the most significant influences here. But sex education cannot simply be understood as the medicalization of sex. Preventive medicine was one, albeit key, element in the network of political alliances which produced the social hygiene movement. This coalition staked out new representations of sex. It constructed concepts of sexual difference, normality and abnormality, and promised a definite range of pleasures and satisfactions to those who heeded the message. Government's relation to these developments was tentative and hesitant – a product of renewed definitions of the sexual as outside the terrain of political intervention. It was the dense schema of voluntary and professional bodies which co-ordinated the move towards sex education in the early twentieth century.

In the context of the longer history of medico-moral politics it is tempting to construct a direct continuity between the sanitary programmes of the early nineteenth century and the hygienics of seventy years later. But there was no direct relation between the two moments, no smooth development of knowledge about sex. Between them lay the sustained challenge of repeal feminism and moral purity. Any examination of the forces which were displaced by social hygiene must record substantial losses. The purity movement – an amalgam of evangelical, patriarchal morality and biting feminist politics – was forced aside by a highly professionalized discourse on sex. Sex education firmly reinstated normalizing hierarchies of knowledge, which set teachers above parents, medics over patients and dismissed competing feminist and popular understandings as lunatic, amateur and irregular. Instruction from above was the keynote. There was none of the emphasis on active self-determination which had characterized the positive side of purity feminism. With the renewed expansion of social policy and state provision in the 1940s and 1950s, social hygiene became written into the rubric of the welfare state.

EPILOGUE

It might be wise to end here. But we began by making a strong claim for the importance of history in understanding sexual politics today; how it can be used to grasp our current dilemmas and discontents. What then has been the relevance of all this? What does it really matter that in the 1830s sanitarians blamed cholera on the moral filthiness of the urban poor? Or that eighty years later a local schoolmistress with feminist sympathies confronted her superiors over sex education? To explain how and why means being explicit about the way we understand history writing. It also means a return to the current state of play around sexual health and disease which opened the book.

Our route into history has been a two-way process. We began with a series of questions about our own situation now. But we were also faced with a number of already constituted historical narratives: an official story telling of the heroic birth of the modern public health movement, the feminist re-discovery of nineteenth-century women's struggles and a popular melodrama of vice and sexual outrage. Hence the book has worked at the interface between the contemporary and the sexual scripts handed down to us. In the process we have tried to construct the genealogy of particular forms of modernity: starting points for the system of medical authority which we still inhabit; the tension within feminist discourse between disciplining and self-determination; regimes of desire incited through the polarities of purity and danger. Our present is caught up in that past, shaped and moulded by the ongoing resonance of some of these deep structures. There are important 'lessons' here. Some are quite precise and direct, pointing to formations with a very long durée indeed. Others are much more fractured and discontinuous. Used self-consciously, a history of the present neither reproduces the faults of evolutionary accounts – a continuous unravelling from past to present – nor should it deliver a blank

211

cheque for every sort of historical analysis. The parameters of where to begin and where to stop are guided by our negotiation with the present. We need to construct modes of history writing which grasp that past/present relation. Let us develop the argument further by returning to the issue which began this history – the narrative of AIDS.

> It is Saturday night at The Stud Saloon and the shadowy back street bar throbs to a deafening disco beat.
> In the crowded dance floor, two young men are locked in a dreamy embrace. Male couples hold hands in quiet corners and a slim-hipped youngster with Boy-George make-up preens coquettishly for an ageing admirer who holds him gently around the waist as he swigs from a long-necked bottle of Budweiser beer. Harassed bartenders can hardly cope with the desperate demand for drinks. It's the same in almost every 'gay' bar in town. 'For Chrissakes, Rick baby, gimme a gin. Better make it a double.'
> Looking for love has always been a high risk undertaking for San Francisco's homosexual community. A few stiff drinks often help before you go out in search of sex with a stranger. Now the nights are filled with alcohol and apprehension. For a four-letter word – AIDS – has brought fresh fears into this city by the bay. ('What the Gay Plague Did to Handsome Kenny', *The Sunday People*, 24 July 1983)

The mythology of AIDS has been constructed through stories like this. These are images, languages, signs of sex which mould and police desire quite as effectively as more overtly coercive regimes of authority. Growing public anxiety in Britain from the autumn of 1982 was the product not just of medical revelations in *The Lancet*, but of a plethora of popular representations. These two genres are not neatly sealed-off from each other. Almost despite itself, official medical language has continually been interrupted by the low, rude noises of the popular, while press and TV coverage fed off and re-worked the discourse of social medicine.

Like other recent panics – drugs, law 'n' order and child

212

abuse – the popular media have played a critical role in shaping opinion over AIDS, setting the parameters for debate, identifying the problem and its potential solutions. This has usually been morality as melodrama, fitting snugly with the long-established tradition of sexual reportage dating back at least as far as Stead's 'Maiden Tribute' scandal of the 1880s. As with many of the journalistic accounts, *The People's* 'Handsome Kenny' worked as exposé, mimicking the language of official inquiry. Like Dr Kay's cholera excursion, we, the 'normal' reader, are invited to descend into a gay sexual underworld. Deviant sex is always at the centre of this spiral, whether in the notorious 'hot house', with its 'black leather harnesses', or in Rock Hudson's desperate search for bathhouse lovers.[1] This type of account is of course always framed by moral condemnation, reaffirming the distance between our own 'normal' sexuality and 'deviant' pleasures. Yet in their voyeuristic fascination with the details of erotica they work to incite sexual desire. The construction of sex as naughty and immoral, but titillating, operates with codes of transgression familiar from our history. Popular sexual pleasures still fixate around moral/immoral opposites. Like the dirty weekend or the proverbial cream cake, sex has to be naughty to be nice. We still need to know more about the genealogy of these structures of desire and their place within the erotica of popular culture.

But the erotic sub-text is always underwritten by the dominant meaning. Promiscuous and 'deviant' sex leads to killer disease. The hyper-realist codes of photographic journalism function as emblems of gay promiscuity. 'Handsome Kenny', his bright eyes showing no hint of the agony to come, as against 'Doomed Kenny', the 'victim', visibly wasting away from AIDS sickness. Rock, 'the hunk who lived a lie', played off against 'the wasted seven-stone shadow'.[2] The very fact that the symptoms can be represented so dramatically, cutting down superstars and handsome young men in their prime, has made AIDS highly accessible to the long-standing protocols of popular investigative journalism. With their sharp polarities between health and disease, good and evil, they set up a direct relation betwen cause and effect and point to simple, graspable solutions.

By late 1986 this repertoire was being subtly re-worked. The second major wave of panic is rooted in the sudden realization that the whole heterosexual population is potentially at risk. Sex per se is now dangerous. The moral frisson has shifted register. No longer is it generated by fascination with deviance – that 'other' sexuality. Danger is everywhere. Like Kay's proverbial thief walking in darkness, AIDS could invade your body, your space.

But tales of sexual outrage have never been told in isolation. Their images of sex and death are read through a wider social and political vocabulary. AIDS has come to occupy a distinctive place in the ideological repertoire of the moral right. Both here and in the USA a fresh generation of ideologues have pushed for a new order of moral absolutes, pointing up links between moral and social and political instabilities. In the wave of panics which have recently swept Britain the moral lobby has been making all the running, orchestrating a language of polarized opposites. More and more, 'sexual undesirables' have been twinned with the 'socially undesirable'. Drug takers, the homeless, down and outs, lesbians and gay men have been run together as outside the healthy body politic.[3]

It is simplistic to see these panics as conspiracies. For public representations to have effects at a popular level they must tap lived experiences. AIDS has done just that. Like the wave of scandals a century ago it focuses genuine fears about current sexual behaviour. Moralists have been quick to exploit the contradictions inherent in 1960s permissiveness and channel them rightwards, demanding a halt to the 'inevitable' by-products of libertarianism – spiralling sexual violence, pornography and disease. At a time of protracted social instability, fundamental truths about right and wrong, good and evil, backed by a socio-biological gloss on our 'true' sexual nature, seem like reassuring certainties.

These popular philosophies of the right do have a history within post-war medico-moral discourse. Since the early 1960s rising VD rates, the increase in viral diseases like herpes and resistant sub-strains of gonorrhea have stimulated renewed scrutiny of sexual disease. Research on the prevention and treatment of infection isolated so-called high risk or target groups. Gay men, black immigrants and young single women were all singled out as potential health hazards.[4] Moreover, it

was their life-style, psychology and 'habits' (i.e. their promiscuity) which were cited as the root cause of the spread of
disease. From the sternest end of social hygiene, moralists like
Dr R. Wilcox of St Mary's Hospital, London, argued that
sexually transmitted diseases among men 'frequently result
from . . . mating with high risk females', women who do not
accept 'the responsibilities of marriage' and who suffer 'from a
sense of inadequacy, loneliness or rejection with an anxiety to
please, or an antagonism to parents or society'.[5]

This is the sharp end of medico-moral discourse. Medics
involved in AIDS research have consciously distanced themselves from any such draconian pronouncements. Yet inevitably their concepts, protocols and procedures continue to
inhabit the historically produced meanings attached to sex,
health and disease. In handling AIDS the medical profession
have slid through a series of hypotheses, which kaleidoscope
different semiologies of disease. When *The Lancet* opened the
debate in 1982 knowledge of the syndrome was very much akin
to knowledge of cholera in the 1830s. Medics were confronted
with an array of symptoms but knew little about the causal
agent of mode of transmission. Problems were exacerbated
because cellular immunodeficiency – the specialism central to
AIDS – was relatively underdeveloped as a field of study. At
this early stage, the absence of any clearly identifiable virus
meant that researchers returned to the 'environmental vari-
ables' which were thought to contribute to the syndrome's
appearance. When medical hypotheses were twinned with
dangerous sex, space was immediately opened up for re-entry of
the medico-moral repertoire.

For gay men, as opposed to other high risk groups, the logic
pointed irresistibly to a link between the homosexual lifestyle
and the spread of AIDS. Was it stimulated by 'poppers', a
recreational drug fashionable on the gay scene? Did it only
attack those who were genetically disposed – a consequence of
some profound defect in immunity? Were levels of promiscuity
to blame?[6] The most comprehensive explanation originally
advanced was the 'immune overload theory', which suggested
that under the impact of a gay lifestyle the body's defences
broke down, exhausted by 'overload', a physiological and moral
protest against excessive bouts of unnatural sex.

Epilogue

This scenario is preserved in the melodrama of the popular media. Medical research, however, propelled by its own internal dynamic, has shifted to another register with the eventual isolation of the HTLV III/LAV virus. We are no longer directed to the moral environment of sufferers, but are now deep into the cellular composition of the organism. There we encounter T-helper/suppressor cell ratios, retro viruses which bud at the plasma membrane and interfere with DNA products.[7] Here is a continuity with the cellular biology glossed by Newman and Newsholme in the early years of this century. Yet unlike those early ideologues, current high prestige research associated with AIDS curiously evacuates the social terrain. The ultimate aim may be altruistic, the elimination of suffering, but the path-breaking romance of pure science circumscribes any excursion into the muddy waters of social relations. This is now carried by the public health agencies – health visitors, social workers, VD clinics – whose explicit brief is with human managment.

Yet when we turn from medicine to those government agencies responsible for public health we encounter official attitudes to sex laid down in the early years of the century. Still, it seems, where sexual health is concerned the state is cautious and has been slow to intervene. The Communicable Diseases Centre at Colindale has monitored the incidence of AIDS, following the 1982 *Annual Report of the Chief Medical Officer of the DHSS* which confirmed outbreaks in Britain and admitted significant under-reporting due to lack of knowledge.[8] Gay activists identified such lethargy as the result of Tory government attacks on the NHS. But as we know administrative lethargy and fiscal stringency have always been enmeshed with the cultural meanings written into the regulation of sexuality. This is the official designation of sex as extra-political, an unwelcome intrusion into the proper business of politics. When the DHSS finally stirred to mount its first publicity campaign in March 1986, the embarrassment was painful. 'Don't Aid AIDS' coyly avoided naming sexual practices considered unsafe (and unsavoury), like anal sex. At this stage traditional arguments held sway. Releasing explicit information ran the risk of inciting that which was to be restrained. Again it is the threat to heterosexuals, plus spiralling statistics, which has pushed government agencies into more decisive action. In late 1986 we saw a high profile Cabinet committee set up under Lord Whitelaw, and a far more sexually explicit media campaign. Leaflets to every household and TV and press coverage warned: 'Don't Die of Ignorance.' The upshot of all this is much more public visibility and talk about sex than ever before. Penetration, condoms and alternative forms of pleasure are chewed over on chat shows. Yet, levels of funding for research and treatment lag behind the rhetoric and still seem inadequate to meet the needs of sufferers and those at risk.

What broader conclusions are thrown up by this encounter between AIDS and the substance of our history? At the most general level, what the book has charted is the continuing power of medical discourse to define the sexual, setting the parameters for what can and cannot be said, for who can speak and who is spoken to. This is crucial to the hierarchy of power around sex. It is the dominance of expertise in all its forms, marking sharp distinctions of power and privilege between male and female, normal and deviant and having real effects on the identities which individuals live out. *But medico-moral discourse is not a conspiracy*. It is not a cabal of white-coated men plotting a string of lies in the interests of capital or patriarchy. It is a distinctive regime of power/knowledge relations, rooted in institutions which circulate authoritative representations of sex.

How to combat such dominant discourses? That task has faced all groups targeted by sanitary interventionism since the feminist campaigns against the Contagious Diseases Acts over a hundred years ago. Today the problems thrown up by AIDS are not just ones for the gay community, but for feminists and progressive forces generally. Confronted by the institutional complexity of the professions, it would be naive to think that a simple anti-professionalism was an adequate response. After all, repealers effectively took on the 'terrible power' of the medical oligarchy precisely by drawing on medical concepts to subvert dominant explanations. Since a large part of medico-moral power lies in the coherence of its discourse, any challenge must engage at the level of ideological struggle. To miss the cultural messages surfacing around AIDS is to fail to grasp an important agenda in current health politics.

The question is what languages to mobilize. This needs asking because resistance is rarely a spontaneous eruption from below. Sanitary politics has always depended on specific languages to articulate demands and endow protests with meaning.

Gay medics and community activists, both here and in the USA, have opted for a politics of information – taking issue with media reporting. The Terrence Higgins Trust, the main gay co-ordinating body in Britain, projects AIDS as essentially a medical issue, distorted by media misrepresentation. Emphasis is laid on empowering individuals to make their own decisions about sex, with the help of adequate medical information which sifts truth from falsity, fact from scare-mongering.

These campaigns mark an important educational offensive, not least because they are run by gay men themselves. The problem is, such a programme can remain trapped inside medical discourse. It may criticize the professional treatment of gay men and the lack of state-funded research, but it does not ultimately confront the medical profession's right to colonize the field. When gay groups make the distinction between medical truth and media falsity they continue to reproduce dominant medical hierarchies. What is urgently needed is a much more extensive challenge to the hegemony of preventive medicine.

Moving beyond AIDS, all of this has implications for a future politics of health generally. Who has the right of access to control the body, to define the parameters of sickness and health and to pronounce on sex – these are pivotal issues. Health politics can no longer afford to inhabit narrow campaigns for increased funding and improvement of facilities, which leave institutional structures and their concepts unchallenged. It must work to mobilize positive representations of health – a new 'Hygeia' – which deals in the real discontents of those disenfranchised by present provision and projects a different vision of needs, beyond a mere defence of the NHS settlement. If this is dismissed as mere utopian rhetoric, then it is a testament to the acute impoverishment of initiatives in the field.

That is one conclusion. But AIDS provokes more than a far-reaching critique of medical authority. It also crystallizes cultural responses from those communities attacked by the virus and its panic – responses to do with lifestyles, desire and sexual practice. For AIDS is not just of the body, it is about the signs and meanings we attach to bodily functions in the head. The disease condenses and magnifies differences among political groupings loosely linked by their opposition to the moral right and their desire to project alternative regimes of sex. In that sense AIDS does indeed represent the front-line of sexual politics.

Responses within the gay community register more widely held positions. Mirroring the right, there are those who tell us to repent and return to monogamy under the threat of disease and death. Pragmatic and liberal voices stress the importance of education into 'safer sex' which need not be unpleasurable.[10] The most consciously theorized position – emerging out of sexual radicalism and utopian socialism – argues that though AIDS demands serious attention, gay men should not lose sight of their long-term objectives.[11] What is ultimately envisaged here is a radical pluralism, capable of uniting various disparate tendencies – gay, feminist, socialist, libertarian – in a progressive sexual alliance. Pluralism will stick because it accepts diversity and choice, avoids moral absolutes and underlines the representational quality of sexual desire. Like the fierce charges and counter-charges of seventy years ago, this bid for sexual hegemony is put together as an explicit challenge both to the moral right and to perceived feminist moralisms.

What is wrong with such a vision of our sexual future is that it is ungendered. As this book has shown, discourses of sex have constructed men and women in terms of difference, difference shot through with power relations. That insight must put the issue of male sexuality firmly on the political agenda. Not, let it be clear, men and their desires as the unified, monolithic oppressor, the source of all power, but men as they appear in this history. Men whose constructed sexualities, identities, pleasures have been complexly written into many of the structures of social and political domination. An alliance of pluralist diversity which refuses this must ultimately flounder.

Our final question then must be how to put together a new settlement around sexual relations. Within this, male sexuality needs to be prioritized, complexly theorized, though not elevated to the status of a negative obsession. If a hundred and fifty years of sexual politics teaches us nothing else, it should be that a large part of winning the argument about groups' and individuals' need to change involves convincing them that their sexuality is capable of changing. At the risk of repetition, this is germane to the book's whole project; that sex is about representations, in the head as well as in the body. But as the contradictions inherent in purity make clear, a strategy for change needs more than biting critique. It needs to project a new vocabulary to speak about masculinity and for men to think about themselves. Such languages do not just drop from the sky, they need to be forged, re-assembled from current images and experience. Like the contest over medical professionalism, the debate about masculinity has only just begun.

NOTES

Abbreviations

BMA	British Medical Association
BMJ	*British Medical Journal*
GBPP	Great Britain Parliamentary Papers; roman numerals refer to bound volume numbers, figures to bound page numbers
HL	House of Lords Sessional Papers, as for Parliamentary Papers
LNA	Ladies' National Association
NCCVD	National Council for Combatting Venereal Disease
NCPM	National Council of Public Morals
NUWSS	National Union of Women's Suffrage Societies
NUWW	National Union of Women Workers
NVA	National Vigilance Association
PRO Adm	Public Record Office, Admiralty Papers, Kew
PRO ED	Public Record Office, Board of Education Papers, Kew
PRO HO	Public Record Office, Home Office Papers, Kew
PRO LG	Public Record Office, Local Government Board Papers, Kew
PRO PC	Public Record Office, Privy Council Papers, Chancery Lane
PRO T	Public Record Office, Treasury Papers, Kew
PRO WO	Public Record Office, War Office Papers, Kew
WSPU	Women's Social and Political Union

Place of publication is London unless otherwise stated.

Narratives of sex.

1 M. Marmoor *et al.*, 'Risk Factors for Kaposi's Sarcoma in Homosexual Men', *The Lancet*, 15 May 1982, vol. 1, pp. 1083–6.
2 M. Gottlieb *et al.*, 'Pneumocystis Carinii Pneumonia and Mucosal Candidiasis in Previously Healthy Homosexual Men', *The New England*

Journal of Medicine, 10 December 1981, vol. 305, no. 24, pp. 1425–31.
3 Commonsense, pre-given assumptions about the meaning of sexuality are a recurrent problem in social histories of the family, sex and marriage. See especially E. Shorter, *The Making of the Modern Family*, 1977 and L. Stone, *The Family, Sex and Marriage in England 1500—1800*, 1977 where sex is assumed to be a basically physiological phenomenon overlaid by changing historical meanings.
4 The Oxbridge school of official or administrative history has been particularly important here. Influenced by post-war debates about the origins of welfarism, the classic texts focus on the early nineteenth century as the period witnessing the growth of modern government. See especially: S. Finer, *The Life and Times of Sir Edwin Chadwick*, 1952; O. MacDonagh, 'The Nineteenth Century Revolution in Government: A Reappraisal', *Historical Journal*, 1958, ii. pp. 59–73; R. Lambert, *Sir John Simon (1816—1904) and English Social Administration*, 1963; J. Hart, 'Nineteenth-Century Social Reform: A Tory Interpretation of History', *Past and Present*, 1965, no. 31, pp. 39–61. Differences of interpretation centre on the understanding of factors influencing transformations within government institutions. 'Tory' accounts, such as MacDonagh's, stress the pragmatic character of state formation, with its often accidental character and effects. Finer's 'Fabian' reading foregrounds the role of Benthamite planning. Both place differing but heavy emphasis on the role of individual experts and civil servants.
5 Social history which has been particularly influential here includes: G. Stedman Jones, *Outcast London*, Harmondsworth, 1984; M. Ignatieff, *A Just Measure of Pain*, 1978; R. Johnson, 'Educating the Educators: "Experts" and the State 1833–9', in A. Donajgrodski (ed.), *Social Control in Nineteenth Century Britain*, 1977; P. Richards, 'State Formation and Class Struggle, 1832–48', in P. Corrigan (ed.), *Capitalism, State Formation and Marxist Theory*, 1980.
6 M. Foucault, *Madness and Civilisation*, 1971; *The Birth of the Clinic*, 1972; *Discipline and Punish*, 1977; *The History of Sexuality. An Introduction*, Vol. I, New York, 1978.
7 For extended discussion of these polarized positions within cultural history and cultural theory see R. Johnson, 'Histories of Culture/Theories of Ideology: Notes on an Impasse', in Michèle Barrett *et al.* (eds), *Ideology and Cultural Production*, 1979.

Moral environmentalism 1830–1860

1 Lords of HM Privy Council, *Papers Relating to the Disease called Cholera Spasmodica in India now prevailing in the North of Europe*, 1831, PRO PCI/105. For general accounts of nineteenth-century cholera epidemics see Margaret Pelling, *Cholera, Fever and English Medicine 1825—1865*, 1978; N. Longmate, *King Cholera. The Biography of a Disease*, 1966. For a detailed account of the 1832 outbreak, attentive to the class-articulated ideology of early social medicine see R. Morris, *Cholera 1832*, 1976.

2 For the impact of cholera in the north-east see Longmate, *op.cit.*, pp. 20–49.

3 King's speech, *Hansard*, 21 June 1831, third series, vol. IV, col. 36.

4 Quoted in Longmate, *op. cit.*, p. 15.

5 Central Board of Health, *Daily Report of Cholera Cases from Central Board of Health, Council Office, Whitehall, London and Vicinity*, 19 April 1832, PRO PC1/4395, Part I.

6 John Marshall to Central Board of Health, 19 July 1831, *Minutes of the Central Board of Health*, 21 June–17 October 1831, PRO PCI/101.

7 Dr Robert Dawn to Doctor Mahony, undated, Mahoney's original letter dated 11 August 1831, *Minutes, op. cit.*

8 Mahony to Central Board of Health, 12 August 1831, *Minutes, op.cit.*

9 Sir Gilbert Blane to Central Board of Health, 30 September 1831, *Minutes, op.cit.*

10 *An Extract from the Proceedings of the Central Board of Health*, 10 December 1831, case no. 3, PRO PCI/2662.

11 Mayor of York to Lord Melbourne, January 1832, *Copies of Certain Papers relating to Cholera together with the Report of the Central Board of Health thereupon*, 1832; GBPP 1831–1832, XXVI, p. 479. See also complaints by Dr W. Haslewood to Central Board of Health, 1 November 1831, *Daily Report of Cholera Cases from Central Board of Health*, PRO PCI/4395, Part II.

12 'Spasmodica Cholera', *The Westminister Review*, 15 October 1831, vol, XV, pp. 485–6.

13 Board of Health, Sunderland, To Central Board of Health, 1 November 1831, PRO PCI/4395.

14 *The Cholera Gazette*, 28 January 1832, preserved in *An Extract from the Central Board of Health*, PRO PCI/2662.

15 'History of the Apothecaries', *The Lancet*, 11 December 1830–1, vol. 1, p. 370.

16 'The Board of Health Job', *The Lancet*, 2 July 1830–1, vol. 2, pp. 433–4. The new board did draft extensive recommendations for dealing with the epidemic, involving the creation of local boards with at least one medical representative. Almost immediately *The Lancet* intervened again, arguing that medics were being deliberately marginalized at a time of national emergency: 'Conduct of the Board of Health', *The Lancet*, 24 September 1830–1, vol. 2, p. 820.

17 Mr Hubbard, Chairman of Durham Board of Health, to Central Board of Health, 15 November 1831, *Minutes of the Central Board of Health 1831—1832*, PRO PC1/105. Also Mr Spooner of Birmingham to the Privy Council, letter not preserved. For reply to Spooner's request see Charles Grenville to Spooner, 19 November 1831, warning that the Privy Council had no legal authority to sanction use of the parish rate, PRO PCI/4395, Part II.

18 T. Spring-Rice to Central Board of Health, 14 November 1831, *Minutes*, 1831–2, *op. cit*.

19 Central Board of Health to Dr Walker, 15 August 1833, PRO PC1/96.

20 F. Smith, *The Life and Times of Sir James Kay-Shuttleworth*, 1923. See also B. Bloomfield (ed.) *The Autobiography of Sir James Kay-Shuttleworth*, Education Libraries Bulletin, supplement 7, 1964. (The text is from Kay's own autobiographical manuscript of 1877.) For a more sophisticated examination of Kay as the agent of early educational professionalism see R. Johnson, 'Educational Policy and Social Control in Early Victorian England', *Past and Present*, November 1970, no. 49, pp. 96–119.

21 Bloomfield, *op. cit.*, p. 5.

22 *Ibid.*

23 *Ibid.*, p. 17.

24 See T.Chalmers, *The Christian and Civic Economy of Large Towns*, Glasgow, 1821–6, 3 vols.

25 Bloomfield, *op.cit.*, p. 12.

26 J. Kay, *The Moral and Physical Condition of the Working Classes Employed in the Cotton Manufacture in Manchester*, 1832, p. 8. There are two editions of the pamphlet which differ significantly. The second edition is used here.

27 *Ibid.*, p. 62.

28 See M. Ignatieff, *A Just Measure of Pain*, 1978, p. 45.

29 Many recent historians, from widely differing intellectual traditions, have stressed the complex technologies of eighteenth-century punishment and incarceration. See especially D. Hay, *et al.* (eds), *Albion's Fatal Tree*, Harmondsworth, 1977; M. Foucault, *Discipline and Punish. The Birth of the Prison*, 1977; Ignatieff, *op.cit.*

30 D. Layard, *Directions to Prevent the Contagion of the Jail—Distemper Commonly Called Jail Fever*, 1772, p. 5; see also Layard's *Hints Respecting the Prison of Newgate*, 1794.

31 Layard, *Directions*, *op.cit.*, p.6.

32 *Ibid.*, p. 8.

33 D. Hartley, *Observations on Man, his frame, his duty and his expectations*, 1749.

34 Ignatieff, *op. cit.*, p. 60. Ignatieff's understanding of eighteenth-century social medicine is generally complex, but there are points where he falls back into a much more conspiratorial explanation of medical ideology.

35 *The Gentleman's Magazine*, 1804, vol. 1, p. 101.

36 T. Percival, *Medical Ethics, or a Code of Institutes and Precepts adapted to the Conduct of Physicians and Surgeons*, 1803, p. 24; also J. Walter, *Practical Observations Concerning the Cure of Venereal Disease by Mercuricals*, 1765.

37 Circular Letter of Instruction to the Assistant Poor Law Commissioners in England, *Report from the Poor Law Commissioners into the Sanitary Condition of the Labouring Population of Great Britain*, 1842; H.L. 1842, XXVI, p. xii. Also Instructions from the Central Board of the Children's Employment Commission to the Subcommissioners, Children's Employment Commission, *First Report of the Commissioners. Mines*, 1842; GBPP 1842, XV, pp. 275–281.

38 Children's Employment Commission, *op.cit.*, p. 3.

39 See M. Jeanne Peterson, *The Medical Profession in Mid-Victorian England*, Berkley, 1978; I. Inkster, 'Marginal Men: Aspects of the Social Role of the Medical Community in Sheffield 1790–1850', in J. Woodward and D. Richards (eds), *Health Care and Popular Medicine in Nineteenth Century England*, 1977; R. Hodgkinson, *The Medical Services of the New Poor Law 1834—71*, unpublished dissertation for the PhD degree, London University, 1950, 2 vols.

40 As late as 1869 the *BMJ* still felt it necessary to warn medics that gentlemanly codes of conduct were essential for professional success, 11 September 1869, p. 286. Elizabeth Gaskell's *Wives and Daughters*, published in 1866 but looking back to the early nineteenth century, was an ironic commentary on the ambiguous status of medics and their wives. George Eliot's study of the doctor Lydgate and his wife Rosamund in *Middlemarch*, 1871, was also acute on medical ambition.

41 See S. Squire Sprigge, *The Life and Times of Thomas Wakley MD*, 1897; N. Humphreys (ed.), *Vital Statistics. A Memorial Volume of Selections from the Reports and Writings of William Farr*, 1885.

42 The new association was established in 1832 to provide a national organization for provincial doctors, with a journal and regular meetings. Reform of entrance to the profession was taken up by Wakley, who had founded *The Lancet* in 1823. As MP for Finsbury after 1835 he acted as the co-ordinator for radical medics. A parliamentary select committee, appointed in 1834 to examine the state of medical education, recommended sweeping reforms but these were systematically blocked until the 1850s. See Sprigge, *op. cit.*, pp. 227–234 and P. Vaughan, *Doctor's Commons, A Short History of the British Medical Association*, 1959, pp. 13–14.

43 'Government Cholera Commission', *The Lancet*, 22 October 1853, vol. 2, p. 393.

44 See R. Lambert, *Sir John Simon (1816—1904) and English Social Administration*, 1963, pp. 48–9. Lambert understands the early dominance of miasma in terms of the internal dynamics of medical discourse and its inter-professional rivalries. Wider social and political determinations on the formation of medical knowledge are generally ignored.

45 T. Southwood Smith, *Treatise on Fever*, 1820, p. 324.

46 Kay, *op. cit.*, p. 5; also Dr H. Gaulter, *The Origins and Progress of the Malignant Cholera in Manchester*, 1833, p. 127.

47 J. Liddle, *On the Moral and Physical Evils resulting from the Neglect of Sanitary Measures. A Lecture*, 1847, pp. 5, 27.

48 *The Evangelical Magazine and Missionary Chronicle*, 1832, new series, vol. 10, p. 22.

49 Rev. C. Girdlestone, *Seven Sermons preached during the Prevalence of Cholera in the Parish of Sedgley*, sermon I, 1833, p. 2. See also Girdlestone's *Farewell Sermons — Preached in the Parish Church of Sedgley*, sermon IV, 1837, p. 55. and E. Miller, *Counsel to the Young. The Substance of a Sermon Preached at Putney Chapel*, 1833, p. 6.

50 Girdlestone, *Letters on the Unhealthy Condition of the Lower Class of*

Dwellings especially in Large Towns, 1845, p. vii.

51 See Inkster, *op. cit.*, p. 128.

52 W. Cooke, *Mind and the Emotions Considered in Relation to Health and Disease*, 1830, pp. 37–8.

53 Lord Brougham, *Paley's Natural Theology with Illustrative Notes*, 1826, pp. 8–9. See also Brougham's, *A Discourse on the Object, Advantages and Pleasures of Science*, 1827, pp. 6, 47. A number of leading scientists saw their work as intimately linked to their religious faith. Michael Faraday was a devout Sandemanian (a small sect believing that ultimately God was only knowable through faith) who stressed that scientific discoveries allowed men better to understand the divine plane. See R. Appleyard, *A Tribute to Michael Faraday*, 1931.

54 See T. Heyck, *The Transformation of Intellectual Life in Victorian England*, 1982, p. 56.

55 *Congregational Magazine*, 1832, vol. 15, p. 72.

56 Health of Towns Association, *Address from the Committee of the Health of Towns Association to the Bishop of London and the Rev. the Clergy*, 1848, p. 32.

57 E. Tilt, *The Serpentine 'as it is' and 'as to ought to be'. And the Board of Health 'as it is' and 'as it ought to be'*, 1848, p. 32. Tilt was physician to the Farringdon General Dispensary and Lying in Charity.

58 For attacks on the General Board see: J. Toulmin Smith, *Centralization or Local Representation? Health of Towns Bill An Address by a Citizen*, 1848; T. Hawksley, *A letter to the most Hon. The Marquis of Chandos MP in relation to some of the Extraordinary Powers Assumed by the General Board of Health*, 1853. The board could only initiate public health measures in areas where the general death-rate had reached twenty three per thousand – elsewhere it had to await a petition signed by local ratepayers. Local authority jurisdiction covered drainage, water-supply and paving, supervised by the central board through circulars and a superintending inspectorate, Public Health Act, 1848, 11 and 12 Vict., ch. 63.

59 Lord Ashley, 26 September 1848, Shaftsbury (Broadlands) manuscript, National Register of Archives, London, SHA/PD/5.

60 Chadwick to Ashley, 25 September 1848, Chadwick manuscript, University College Library, London.

61 Ashley to the Duchess of Beaufort, November 1849, Shaftsbury manuscript, *op.cit.*, SHA/PC/18/1.

62 Ashley to Chadwick, 29 October 1849, Chadwick manuscript, *op.cit.*

63 These differences are discussed in M. Cullen, *The Statistical Movement in Early Victorian Britain*, Hassocks, 1975, p. 62.

64 Kay, *op. cit.*, 63–4.

65 See *Report into the Sanitary Condition of the Labouring Population*, *op.cit.*, pp. 233–78.

66 Kay, *op. cit.*, p. 15. See also R. Johnson, 'Educating the Educators: "Experts" and the State 1833–9', in A. Donajgrodski (ed.), *Social Control in Ninetenth Century Britain*, 1977.

67 Ashley, *Moral and Religious Education of the Working Classes*, 1843, pp.10–11.

68 Evidence of Dr Gilly, Canon of Durham, *Report into the Sanitary Condition of the Labouring Population*, *op. cit.*, p. 124.
69 Evidence of Mr Ridall Wood, *ibid.*, p. 125.
70 See evidence of Mr Baker, assistant commissioner for Leeds, *ibid.*, p. 126. For discussion of incest within the working-class family see A. Wohl, 'Sex and the Single Room: Incest among the Victorian Working Classes' in Wohl (ed.), *The Victorian Family*, 1978.
71 *Report into the Sanitary Condition of the Labouring Population*, *op.cit.*, p. 127. For analysis of the sexual dimensions of sanitary reform see: F. Mort, 'The Domain of the Sexual', *Screen Education*, 1980, no. 36, pp. 69–84; Wohl, 'Unfit for Human Habitation', in H. Dyos and M. Woolf (eds), *The Victorian City. Images and Realities*, 1973, vol. 2.
72 Evidence of Dr Scott Alison of Tranent, *Report into the Sanitary Condition of the Labouring Population*, *op.cit.*, p. 142.
73 Girdlestone, *Farewell Sermons*, *op.cit.*, p. 55. For feminist appropriations of evangelical discourse see Barbara Taylor, *Eve and the New Jerusalem*, 1983. Charlotte Brontë's, *Jane Eyre*, 1847, not only contains a lengthy debate on evangelical morality, via the character St John Rivers, but also employs evangelical language to convey women's sexual and emotional experience.
74 Girdlestone, *Farewell Sermons*, *op. cit.*, pp. 138–9.
75 Health of Towns Association, *op. cit.*, p. 6.
76 Foucault, *The History of Sexuality*, Volume I, New York, 1978, pp. 120–7.
77 Kay, *op.cit.*, pp. 7–8.
78 Anon., *Twenty Minutes Advice on Diet, Regimen and all other matters connected with health*, undated, pp. 8–9.
79 'Impotence and Sterility', *The Lancet*, 28 August 1840–41, vol. 2, p. 779.
80 Anon., *Tables Dorsalis or, the Causes of Consumption in Young Men and Women*, 1832, p. 8.
81 *Ibid.*, p. 31.
82 Anon., *Twenty Minutes Advice*, *op.cit.*, p. 34; see also anon., *The Book of Matrimony*, undated.
83 Cooke, *Mind and the Emotions Considered in Relation to Health and Disease*, 1830, p. 5.
84 M. Ryan, *The Philosophy of Marriage in its Social, Moral and Physical Relations*, 1837. Also Cooke, *An Address to British Females on the Moral Management of Pregnancy and Labour*, 1817.
85 H. Macrosty and J. Bonar, *Annals of the Royal Statistical Society 1834—1934*, 1934, pp. 52–5. See also Cullen, *op. cit.*, part II; T. Ashton, *Economic and Social Investigations in Manchester, 1833—1933*, Hassocks, 1977.
86 J. Roberton, *The Relative Proportion of Male and Female Population*, Report of the Manchester Statistical Society, session 1839–40; also Roberton, *On the Alleged Influence of Climate on Female Puberty in Greece*, session 1843–4, quoted in Ashton, *op. cit.*, appendix C.

87 The act established a system of local and superintendent registrars, though the local administrative structure was based initially on the poor law. Registrars were to make quarterly returns on the number of births, deaths and marriages to the Registrar-General, who was responsible for the compilation of an annual population abstract to be laid before Parliament. See J. McCulloch (ed.), *A Statistical Account of the British Empire*, vol. 1, 1839, pp. 407–12.

88 W. Farr, 'Lecture Introductory to a Course on Hygiene', *The Lancet*, 14 November, 1835–6, vol. 1, p. 241; also Farr, 'Lecture on the History of Hygiene', *The Lancet*, 13 February, 1835–6, vol. 1, pp. 773–6.

89 Farr, Letter to the Registrar-General, *Appendix to the Fourth Annual Report of the Registrar-General of Births, Deaths and Marriages*, 1842; GBPP 1842, XIX, p. 525.

90 *Appendix to the Fifth Annual Report*, 1843; GBPP 1843, XXI, pp. 574–5.

91 Parliamentary divorces, introduced in the 1660s, had always been concerned with the correct transmission of aristocratic inheritance in the male line. The extension of divorce facilities to the middle-class via the recommendations of the *Report of the Commissioners on the Law of Divorce, and on the mode of obtaining Divorces à vinculo matrimonii*, 1853; GBPP, 1852–53, XL, and the Divorce and Matrimonial Causes Act, 1857, 20 and 21 Vict., ch. 85, preserved that concern with property transmission, by insisting that one of the principal reasons for divorce by the husband was the danger of an adulterous wife palming spurious offspring on the husband. The 1868 *Report of the Royal Commission on the Laws of Marriage*, 1868; GBPP, 1867–68, XXXII, addressed itself to working-class immorality, recommending a tightening of the regulations governing the solemnization and registration of marriage to promote sound moral principles among the poor. See O. McGregor, *Divorce in England*, 1957 and Rachel Harrison and F. Mort, 'Patriarchal Aspects of Nineteenth Century State Formation: Property Relations, Marriage and Divorce and Sexuality', in P. Corrigan (ed.), *Capitalism, State Formation and Marxist Theory*, 1980, pp. 93–100.

92 Foucault, *History of Sexuality*, *op cit.*, pp. 122–7.

93 Evidence of Mr George Armitage, Children's Employment Commission, *First Report, Mines*; GBPP 1842, XV, p. 43; see also evidence of John Cawthra, p. 44. For a study of women in the mining industry in the nineteenth century see Angela John, *By the Sweat of their Brow. Women Workers at Victorian Coal Mines*, 1984.

94 Children's Employment Commission, *op. cit.*, p. 268.

95 From fragment contained in Chadwick manuscript, London.

96 *Ibid.*

97 Report by Jelinger Symons, Yorkshire Coalfield, Children's Employment Commission, *op. cit.*, XVI, p. 189. Symons' evidence is discussed by Jane Humphries in 'Protective Legislation, the Capitalist State and Working Class Men. The Case of the 1842 Mines Regulation Act', *Feminist Review*, no. 7, 1981, pp. 1–34.

98 Children's Employment Commission, *op. cit.*, XVI, p. 189.
99 *Ibid.*
100 *Ibid.*
101 Evidence of Edward Newman, Childen's Employment Commission, *op. cit.*, XVI, p. 258.
102 Instructions to sub-Commissioners, Children's Employment Commission, *op. cit.*, XV, p. 278.
103 Evidence of J. Leifchild, Children's Employment Commission, *op. cit.*, XVI, pp. 747–8.
104 Girdlestone, *Farewell Sermons*, *op. cit.*, p. 54.
105 S. Finer, *The Life and Times of Sir Edwin Chadwick*, 1952, p. 5.
106 *Ibid.*, p. 4. All the standard biographies of these civil servants reproduce traditional distinctions between the public and private spheres, refusing to examine the inter-relation of the two domains.
107 See Sir J. Simon, *Personal Recollections*, 1894, p. 13; also Lambert, *op. cit.*, pp. 27–9, 485–7.
108 Before and after the marriage Jane Simon mixed freely in artistic and scientific circles and later became a close friend of Ruskin: Lambert, *op. cit.*, 27–9 and 489–90.
109 J. Kay-Shuttleworth to Lady Kay-Shuttleworth, Stockbridge, 9 February 1851. Kay Shuttleworth papers, John Ryelands Library, Manchester.
110 Lady JKS, Capesthorne, 7 December 1841, *ibid.*
111 JKS to his children, Fleetwood, 28 April 1858, *ibid.* A number of the Kay papers remain closed, especially those relating to the couple's estrangement. See Bloomfield, *A handlist of papers in the deed box of Sir J.P. Kay Shuttleworth*, College of St Mark and St John, occasional paper no. 2, 1961.
112 See Catherine Hall, 'The Early Formation of Victorian Domestic Ideology', in Sandra Burman (ed.), *Fit Work for Women*, Oxford, 1979.
113 For a study of the role of women in philanthropic charities see: F. Prochaska, *Women and Philanthropy in Nineteenth Century England*, Oxford, 1980; Anne Summers, 'A Home from Home – Women's Philanthropic Work in the Nineteenth Century', in Burman, *op. cit.* Also J. Pringle, *Social Work of the London Churches. Being some Account of the Metropolitan Visiting and Relief Association 1843—1937*, 1937, pp. 116–208.
114 Farr, *Appendix to the Fifth Annual Report of the Registrar-General*, *op.cit.*, p. 575.
115 Edward Sieveking, 'On Dispensaries and Allied Institutions', in Rev. F. Maurice (ed.), *Lectures to Ladies*, Cambridge, 1855, p. 92.
116 *Ibid.*, p. 106.
117 Maurice, 'The College and the Hospital', in Maurice, *op.cit.*, p. 47.
118 *Ibid.*, p. 13.
119 *Ibid.*
120 Judith Walkowitz notes how many of the leaders of the Ladies' National Association had a history of involvement in charity and philanthropic

work, *Prostitution and Victorian Society. Women, class and the state*, Cambridge, 1980, pp. 126–7.

121 See Elspeth Platt, *The Story of the Ranyard Mission 1857—1937*, 1937; Kathleen Heesman, *Evangelicals in Action. An Appraisal of Their Social Work in the Victorian Era*, 1962, p. 36. For Ranyard's own account of her work see LNR, *London and Ten Years Work in It*, 1868. The St Giles Rookery in Holborn was an early target for sanitary clearance schemes under the direction of the local medical officer of health.

122 LNR, *Life Work; or the Link and the Rivet*, 1861, p. 158.

123 *Ibid.*, p. 9.

124 *Ibid.*, p. 269.

125 LNR, *London, op. cit.*, p. 7. Ranyard's journal of the London Bible and Domestic Mission was aptly called *The Missing Link*.

126 LNR, *Life Work, op.cit.*, p. 40.

127 *Ibid.*, p. 141.

128 *Ibid.*, pp. 117–18.

The sanitary principle in dominance: medical hegemony and feminist response 1860–1880.

1 The life of the General Board of Health was not extended by Parliament in 1854. Instead a new, drastically curtailed board was set up, prompting Chadwick's resignation. John Simon entered this second General Board of Health in 1855 as Medical Officer. The Board lasted until 1859 when it was replaced under the terms of the Public Health Act of that year by the Medical Office within the Privy Council, with Simon again holding the officership.

2 *The Times*, 1 August 1854.

3 Simon's research team at the Medical Office functioned as part of the system of public health administration. The results of this work, which focused on many of the pressing and unresolved medical issues of the day, and in particular the problems of contagious and infectious diseases, were attached to Simon's annual reports at the Privy Council and the Local Government Board between 1859 and 1877. See 'Dr Buchanan on the Distribution of Phthisis as affected by the dampness of soil', *Tenth Annual Report of the Medical Officer of the Privy Council*, 1867, GBPP 1867–8, XXXVI, p. 471; 'Dr Sanderson on the Communicability of the Tubercule by Innoculation', *Tenth Annual Report*, p. 525; 'Dr Thudichum on Researches Intended to Promote an Improved Chemical Identification of Diseases', *Tenth Annual Report*, p. 568.

4 See *Thirteenth Annual Report of the Medical Officer of the Privy Council*, 1870; GBPP 1871, XXI, p. 771.

5 For the impact of technological changes on medical science in the mid-Victorian period see G. 1 'E. Turner, *Historial Aspects of Microscopy: papers read at a one-day conference held at the Royal Microscopical Society at Oxford*, Cambridge, 1967; H. Malies, *A Short History of the English Microscope*, Chicago, 1981. Both accounts adopt a technicist and evolutionist reading of the new technology.

6 *Tenth Annual Report of the Medical Officer of the Privy Council*, 1867; GBPP 1867–8, XXXVI, p. 434.
7 See: The Public Health Act, 1848, 11 and 12 Vict., ch. 63; The Nuisance Removal Act, 1855, 18 and 19 Vict., ch. 121; The Sanitary Act, 1866, 20 and 21 Vict., ch. 41; The Public Health Act, 1875, 38 and 39 Vict., ch. 55.
8 The effects of these negative street clearance schemes intensified the housing crisis in central London in the late 1860s and 1870s, See G. Stedman Jones, *Outcast London*, Harmondsworth, 1984, chs 9, 10.
9 *Thirteenth Annual Report of the Medical Officer of the Privy Council*, op. cit., p. 771.
10 An Act for the Prevention of Contagious Diseases at Certain Naval and Military Stations, 1864, 27 and 28 Vict., ch. 85; An Act for the Better Prevention of Contagious Diseases at Certain Naval and Military Stations, 1866, 29 and 30 Vict., ch. 96; An Act to Amend the Contagious Diseases Acts 1866, 1869, 32 and 33 Vict., ch. 86.
11 Since 1823 military returns had reported a steady incease in VD. By 1864 one out of every three sick cases were venereal in origin, while admission to hospitals for gonorrhea and syphilis reached 290.7 per 1,000 of total troop strength. In the navy one out of eleven hospital patients was suffering from VD, and VD patients constituted 125 admissions per 1,000 troops. See W. Sloggett, *History and Operation of the Contagious Diseases Acts in the Home Ports*, 10 April, 1873, PRO Adm 1/6418, p. 2.
12 See *Report of the Royal Commission on the Health of The Army*, 1857; GBPP 1857, XVIII, p. xv.
13 There is an expanding body of research on the Contagious Diseases Acts and nineteenth-century prostitution, especially from feminist historians. This section relies heavily on the material covered by Judith Walkowitz in *Prostitution and Victorian Society. Women, class and the State*, Cambridge, 1980. But see also P. McHugh, *Prostitution and Victorian Social Reform*, 1980; E. Sigsworth and T. Wyke, 'A Study of Victorian Prostitution and Venereal Disease', in Martha Vicinus (ed.), *Suffer and Be Still: Women in the Victorian Age*, Bloomington, 1972; Jean L' Esperance, 'The Work of the Ladies' National Association for the Repeal of the Contagious Diseases Acts', *Bulletin of the Society for the Study of Labour History*, spring, 1973, pp. 14–16; K. Nield (ed.), *Prostitution in the Victorian Age: Debate on the Issues from Nineteenth Century Critical Journals*, Farnborough, 1973; Judith Walkowitz and D. Walkowitz, 'We are Not Beasts of the Field: Prostitution and the Poor in Plymouth under the Contagious Diseases Acts', *Feminist Studies*, 1973, no. 1, pp. 73–106; Nancy Wood, 'Prostitution and Feminism in Nineteenth-Century Britain', *m/f*, 1982, no. 7, pp. 61–78.
14 'The Contagious Diseases Act', *The Lancet*, 29 July 1871, vol. 2, pp. 166–7. For similar appeals to the sanitary principle see 'Venereal Disease in the Army and Navy', *The Lancet*, 19 March 1864, vol. 1, p. 329.
15 *The Westminister Review*, 1850, vol. 53, p. 502.
16 See *Report of the Committee to Inquire into the Prevalence of Venereal*

Disease in the Army and Navy, 1862, PRO WO 33/12.

17 See especially A. Parent-Duchâlet's *De la prostitution dans la ville de Paris, considerée sous le rapport de l'hygiène publique de la morale et de l'administration*, Paris, 1836. Paris had a comparatively extensive network of public health regulation, controlled by the Prefect of the Seine and established under the First Empire.

18 Harveian Medical Society of London, *Report of the Committee for the Prevention of Venereal Diseases*, 1867. for medical campaigns to extend the acts to the civilian population see: *The Lancet*, 26 January 1867, vol. 1, p. 127; *The Lancet*, 15 February 1868, vol. 1, pp. 232–4.

19 *The Lancet*, 3 March 1860, vol. 1, p. 226.

20 W. Acton, *Prostitution Considered in Its Moral, Social and Sanitary Aspects in London and Other Large Cities; with Proposals for the Mitigation and Prevention of Its Attendant Evil*, 1857, p. viii.

21 'Out-Patient Administrative Reform', *The Lancet*, 6 May 1871, vol. 1, p. 619.

22 *The Lancet*, 3 March 1860, vol. 1, p. 226; also *The Lancet*, 16 July 1864, vol. 2, pp. 75–6.

23 *Report from the Royal Commission on the Administration and Operation of the Contagious Diseases Acts 1866–69*, 1871; GBPP 1871, XIX, p. 11.

24 See G. Plarr, *Lives of the Fellows of the Royal College of Surgeons of England*, 1930, vol. 1, pp. 537–8. See also Deborah Gorham, 'Victorian Reform as A Family Business: the Hill Family', in A. Wohl (ed.), *The Victorian Family*, 1978.

25 For changing mid-century attitudes to the problem of poverty see Stedman Jones, *Outcast London*, *op. cit*. For an account of the pathologization of criminals and the insane see J. Tagg, 'Power and Photography: Part One. A Means of Surveillance: The Photograph as Evidence in Law', *Screen Education*, 1980, no. 36, pp. 17–55.

26 See *Report on the organization of the permanent civil service*, 1854; GBPP *1854, XXVII*. Recommendations included the introduction of a system of open competitive examination and the abolition of political jobbery and aristocratic influence. The aim was to create a new cadre of intellectuals within the state, backed by an ideology of neutral administrative expertise. See G. Kitson Clark, ' "Statesmen in Disguise": Reflections on the History of Neutrality of the Civil Service', *The Historical Journal*, 1959, II, 1, pp. 19–40.

27 See P. Abrams, *The Origin of British Sociology 1834—1914*, 1968, pp. 42, 47–8.

28 *Report of the Royal Commission on the Health of the Army*, *op. cit*.

29 Evidence of William Hinkman, *Report of the House of Commons Select Committee to Inquire into the Pathology and Treatment of the Venereal Disease, with a View to Diminish the Injurious Effects on the Men of the Army and Navy*, 1868; GBPP 1867–8, XXXVII, p. 1058.

30 Evidence of Dr Barclay, *ibid*., p. 707. *The Report of the Royal Commission*, 1871, *op cit*., dismissed appeals for the periodic examination of the lower ranks of the Army and Navy, insisting that there was no compari-

son between the 'irregular indulgence' of the men and the crime committed by the prostitute (p.17).

31 J. Curgenven, *The Contagious Diseases Act of 1866, and its Extension to the Civil Population of the United Kingdom*, 1868.

32 *BMJ*, 16 May 1868, vol. 1, p. 489. See also evidence of William Sloggett, *Report from the Select Committee on the Contagious Diseases Act (1866)*, 1869; GBPP 1868–9, VII, p. 23.

33 Many local acts and by-laws contained clauses designed to regulate sexual immorality among the urban poor. The Metropolitan Police Acts, 1829 and 1839, were frequently used against prostitutes, as were the Manchester Police Act, 1844 and the Town Police Clauses Act, 1847. See J. Walkowitz, *op. cit.*, ch. 10.

34 J. Walkowitz, *op. cit.*, pp. 197–201.

35 See W. Tait, *Magdalenism: An Inquiry into the Extent, Causes and Consequences of Prostitution*, Edinburgh, 1840, pp. 4–33; similarly R. Wardlaw, *Lectures on female prostitution; its nature, extent, effects, guilt, causes and remedy*, Glasgow, 1842, pp. 8–9.

36 W. Acton, *The Functions and Disorders of the Reproductive Organs in Childhood, Youth, Adult Age and Advanced Life*, 1875, p. 142.

37 *Ibid.*, p. 74.

38 *Ibid.*, p. 189.

39 See P. Cominos, 'Late-Victorian Sexual Respectability and the Social System', *International Review of Social History*, 1963, vol. 8, pp. 18–48 and 216–250.

40 *Report of the Royal Commission*, *op. cit.*, p. 17.

41 Acton, *The Functions*, *op. cit.*, p. 184.

42 *Ibid.*, p. 183.

43 See especially Abraham Solomon's *Drowned! Drowned!*, 1860. Other paintings, like Alfred Elmore's *On the Brink*, 1865 and William Frith's *At Homburg*, 1869, emphasized that it was only when women left the protection of the home that they put themselves at risk: Lynda Nead 'Seduction, Prostitution, Suicide: *On the Brink* by Alfred Elmore', Art History, 1982, vol. 5, pp. 310–22.

44 See Wardlaw, *op.cit*: M. Ryan, *The Philosophy of Marriage, in its social, moral and physical relations*, 1837; Ryan, *Lectures on Population, Marriage and Divorce*, 1831.

45 Wardlaw, *op. cit.*, pp. 68–9.

46 Ryan, *Lectures on Population*, *op. cit.*, p. 54. See also A. Walker, *Women Physiologically Considered as to Mind, Morals, Marriage, Matrimonial Slavery, Infidelity and Divorce*, 1839, p. 91.

47 Acton, *op. cit.*, p. 112.

48 For partisan accounts of the improving effects of lock-hospitals see Acton, *The Contagious Diseases Act, Shall the Contagious Diseases Act be Applied to the Civil Population?*, 1870, pp. 17, 24; 'Contagious Diseases Acts', *The Lancet*, 29 July 1871, vol. 2, p. 166.

49 See Stedman Jones, *op. cit.*, ch. 9.

50 'Association of Medical Officers of Health', *BMJ*, 8 January 1870, vol. 1, p. 35.

51 Acton, *The Functions and Disorders*, *op. cit.*, p. 142.

52 Speech of Mr Morgan, Women's Disabilities Removal Bill, Commons, *Hansard*, 1 May 1872, third series, vol, 211, col. 55.

53 'A Lady Among the Students', *The Lancet*, 6 July 1861, vol. 2, p. 16. See also 'Female Obstetricians', *The Lancet*, 23 January 1875, vol. 1, p. 139; 'Female Graduates at the University of London', *The Lancet*, 22 January 1876, vol. 1, p. 147.

54 See J. and Olive Banks, *Feminism and Family Planning in Victorian England*,. Liverpool, 1964, pp. 95–6.

55 Annie Besant, *Autobiography*, 1908, p. 207.

56 *The Lancet*, 22 January 1859, vol. 1, p. 89.

57 'Walter', *My Secret Life*, quoted in S. Marcus, *The Other Victorians. A Study of Sexuality and Pornography in Mid-Nineteenth Century England*, 1966, pp. 91–2.

58 *Ibid.*, pp. 122–3.

59 Flora Tristan, *Flora Tristan's London Journal*, translated by D. Palmer and Giselle Pincet 1, 1980, pp. 75–6.

60 Quoted in D. Hudson, *Munby Man of Two Worlds. The Life and Diaries of Arthur J. Munby 1828–1910*, 1974 p. 195. For discussion of the dynamics of the Munby–Cullwick relationship see Leonore Davidoff, 'Class and Gender in Victorian Britain. Arthur J. Munby and Hannah Cullwick', *Feminist Studies*, 1979, vol. 5, no. 1, pp. 87–133.

61 Brian Harrison identified the repeal campaign as a key mid-Victorian pressure group in *Drink and the Victorians: The Temperance Question in England 1815—1872*, 1971, pp. 174–5, 224, 381 and more especially in his 'State Intervention and Moral Reform', in Patricia Hollis (ed.),*Pressure from without in Early Victorian England*, 1974, pp. 319, 321. But see the feminist response to this approach in J. Walkowitz, *op cit*., p. 6.

62 See G. and Lucy Johnson (eds), *Josephine E. Butler An Autobiographical Memoir*, 1928, pp. 65–72.

63 *Ibid.*, p. 72.

64 Speech of Mr Divett, Divorce Bills, Commons, *Hansard*, 22 April 1836, third series, vol. 33, col. 116.

65 Speech of Mr Fowler, Contagious Diseases Act (1866–69) Repeal Bill, Commons, *Hansard*, 21 May 1873, third series, vol. 216, col. 218.

66 See G. Finlayson, *The Seventh Earl of Shaftesbury*, 1981, pp. 43–4. The court of the young Queen Victoria, dominated by Lord Melbourne and the big Whig families, was renowned as being morally lax. When Peel tried unsuccessfully to form a government in 1839 he insisted on appointing his own personal attendant to the royal household, in an effort to improve the moral culture of the court.

67 T. Biggs, *The Proposed Extension of the Contagious Diseases Act in Its Moral and Economic Aspects*, 1870, p. 11.

68 See for example J. Wilkinson, *The Forcible Introspection of Women for the Army and Navy by the Oligarchy Considered Physically*, 1870; Ladies' National Association, *Report for the Year Ending November 1871*, 1871; C.Taylor, *The Statistical Results of the Contagious Diseases Acts . . . showing their Total Failure from a Sanitary Point of View*, Nottingham, 1872.

69 J. Stansfield, *Speeches . . . on the Contagious Diseases Acts*, 1875, p. 11.
70 *Ibid.*, p. 2.
71 Josephine Butler, *Personal Reminiscences of a Great Crusade*, 1896, p. 294.
72 Stansfield,*op. cit.*, p. 12.
73 *Eleventh Annual Report of the Medical Officer of the Privy Council*, 1868; GBPP 1868–9, XXXII, pp. 3–13.
74 George Butler to Josephine Butler, 13 July 1856, quoted in G. Johnson, *op. cit.*, p. 29.
75 See W. Fowler, *A Study in Radicalism and Dissent: The Life and Times of Henry Joseph Wilson 1833—1914*, 1961, pp. 25–7.
76 Butler to Joseph Edmondson, 28 April 1872, Josephine Butler Collection, Fawcett Library, London, no. 3136.
77 Butler, *Personal Reminiscences*, *op.cit.*, p. 73.
78 Barbara Taylor, *Eve and the New Jerusalem*, 1983, ch. V.
79 Butler, *Personal Reminiscences*, *op. cit.*, p. 319.
80 Butler, *Social Purity. An Address Given at Cambridge*, 1879, p. 5.
81 Butler, *A Letter to the Members of the Ladies' National Asociation*, 1875, p. 5.
82 Mrs Hume-Rothery, *A Letter Addressed to the Right Hon. W.E. Gladstone, M.P., and Other Members of Her Majesty's Government*, Manchester, 1870, pp. 16–17.
83 Wilkinson, *op. cit.*, p. 15.
84 See Kell's evidence to the *Report of the Royal Commission*, *op. cit.*, pp. 690–7.
85 G. Johnson, *op. cit.*, pp. 44–5.
86 Butler, 'Introduction', in J. Butler (ed.), *Women's Work and Women's Culture*, 1869, pp. xxv-xxxvii.
87 Rothery, *op. cit.*, pp. 8–9.
88 *Report of the Royal Commission*, *op. cit.*, pp. 690–3.
89 *The Shield*, 21 October 1876, p. 313–4.
90 *The Shield*, 20 January 1877, pp. 9–10. For similar accounts see *National League Journal*, August 1883, pp. 1,4.
91 See *The Shield*, 25 February 1882, p. 39. For similar misgivings from Mrs Hampson see *The Shield*, 1 October 1870, p. 240.
92 See *National League Journal*, 1 January 1881, pp. 12–13.
93 *Report of the Royal Commission*, *op. cit.*, pp. 691–2. Butler herself tended to stress the penitence shown by reformed prostitutes, as she put it in her letter to James Wilkinson: 'I believe at this moment that there is a general feeling of penitence on the part of the women', quoted in Wilkinson, *op. cit.*, p. 25.
94 Butler, *Women's Work*, *op cit.*, p. xxxvii.
95 *Ibid.*

From state medicine to criminal law. Purity, feminism and the state 1880–1914.

1 *The Times*, 31 July 1885, p. 11.

2 'The Maiden Tribute of Modern Babylon', *Pall Mall Gazette*, 6, 7, 8, 10 July 1885.

3 *Pall Mall Gazette*, Special Morning Edition, 22 August 1885.

4 NVA, *Objects, Constitution and Rules of the National Vigilance Association*, 1885, p. 3. See also *Minutes of the National Vigilance Association*, 1885, Fawcett Library, London.

5 W. Coote, 'Law and Morality', in J. Marchant (ed.), *Public Morals*, 1902, p. 45. See also A. Barry, 'The Duty of the Church of Christ Against Impurity', in *Public Morals*, pp. 26–7.

6 Coote, *op cit.*, p. 69.

7 Legislation included the Indecent Advertisements Act, 1889, 52 and 53 Vict., ch. 18; the Vagrancy Act, 1898, 61 and 62 Vict., ch. 39, criminalizing male pimping and importuning; the Incest Act, 1908, 8 Ed. 7, ch. 45; the Criminal Law Amendment Act, 1912, 2 and 3 Geo. 5, ch. 20, increasing penalties and police powers against procurers and brothel-keepers and clarifying the scope of the 1898 act to include male homosexuals; the Criminal Law Amendment Act, 1922, 12 and 13 Geo. 5, ch. 56, abolishing the 'reasonable cause to believe' clause in cases of indecent assault on girls under sixteen and again increasing penalties for brothel-keeping.

8 See G. Stedman Jones, *Outcast London*, Harmondsworth, 1984, chs. 9–13.

9 See especially the fictional and journalistic accounts by J. Greenwood in *The Wilds of London*, 1874; *Low Life Deeps and an Account of the Strange Fish to be found there*, 1876, and by G. Sims, *How the Poor Live in Horrible London*, 1883, and J. London, *The People of the Abyss*, 1903.

10 Rev. A. Mearns, *The Bitter Cry of Outcast London*, 1883.

11 Evidence of the Rev. R. Billing, Royal Commission on the Housing of the Working Classes. *First Report of the Commissioners, England*, 1884; GBPP 1884–5, XXX, p. 254. For opposing arguments which ascribed incest primarily to drunkenness see Rev. A. Fryer, curate of St Philip's, Clerkenwell, *ibid.*, p. 169.

12 Evidence of Mearns, *ibid.*, p. 268.

13 See *The Lancet*, 17 March, 1883, vol. 1, p. 486 and 4 August, 1883, vol. 2, p. 192.

14 The Royal Commission on the Sanitary Laws, 1868 recommended the creation of one responsible administrative body for public health. Under the Local Government Act, 1871 the staff at the Poor Law Board, the General Register Office, the Local Government Office, and, subsequent to a limitation, the staff of the Privy Council Medical Department, were amalgamated to form the new Local Government Board. But the Act in no way defined the character, internal structure and relations of the new board. The direction of central health administration was left to the discretion of ministers and permanent officials. See Sir J. Simon, *Sanitary Institutions Reviewed in the Course of their Development and in Some of their Political and Social Relations*, 1890, pp. 348–9.

15 J. Brand, *The British Medical Profession and State Intervention in Public Health, 1870—1911*, unpublished dissertation for the PhD degree, London University, 1953, p. 86. See also J. and Barbara Hammond, *James Stansfield: A Victorian Champion of Sex Equality*, 1932, pp. 108–11.

16 For Lambert's work at the Local Government Board see H. Preston Thomas, *Work and Play of a Government Inspector*, 1909. Also *Miscellaneous Correspondence*, 1876, PRO LGB 58096/76 and *Government Office Correspondence*, 1873, PRO LGB 78178/73.

17 For *The Lancet*'s support for Simon's embattled position see *The Lancet*, 25 July 1874, vol. 2, pp. 134–5 and 15 April 1876, vol. 1, pp. 576–7.

18 *The Lancet*, 27 May 1876, vol. 1, pp. 782–3.

19 Administrative historians explain the eclipse of state medicine in terms of the clash of personalities of Simon and Lambert, and more broadly that the movement for public health reform had run out of steam. See especially R. Lambert, *Sir John Simon (1816—1904) and English Social Administration*, 1963, ch. XXIII, and Brand, *op.cit.*

20 Lingen, Treasury minute, 1 June 1871, PRO T1/18, 953.

21 The secretariat at the board conformed to the new civil service model and worked to circumscribe medical authority. The majority were Oxbridge graduates, recruited by public examination, whose subsequent experience was primarily 'paper experience', acquired by minutes, correspondence and occasional conferences.

22 Buchanan to Newsholme, quoted in A. Newsholme, *The Last Thirty Years in Public Health*, 1936, p. 34.

23 Ellice Hopkins, *Work in Brighton*, 1877, p. 49.

24 Elizabeth Blackwell, *How to Keep a Household in Health*, 1870; *The Religion of Health*, 1889. See also Rachel Baker, *The First Woman Doctor. The Story of Elizabeth Blackwell*, 1946.

25 Blackwell, *The Human Element in Sex: being a medical enquiry into the relation of sexual physiology to Christian morality*, 1884, pp. 11–12. 57.

26 For the impact of Darwinism on the mid-Victorian church see O. Chadwick, *The Victorian Church*, 1966, vol. 1, pp. 527–72, and T. Heyck, *The Transformation of Intellectual Life in Victorian England*, 1982.

27 *BMJ*, 12 October 1872, vol. 2, p. 416. Many scientists were arguing for a similar compromise in the 1870s. At the annual meeting of the British Association in 1871 Sir William Thompson, the president, affirmed that God's divine plan was manifest in the formal beauty of creation, *BMJ*, 12 August 1871, vol. 2, p. 187.

28 C. Darwin, *The Descent of Man. Selection in Relation to Sex*, 1871, vol. 1, chs. III and IV.

29 Social Party Alliance, *Schoolboy Morality. An Address to Mothers*, 1884, pp. 8–9.

30 Blackwell, *The Human Element*, *op. cit.*, p. 17.

31 *Ibid*.

32 Hopkins, *Village Morality, A Letter to Clergymen's Wives and Christian*

Workers, 1882, pp. 18–19. See also Frances Power Cobbe, 'The Causes of Evil', in Marchant, *op. cit.*, p. 25. Stedman Jones has argued strongly that renewed anxiety over the urban poor in the 1880s ruptured moral and environmental explanations of poverty and prepared the ground for new theories of urban degeneracy, based on the heredity transmission of characteristics. Yet the move away from traditional solutions was extremely uneven. In many areas of social reform a modified version of moral environmentalism remained dominant. Purists' practical religion of rescue and reclamation militated against any wholesale adoption of social Darwinism.

33 See for example 'Cases of Conversion', *Quarterly Record of the Tower Hamlets Mission*, 1881, no. 1, p. 5; *ibid.*, 1881, no. 2, p. 6. The mission was founded by Frederick Charrington, from the prominent brewing family.

34 A. Dyer, *Facts for Men on Moral Purity and Health*, 1884, p. 6.

35 Other similar groups included the Metropolitan Association for Befriending Young Servants, 1877 and the Travellers' Aid Society, 1885. See E. Bristow, *Vice and Vigilance: Purity Movements in Britain since 1700*, 1977, ch. 5.

36 See Hopkins, *Village Morality*, *op. cit.*, pp. 9–10, and her *The Early Training of Girls and Boys – An Appeal to Working Women*, 1902, pp. 18, 22–23. Purists were also encouraged to co-operate with the new elementary school-teachers created under the Education Act, 1870; see Hopkins, *The Girls' Friendly Society — An Appeal to the Mistresses of Elementary Schools*, 1882, pp. 9–10.

37 Purity campaigns against the London music halls consistently attacked the perceived immoral alliance between the aristocracy, big business and the urban working-class. The most famous campaign was against the Empire Theatre in 1894, see Laura Ormiston Chant, *Why We Attacked the Empire*, 1895.

38 See NVA, *Pernicious Literature. Debate in the House of Commons. Trial and Convictions for Sale of Zola's Novels with Opinion of the Press*, 1889.

39 *The Daily Telegraph*, 6 April 1895 and 27 May 1895.

40 *The Evening News*, 27 May 1895.

41 Speech of the Earl of Halsbury, Incest Bill, Lords, *Parliamentary Debates*, 16 July 1903, fourth series, vol. 125, col. 822; also speech of Mr Rawlinson, Incest Bill, Commons, *Parliamentary Debates*, 26 June 1908, fourth series, vol. 191, cols 278–9.

42 Hopkins, *The White Cross Army, A Statement of the Bishop of Durham's Movement*, 1883, p. 3. See also Blackwell, *The Human Element*, op. cit., p. 32.

43 Rev J. Wilson, *Sins of the Flesh. A Sermon preached in Clifton College Chapel*, 1883, p. 5. See also Wilson's, *An Address*, 1884, p. 12.

44 A. Dyer, *op. cit.*, p. 12.

45 See Rosa Barrett, *Ellice Hopkins: A Memoir*, 1907, p. 157.

46 Darwin was ambiguous about the evolutionary potential of women. While acknowledging that women's maternal instincts gave them a greater capacity for tenderness and selflessness, he insisted that men had

attained a higher stage of evolution. Yet Darwin was aware that women were more advanced on moral issues: *The Descent of Man*, *op. cit.*, vol. 2, ch. XIX.

47 Blackwell, *The Human Element*, *op. cit.*, p. 22.
48 *Ibid.*, p. 46.
49 See Judith Walkowitz, 'Science, Feminism and Romance: The Men and Women's Club 1885–1889', *History Workshop*, 1986, no. 21, pp. 36–59; also Lucy Bland, 'Marriage Laid Bare: Feminists Take Issue with Marital Sex, 1880– 1st World War', in Jane Lewis (ed.), *Labour and Love*, Oxford, 1986.
50 In the 1890s Butler expressed strong opposition to the new purity campaigns: 'I continue to protest that I do not believe that any reforms will ever be reached by outward repression', Butler to Miss Priestmann, 5 November 1894, Josephine Butler Correspondence, Fawcett Library, London.
51 J. Weeks, *Sex, Politics and Society*, 1981, ch. 5.
52 Judith Walkowitz, 'Male Vice and Feminist Virtue: Feminism and the Politics of Prostitution in Nineteenth Century Britain', *History Workshop*, 1982, no. 13, p. 89.
53 Sheila Jeffreys, *The Spinster And Her Enemies. Feminism and Sexuality, 1880—1930*, 1985.
54 Barrett, *op. cit.*, p. 157.
55 Hopkins, *An Englishwoman's Work among Workingmen*, 1875, pp. 4–5.
56 *Ibid.*, p. 5.
57 Hopkins, *Work in Brighton*, *op cit.*, p. 16.
58 Barrett, *op. cit.*, p. 254.
59 Hopkins, *Village Morality*, *op. cit.*, p. 13.
60 Barrett, *op. cit.*, pp. 173–4.
61 Hopkins, *The Power of Womanhood: or Mothers and Sons*, 1899, p. 2.
62 *Ibid.*, p. 19.
63 Hopkins, *Work in Brighton*, *op. cit.*, p. 60.
64 Hopkins, *The Power of Womanhood*, *op. cit.*, p. 160.
65 See T. Green, *Lectures on the Principles of Political Obligation and Freedom of Contract*, 1885; L. Hobhouse, *Democracy and Reaction*, 1904, and his *Mind in Evolution*, 1901. New liberal philosophies of the organic state are discussed in M. Freeden, *the New Liberalism: an Ideology of Social Reform*, 1978.
66 Hopkins, *The Early Training*, *op. cit.*, pp. 5–6.
67 Hopkins, *Work in Brighton*, *op. cit.*, p. 86.
68 Hopkins, *The Power of Womanhood*, *op.cit.* pp. 46, 127.
69 *Journal of the Vigilance Association for the Defence of Personal Rights*, 15 November 1882, no. 11, p. 90.
70 *Minutes of the National Association for the Repeal of the Contagious Diseases Acts*, 15 December 1879, no. 2184, see also 12 January 1880, no. 2201, Fawcett Library, London.
71 Mrs Jerome Mercier, 'The Bonds of Union between Women of Different Ranks', in the Girls' Friendly Society, *A Special Report*, 1879, p. 29.

72 Hopkins, *Work in Brighton*, p. 23.
73 For a retrospective account of the Brussels scandal see *The Shield*, January 1909, p. 52.
74 *Ibid*.
75 *Report from the Select Committee on the State of the Law relating to the Protection of Young Girls*, 1882; GBPP 1882, XIII, p. 841.
76 *Ibid*., *First Report*, 1881; GBPP 1881, IX, pp. 436–47.
77 Bath Preventive Mission and Ladies' Association for the Care of Friendless Girls to Sir Vernon Harcourt, 23 February 1884, PRO HO45/59343 G.
78 London Women's Christian Association to W. Gladstone, 22 February 1884, PRO HO45/59343 G.
79 Hartington to Roseberry, 30 May 1883, PRO HO45/59343 G.
80 Town Clerk of Hereford to Sir R. Cross, Under Secretary of State, Home Office, 29 September 1885, PRO HO45/A40683.
81 See Broadhurst's speech in the debate on the Criminal Law Amendment Bill, Commons, *Hansard*, 9 July 1885, third series, vol. 299, cols. 203–4, also similar opposition from the radical liberal C. Hopwood in the same debate, cols 199–202.
82 J. Stuart to S. Smith, 8 July 1884, PRO HO45/59343 I. For similar protests by the Vigilance Association see H. Beaumont, 'The Criminal Law Amendment Bill', *Journal of The Vigilance Association for the Defence of Personal Rights*, 15 June 1885, no. 51, p. 493.
83 *Pall Mall Gazette*, *The Maiden Tribute of Modern Babylon. The Report of the* Pall Mall Gazette*'s Secret Commission*, 1885, pp. 13–14.
84 Evidence of Mrs Anna Wilkes, *Report of the Select Committee on the Protection of Girls*, 1882, *op. cit.*, pp. 872–4.
85 Criminal Law Amendment Act, 1885, 48 and 49 Vict., ch. 69, section 11. The legislation criminalized all acts of gross indecency between males with a penalty of up to two years imprisonment. See J. Weeks, *Coming Out. Homosexual Politics in Britain from the Nineteenth Century to the Present*, 1977, pp. 14–16 H. Montgomery Hyde, *The Other Love: a historical and contemporary survey of homosexuality in Britain*, 1972, p. 325.
86 *The Times*, 11 June 1885.
87 *The Times*, 18 August 1885.
88 Coote, *A Romance of Philanthropy*, 1916, p. 27.
89 Clapham Vigilance Association to the Under Secretary of State, Home Office, 4 December 1886, PRO HO45/A45364.
90 Assistant Metropolitan Commissioner of Police to the Under Secretary of State, 19 December and 27 December 1886, PRO HO45/A45364.
91 Metropolitan Police Office to Under Secretary of State, 18 February 1889, PRO HO 45/X15663.
92 A. Gardiner, *The Life of Sir William Harcourt*, 1923, vol. 1, pp. 607–8.
93 Wilson to Robert Eadon Leader, 13 December 1882, quoted in P. McHugh, *Prostitution and Victorian Social Reform*, 1980, p. 239. For evangelical influence on the Liberal Party in the 1880s see D. Hamer,

Liberal Politics in the Age of Gladstone and Roseberry, 1971, pp. 5–9.

94 Coote, *A Romance*, *op. cit.*, pp. 156–60.

95 'Report on Application from St George's Vigilance Association for the appropriation of fines imposed on brothel-keepers', 9 July 1887, PRO HO45/X14891. For purists' reactions see Coote, *A Romance*, *op cit.*, p. 27.

96 Coote, *A Romance*, *op. cit.*, p. 95.

97 NVA annual reports noted with satisfaction the growing help and encouragement received from the police and the watch committees of local councils. See NVA, *Eleventh Annual Report*, 1896, p. 33.

98 NVA, *Sixteenth Annual Report*, 1901, p. 27. For Home Office response to mounting pressure for law reform see PRO HO45/A57406/1. Also V. Bailey and Sheila Blackburn, 'The Punishment of Incest Act 1908: A Case Study of Criminal Law Creation', *Criminal Law Review*, November 1979, pp. 708–18.

99 See NUWW, *Handbook and Report*, 1909–10, pp. 60–1, 125.

100 Until the creation of the new tier of borough councils in 1889 responsibility for prosecution lay with the old parish vestries who displayed a reluctance to prosecute, Bristow, *op. cit.*, p. 163.

101 See *Report of the Royal Commission upon the Duties of the Metropolitan Police*, 1908; GBPP 1908, L, p. 478.

102 *Ibid.*, p. 94.

103 *Ibid.*, p. 135.

104 *Ibid.*

105 *Ibid.*, p. 686.

106 Between 1895 and 1912 the NUWW passed a series of annual conference resolutions calling for criminal law amendments to protect women and children, see NUWW, *Handbook and Report*, 1909–10, pp. 60–1; NUWW, *Occasional Paper*, September 1910, special no., p. 37.

107 *The Shield*, November 1903, pp. 59–60.

108 'To Suppress the White Slave Traffic', *The Suffragette*, 11 July 1913, p. 660. See also 'The Lessons of the Great Crusade', *The Common Cause*, 11 May 1910.

109 See Jeffreys, 'Free From all Uninvited Touch of Man: Women's Campaigns around Sexuality, 1880–1914', *Women's Studies International Forum*, 1982, vol. 5, no. 6, p. 641.

110 See especially 'Decadence and Civilization', *The Hibbert Journal*, October 1911.

111 Lucy Re-Bartlett, *Sex and Sanctity* 1912, p. 26.

112 Cicely Hamilton, *Marriage as a Trade*, 1909, pp. 37–8.

113 Medics, psychiatrists and criminologists frequently explained the physical and mental diseases of women in terms of excessive sexuality or a malfunctioning of the reproductive system. See H. Maudsley, *Body and Mind*, 1870; Dr H. Tuke (ed.), *Dictionary of Psychological Medicine*, 1892; C. Lombroso and W. Ferrero, *The Female Offender*, 1895. Ellis and Carpenter worked with a notion that women's sexuality was repressed and needed to be liberated by the care and skill of the man, see H.

Havelock Ellis, *Studies in the Psychology of Sex*, vol. III, *Analysis of the Sexual Impulse Love and Pain. The Sexual Impulse in Women*, 1903 and E. Carpenter, *Love's Coming of Age*, 1896.

114 Christabel Pankhurst, *The Great Scourge and How to End It*, 1913, p. 20. See also Hamilton, *op. cit.*, p. 183.

115 Frances Swiney, *The Bar of Isis; or the Law of the Mother*, 1907, pp. 48, 51. For a contemporary account of Swiney's work see *The Suffrage Annual and Women's Who's Who*, 1913.

116 Swiney, *The Mystery of the Circle and the Cross; or the Interpretation of Sex*, 1908, p. 64.

117 Bartlett, *The Coming Order*, 1911, p. 33.

118 C. Pankhurst, *op. cit.*, p. viii.

119 Bartlett, *op. cit.*, p. 28.

120 Hamilton, *op. cit.*, p. 135.

121 C. Pankhurst, *op. cit.*, pp. 118–9; also Hamilton, *op. cit.*, p. 135.

122 'A Case of Child Assault', *The Vote*, 28 October 1911, p. 27; 'How Men Protect Women', *The Vote*, 23 March 1912, p. 26.

123 'A Wronged Woman', *The Common Cause*, 9 November 1911, p. 530.

124 'Scapegoats of Our Respectability', *The Vote*, 20 March 1912, p. 276.

125 Home Office Memorandum on the White Slave Traffic Bill, 24 May 1911, PRO HO445/178486.

126 Home Office Memorandum in response to parliamentary question from Mr France on the Criminal Law Amendment Bill, 8 May 1912, PRO HO45/178486.

127 NUWW, *Occasional Paper*, no. 54.

128 *The Shield*, June 1912, p. 121; and *The Shield*, November – December 1911, pp. 78–9. See also Wolverhampton Women's Suffrage Societies to G. Thomas MP, 20 May 1912, PRO HO45/178486.

129 NUWW, *Handbook and Report*, 1912–13.

130 *The Common Cause*, 13 June 1912.

131 *The Shield*, January 1911, pp. 14–15.

132 *The Suffragette*, 11 April 1913.

133 Teresa Billington-Grieg, 'The Truth About White Slavery', *The English Review*, June 1913, p. 445.

134 *Ibid.*

135 'Protecting Women', *Women's Dreadnought*, 19 December 1914, p. 159.

136 *The Freewoman* was established in November 1911, edited by Dora Marsden and Mary Gawthorpe. It was dedicated to developing the 'subjectivist side of feminist politics'. Discussion of sexuality was high on the agenda because readjustment of relations betwen men and women was seen as central to women's freedom and the evolution of a higher stage of civilization. See Jane Lidderdale and Mary Nicholson, *Dear Miss Weaver. Harriet Shaw Weaver, 1876—1961*, 1970.

137 See, for example, Gertrude Slater, 'Champions of Morality', *The Freewoman*, 13 June 1912, p. 79; Katherine Vulliamy, 'Pass the Bill', *The Freewoman*, 20 June 1912, p. 96. For attacks on the purity position, see: C. Norman, 'Champions of Morality', *The Freewoman*, 6 June 1912, pp. 45–6.

138 See the Legitimation League, *Aims and Objects* (undated), p. 3. Also 'GDL', 'Free Love and Sexual Relations, *The Adult*, December 1898, vol. 2, no 11, pp. 293–4 and G. Moore, 'The Logic of Free-Love', *The Adult*, September 1898, vol. 2, no. 8, p. 240.

139 O. Northcote, 'The Mutability of Sex Love', *The Adult*, September 1897, vol. 1, no. 2, p. 24.

140 Anon., 'Eve and her Eden', *The Adult*, 2 March 1898, vol. 2, no. 2, p. 30.

141 *The Adult*, January 1898, vol. 1, no. 6, p. 138.

142 Lillian Harman, 'Some Problems of Social Freedom', *The Adult*, 1898, extra no., 2, p. 7.

143 See especially F.W. Stella Browne, *Sexual Variety and Variability Among Women and their Bearing upon Social Reconstruction*, 1917. Also Sheila Rowbotham, *A New World for Women: Stella Browne — Socialist Feminist*, 1978, section 1.

144 'A New Subscriber', *The Freewoman*, 22 February 1912.

145 See for example: Winifred Carey, 'The Idealism of Sex Relations', *The Freewoman*, 22 February 1912, pp. 273–4; Kathryn Oliver, 'Chastity and Normality', *The Freewoman*, 29 February 1912, p. 290.

146 See Mary and S. Randolph, 'Free Unions', *The Freewoman*, 13 January 1912, p. 79.

147 The point is made by A. Hussain in his critique of Foucault's distinction between juridical and discursive forms of power, 'Foucault's History of Sexuality', *m/f*, 1981, nos 5 and 6, pp. 168–91.

From purity to social hygiene: early twentieth century campaigns for sex education.

1 The whole account of the Dronfield sex education case is preserved in the Public Record Office at PRO ED50/185.

2 PRO, *op. cit.*

3 Deposition of Doris Harrison, pupil at Dronfield School, taken by the school managers and sent to the Board of Education on 6 March 1914, as evidence against Outram, PRO, *op. cit.*

4 Evidence of Mrs S. Milnes, Dronfield School managers' meeting, 27 January 1914, PRO, *op. cit.*

5 Evidence of Mr Bradwell, Dronfield School managers' meeting, 14 January 1914, PRO, *op. cit.*

6 Speech of Miss Outram, managers' meeting, 14 January 1914, PRO *op. cit.*

7 *Ibid.*

8 Managers' meeting, 14 January 1914, *op. cit.*

9 Derbyshire Education Committee to Rt Hon J. Pease, MP, President of the Board of Education, 6 March 1914, PRO, *op. cit.*

10 Evidence of Mrs Milnes, managers' meeting, 14 January 1914, PRO, *op. cit.*

11 Evidence at Dronfield School managers' meeting, 27 January 1914, PRO *op. cit.*

12 *The Weekly Dispatch*, undated, cutting preserved in PRO file; also *The Derbyshire Times*, 7 February 1914.

13 F. Oakes, Private Secretary to the President, to Pease, 23 March 1914 and Oakes to H. Lucas, Clerk to Dronfield School Managers, 26 March 1914, PRO, *op. cit*.

14 'Dronfield Scholars on Strike', *The Derbyshire Times*, 25 April 1914.

15 National Council of Public Morals, *Manifesto*, 1910, pp. 3–4.

16 The most notable of the auxiliary studies sponsored by the board were the series undertaken by Dr L. Thudichum on the chemistry of the brain. The main research was disease-orientated, carrried out under the direction of Sir. J. Burdon Sanderson. See Jeanne L. Brand, *Doctors and the State: The British Medical Profession and Government Action in Public Health, 1870—1912*, Baltimore, 1965.

17 *BMJ*, 19 June 1897, vol. 1, p. 1571.

18 Between 1870 and 1905 many of the bacilli of the infectious and contagious diseases were isolated, including leprosy, typhoid, tuberculosis, cholera, diptheria and tetanus, together with the development of vaccines and anti-toxins. See Sir G. Newman, *An Outline of the Practice of Preventive Medicine*, 1919; GBPP 1919 XXXIX, p. 681.

19 *Ibid.*, p. 695. See also *BMJ*, 10 June 1897, vol. 1, pp. 1547–50.

20 Newman, *op. cit.*, pp. 682, 735–6; see also J. Burns, 'An Address on the Relationship Between Medicine and Health', *The Lancet*, 16 August 1913, vol. 2, pp. 455–61; Sir C. Allbutt, 'The New Birth of Medicine', *BMJ*, 12 April 1919, vol. 1, pp. 433–8.

21 See for example: The Sale of Food and Drugs Acts, 1879, 1899; The Factory and Workshops Acts, 1901 and 1907; The Housing of the Working Classes Acts, 1900 and 1903; The National Insurance Acts, 1911, 1917 and 1918.

22 Brand in *Doctors and the State*, *op. cit.*, loosely ascribes this medical resurgence to the growing trend towards collectivism, while Anna Davin ties it too directly to the political and military exigencies of the conjuncture, 'Imperialism and Motherhood', *History Workshop*, 1978, no. 5, pp. 9–12.

23 See especially the *Annual Reports of Inspector General of Recruiting*, 1900–03; GBPP 1901, IX, 1902, X, 1903, XXXVIII. Also A. White, *Efficiency and Empire*, 1901 and the *Interdepartmental Committee on Physical Deterioration*, 1904; GBPP 1904, XXXII. For discussion see Anne Summers, 'Militarism in Britain before the Great War', *History Workshop*, 1976, no. 2, pp. 104–23.

24 See Major General Sir F. Maurice, 'National Health; A Soldier's Study', *The Contemporary Review*, January 1903, pp. 41–55. See also: 'Pretorious', 'The Army and the Empire', *Empire Review*, March 1901, pp. 189–94; T. Macnamara, 'In Corpore Sano', *The Contemporary Review*, February 1905, pp. 239–48; C. Ewart, 'National Health, *Empire Review*, May 1910, pp. 255–63.

25 'The Medical Service of the Army', *BMJ*, 20 February 1904, vol. 1, pp. 445–6. Medics had first voiced these anxieties during the Boer War campaign, see: *The Lancet*, 28 April 1900, vol. 1, pp. 1218–19.

26 'The Physique of the Japanese', *BMJ*, 12 March 1904, vol. 1, pp. 622–3.

27 The 1902 syllabus was closely based on military drill which had first been

introduced for army recruits in the 1860s. Subsequent revisions between 1904 and 1909 moved to a broader conception of PT. See Board of Education, *Syllabus of Physical Exercises for Use in Public Elementary Schools*, 1904 and *Report of the Interdepartmental Committee on Physical Exercises*, 1904; GBPP 1904, XIX p. 411. Also W. Smith, *Stretching Their Bodies. The History of Physical Education*, Newton Abbott, 1974, chs 5 and 6.

28 *Annual Report for 1900 of the Chief Medical Officer of the Board of Education*, 1910; GBPP 1910, XXIII, pp. 359–61.

29 Board of Education, *Syllabus*, 1909, p. vii.

30 Despite a decline in the general death-rate for England and Wales between 1851 and 1901, infant mortality had increased. By 1900 it was almost as high as it had been fifty years before. Coupled with this problem was the rapid decline in Britain's birth-rate over the same period. In an extensive statistical study Arthur Newsholme, medical officer to the Local Government Board, drew on the recent annual reports of the Registrar-General to compare the average rates of population increase of 11.2 per cent for England and Wales with 14.8 per cent for the German Empire (A. Newsholme, *The Declining Birth Rate. Its National and International Significance*, 1911, p. 10). But, as Newsholme noted, the birth-rated was not declining uniformly, it was most marked among the upper classes, who had more than halved their fertility rate in fifty years. In the face of both sets of problems, the call was for a greater focus on the health of the mother and child in the interests of qualitative and quantitative population increase. See Davin, *op. cit*: Jane Lewis, *The Politics of Motherhood: Maternal and Child Welfare in England 1900—39*, 1980; Carol Dyhouse, 'Working Class Mothers and Infant Mortality in England, 1895–1914', *Journal of Social History*, 1978, vol. 12, no 2, pp. 248–67.

31 See especially Dr J. Ballantyne, *Manual of Ante-natal Pathology and Hygiene, The Embryo*, Edinburgh, 1904 and Newsholme, 'Infant Mortality – A Statistical Study from the Public Health Standpoint', *The Practitioner*, October 1905, pp. 489–500.

32 Newsholme, *The Declining Birth Rate, op. cit.*, p. 57.

33 Quoted in K. Pearson, *Darwinism, Medical Progress and Eugenics*, 1912, pp. 4–5. For an account of the take-up of eugenics in Britain see G. Searle, *Eugenics and Politics in Britain 1900—1914*, Leyden, 1976.

34 The most sustained attack on medical environmentalism came from Pearson. See Pearson, *Eugenics and Public Health*, 1912, pp. 32–4, and his *The Problem of Practical Eugenics*, 1909, p. 31. Also Ethel Elderton *The Relative Strength of Nature and Nurture*, 1909, pp. 32–3.

35 H. Havelock Ellis, *The Task of Social Hygiene*, 1912, p. 15.

36 C. Saleeby, *The Methods of Race-Regeneration*, 1911, p. 63.

37 Pearson, *The Scope and Importance to the State of the Science of National Eugenics*, 1909, pp. 16, 43. The new statistical approach to theories of probability and error was also registered by the statistical societies: see H. Macrosty and J. Bonar, *Annals of the Royal Statistical*

Society, 1834—1934, 1934, pp. 177–83. The whole debate is summarized in N. Rose, *The Psychological Complex*, 1985.

38 In the 1880s the German biologist Weismann argued that there was a clear distinction between the germ cells and the somatic cells. The germ plasm could not be affected by any modification of the bodily organs. Acceptance of this logically entailed a rejection of Lamarck's belief that acquired characteristics could be inherited, see Searle, *Eugenics and Politics*, *op. cit.*, p. 6.

39 Pearson, *Eugenics and Public Health*, *op. cit.*, pp. 32–4.

40 R. Rentoul, *Race Culture or Race Suicide? A Plea for the Unborn*, 1906. For medical attacks on Rentoul's proposals see *BMJ*, 12 March 1904, vol. 1, pp. 625–6.

41 E. Schuster, 'The Scope and the Science of Eugenics', *BMJ*, 2 August 1913, vol. 2, pp. 223–4 and H. Cambell, 'Eugenics from the Physical Standpoint', *BMJ*, *ibid.*, pp. 225–7.

42 'Eugenics', *BMJ*, 23 August 1913, vol. 2, pp. 508–9.

43 For the influence of eugenic thinking on these major social inquiries see: *Interdepartmental Committee on Physical Deterioration*, *op. cit.*, pp. 44–5; *Report on the Royal Commission on the Care and Control of the Feeble-Minded*, 1908; GBPP 1908, XXXIX, pp. 363–86; *Report of the Royal Commission on Divorce and Matrimonial Causes*, 1912; GBPP 1912–13, XVIII, p. 313; Royal Commission on Venereal Diseases. *Final Report of the Commissioners*, 1916; GBPP 1916, XVI, pp. 49–56.

44 Newman, *An Outline*, *op. cit.*, p. 682.

45 J. Marchant, *The Master Problem*, 1917, pp. 128–9: see also his *Aids to Purity*, 1909, pp. 36, 44.

46 NCPM, *The Nation's Morals*, 1910, pp. 3–4.

47 Searle, *The Quest for National Efficiency: a study in British politics and political thought, 1899—1914*, Oxford, 1977, p. 97.

48 Rev W. Inge, 'Some Moral Aspects of Eugenics', *Eugenics Review*, April 1909–January 1910, vol. 1, no. 1, pp. 30–1. For similar arguments see *BMJ*, 8 March 1913, vol. 1, pp. 521–2.

49 See S. Dark, *Five Deans*, 1928, p. 223, also Inge, *The Diary of a Dean of St Pauls 1911—1934*, 1949.

50 Newman, *An Outline*, *op. cit.*, p. 692.

51 See especially Newman, *The Place of Public Opinion in Preventive Medicine*, 1920; also C. Addison, *Politics from Within 1911—1918*, 1924, vol. 1, pp. 221–2. For health education programmes in the inter-war period see the work of the Central Council for Health Education, *Minute Book*, 1935–9, PRO MH82/1. The council was established in 1927 to co-ordinate propaganda for health improvement.

52 The People's League of Health, *Second Report for the Years 1922, 1923, 1924 and 1925*.

53 *Ibid.*

54 Newman, *Infant Mortality. A Social Problem*, 1906, p.v.

55 For moralists' continuing suspicion of the medical profession over VD see: Blanche Leppington, 'Neo-Regulationism – Its Principles, Its

Practice and Its Prospects', *The Shield*, November–December 1904, new series, p. 72; 'The Need for Watchfulness', *The Shield*, October 1909, p. 1.

56 *The Shield*, April 1899, pp. 17–18; *The Shield*, November 1899, pp. 56–7. For an account of regulationism in India see K. Ballhatchet, *Race, Sex and Class under the Raj*, 1980.

57 For changing medical conceptions of the regulation of VD see: Local Government Board, *Report on Venereal Diseases by Dr R.W. Johnstone*, 1913; GBPP 1913, XXXII, p. 423; Sir M. Morris, 'A plea for the appointment of a Royal Commission', *The Lancet*, 28 June 1913, vol. 1, p. 1817–19. For analysis of the changes see Lucy Bland, "Cleansing the portals of life', the venereal disease campaign in the early twentieth century', in Mary Langan and B. Schwarz (eds), *Crises in the British State 1880—1930*, ch. 9. The general call was for the confidential notification of syphilis, together with systematic diagnosis and treatment. Medical pressure led to the setting up of a royal commission in October 1913.

58 Leppington, 'Public Morals and the Public Health', in Marchant (ed.), *Public Morals*, 1902, p. 229. For the gradual shift in the position of the British Branch of the International Abolitionist Federation and the LNA on science see: *The Shield*, November–December 1904, p. 74; *The Shield*, January 1910, p. 1; also International Abolitionist Federation, *Morals and Public Health, Report of the Portsmouth Conference*, June 1914.

59 'The Federation and Hygiene', *The Shield*, January 1906, p. 5.

60 *The Shield*, October 1913, p. 69.

61 *The Shield*, October 1915, p. 63.

62 *Ibid*.

63 F. Gould, 'Some Vital Principles of Moral Education', *The Shield*, June 1917, p. 292. See also NUWW, *Handbook and Report*, 1909–10, pp. 106–8; *The Vote*, 20 January 1912, p. 155.

64 See Mary Scharlieb, *Womanhood and Race Regeneration*, 1912, p. 7; Scharlieb, *The Seven Ages of Woman*, 1915, p. 76.

65 Alice Ravenhill, 'Eugenic Ideals for Womanhood', *Eugenics Review*, April 1909–January 1910, vol. 1, no. 4 pp. 267–73.

66 Christabel Pankhurst, *The Great Scourge and how to end it*, 1913, p. vi.

67 Frances Swiney, *Women and Natural Law*, 1912, p. 12.

68 Swiney, *The Mystery of the Circle and the Cross; or the Interpretation of Sex*, 1908, p. 27. For Geddes' and Thomson's original theories see P. Geddes and J. Thomson, *Sex*, 1911.

69 Swiney, *The Bar of Isis; or, the Law of the Mother*, 1907. p. 38. Swiney claimed that under favourable environmental conditions mothers only produced daughters. Self-fertilization, using modern science, would be a real possibility for women as the race developed: *The Mystery of the Circle*, *op. cit.*, p. 55.

70 'Sexual Hygiene', *The Lancet*, 4 January 1913, vol. 1, p. 5.

71 Gould *op. cit.*, pp. 292–3; also Norah March, 'Education of the Young in

the Morals of Sex', *The Shield*, July 1916, pp. 79–80.

72 Havelock Ellis, *Studies in the Psychology of Sex*, vol. III, *Analysis of the Sexual Impulse, Love and Pain. The Sexual Impulse in Women*, 1903, pp. 16–17. By the early twentieth century many of these debates were registering research into hormonal theory. See especially W. Blair Bell, *The Sex Complex; A Study of the Relationships of the Internal Secretions to the Female Characteristics and Functions of Health and Disease*, 1916. For a summary of this research see E. Seligman (ed.), *Encyclopedia of the Social Sciences*, 1930–5, vol. 8, pp. 81–3.

73 Havelock Ellis, *Analysis of the Sexual Impulse, op. cit.*, pp. 3, 58. See also 'Chastity and Sexual Discipline', *The Lancet*, 22 December 1900, vol. 2, pp. 1819–20.

74 See especially NCPM, *Manifesto, op. cit.*, pp. 6–7 and National Birth Rate Commission, *Youth and the Race. The Development of Young Citizens for Worthy Parenthood*, 1923, pp. 3–7.

75 Dr A. Schofield, *Continence*, 1909, p. 11.

76 Dr Helen Wilson, 'Ideals of Parenthood', *The Shield*, July 1916, p. 83. See also Gould, *On the Threshold of Sex*, 1909, p. 7.

77 Elizabeth Sloan Chesser, *From Girlhood to Womanhood*, 1913, p. x.

78 National Birth Rate Commission, *op. cit.*, pp. 10–11.

79 For details of the NCCVD's educational and propaganda work see NCCVD, *Fifth Annual Report*, p. 34, 145; NCCVD, *Sixth Annual Report*, p. 134.

80 Geddes and Thomson, *op.cit.*, pp. 16, 20; also Havelock Ellis, *Little Essays of Love and Virtue*, 1922, p. 61.

81 See Havelock Ellis, *The Criminal*, 1889, and C. Lombroso and G. Ferrero, *The Female Offender*, 1895.

82 W. McDougall, *An Introduction to Social Psychology*, 1908, p. vi.

83 *Ibid.*, pp. 150, 359. See also McDougall's *An Outline of Abnormal Psychology*, 1926.

84 Scharlieb, *The Seven Ages of Women, op. cit.*, p. 25. For early medical responses to Freud's work see: *The Lancet*, 21 May 1909, vol. 1, pp. 1424–5; *The Lancet*, 4 May 1912, vol. 1, p. 1238.

85 See especially the work of the Institute for the Scientific Treatment of Delinquency in Edward Glover, *The Diagnosis and Treatment of Delinquency*, 1944; also National Council for Mental Hygiene, *Eleventh Report*, 1934.

86 Scharlieb, *The Seven Ages of Women, op. cit.*, p. 25.

87 Evidence of Mrs M. McMillan, Headmistress, Moberly Elementary School, Paddington, London County Council, *Report of the Education Committee on the Teaching of Sex Hygiene*, 1914, LCC no. 176, p. 15. For discreet warnings about lesbianism see Scharlieb, 'Adolescent Girlhood under Modern Conditions', *Eugenics Review*, April 1909– January 1910, vol. 1, no. 2, p. 174.

88 Evidence of Mr W. Nicholls, late Head Boy's Department, Ruby St School, Peckham, London Country Council, *op. cit.*, p. 21.

89 Bland, ' "Guardians of the race" or "Vampires upon the nation's

health"?: Female sexuality and its regulation in early twentieth-century Britain', in Elizabeth Whitelegg *et al.* (ed.), *The Changing Experience of Women*, Oxford, 1982. For contemporary panics over 'the amateur' see *The Weekly Dispatch*, 2 June 1917; *The Daily Mail*, 29 June 1917; evidence of J. Dickenson, Chief Magistrate, *Report of the Joint Select Committee on The Criminal Law Amendment Bill and Sexual Offences Bill* [H.L.], 1918; GBPP 1918, III, p. 333.

90 Mary Douie, *How Girls can help towards Social Hygiene*, 1924, pp. 16–17. See also Louise Creighton, *Successful and Unsuccessful Marriages*, 1916, p. 29.

91 Evidence of Mrs McMillan, London County Council, *op.cit.*, p. 26

92 Chesser, *op. cit.*, p. 23.

93 Havelock Ellis, *Analysis of the Sexual Impulse*, *op. cit.*, pp. 229, 241.

94 *Ibid.*, p. 18.

95 Marie Stopes, *Married Love: a new contribution to the solution of sex difficulties*, 1918, p. 21. See also her *Contraception — Its Theory, History and Practice*, 1923.

96 See E. Lyttleton's evidence to the Royal Commission on Venereal Diseases, *Final Report*, 1916; GBPP 1916, XVI, p. 359. For older style prohibitions see F. Sibly and Scharlieb, *Youth and Sex Dangers and Safeguards for Girls and Boys*, 1912, pp. 59–60.

97 Schofield, *op. cit.*, p. 3.

98 Evidence of Sir Robert Baden-Powell, National Birth Rate Commission, *op. cit.*, p. 206.

99 Schofield, *op. cit.*, p. 3.

100 *Ibid.*

101 See Tansley's evidence, National Birth Rate Commission, *op.cit.*, p. 78.

102 Evidence of Lyttleton, Royal Commission on Venereal Diseases, *Final Report*, p. 353.

103 Sibly and Scharlieb, *op. cit.*, p. 109.

104 See E. Hughes, 'Sex Teaching in Girls' Schools', *Eugenics Review*, April 1910–January 1911, vol II, no. 1, pp. 144–6.

105 London County Council, *op. cit.*, pp. 9–12.

106 *Ibid.*, p. 15.

107 Scharlieb, *Womanhood and Race Regeneration*, 1912, p. 21.

108 See Wilson's evidence to the Royal Commission on Venereal Diseases, *First Report*, 1914; GBPP 1914, XLIX, pp. 295–6.

109 London County Council, *op. cit.*, pp. 4–5.

110 Royal Commission on Venereal Diseases, *Final Report*, *op.cit.*, pp. 82–3.

111 *Ibid.* See also *Forty-Sixth Annual Report of the Local Government Board for 1916—1917, Supplement containing the Report of the Medical Officer*, 1917; GBPP 1917–18, XVI, pp. 220–1.

112 NCCVD, *Fifth Annual Report*, 1920, p. 10. The Royal Commission on Venereal Diseases had recommended that the NCCVD should be recognized as an authoritative body for the purpose of spreading knowledge and giving advice on VD. During 1918 grants totalling £13,000 were made to it by the Local Government Board. These funds were continued by the Ministry of Health throughout the 1920s.

113 See British Social Hygiene Council, *Empire and Social Hygiene Yearbook*, 1934, p. 97.

114 In 1922 the Ministry of Health upheld the dismissal of Nurse E. Daniels, a health worker in Edmonton, London, for giving contraceptive advice to local maternity clinics. See Sheila Rowbotham, *A New World for Women: Stella Browne— Socialist Feminist*, 1978. Under a memorandum of July 1930, 153/MCW, the Minister of Health permitted maternity centres to give contraceptive advice to married women 'in cases where further pregnancy would be detrimental to health'. For politicians ambiguity over the issue, see Mr Broad to the Minister of Health, *Parliamentary Debates*, Commons, 25 July 1923, fifth series, vol. 167, col. 480.

115 See B. Schwarz, 'The Language of Constitutionalism: Baldwinite Conservatism', in *Formations of Nation and People*, 1984, pp. 1–18.

116 National Birth Rate Commission, *op. cit.*, p.v.

117 Jeffrey Weeks discusses the relation between new patterns of consumption and changes in sexual and marital behaviour in *Sex, Politics and Society*, 1981, ch. 11. For the impact of the new consumerism on women's lives see Catherine Hall, 'Married Women at Home in Birmingham in the 1920s and 1930s', *Oral History*, 1977, vol. 5, no. 2, pp. 62–83. For women's magazines, see Cynthia White, *Women's Magazines 1693—1968*, 1970.

118 See Stevenson to Stopes, 3 March 1921, quoted in Ruth Hall (ed.), *Dear Dr. Stopes. Sex in the 1920s,* Harmondsworth, 1978, p. 202.

119 Speech of Viscountess Astor on the Ministry of Health Supply Committee, *Parliamentary Debates*, Commons, 17 July 1935, fifth series, vol. 304, col. 1135.

120 See especially: 'Birmingham Cinema Enquiry Committee', NVA, *Executive Committee Minutes*, 26 April 1932, Fawcett Library, London, p. 127; 'Mother's Union, Cinema Films', *ibid.*, 27 June 1933, p. 175.

121 NVA, *Executive Committee Minutes*, 25 March 1919.

122 Dame Katherine Furse, Biological Education Congress, 1928, in NVA, *Papers*, box 98, 10A, Fawcett Library, London.

123 Sex Education, NVA, *Minutes*, 23 February 1932, pp. 115–16.

124 Sir W. Arbuthnot Lane, 'What are the Disabilities and the Compensations entailed by the Reproductive Function of the Female?', *The Lancet*, 9 November 1918, vol. 2, p. 622.

125 *The Lancet*, 28 December 1918, vol. 2, p. 886; *BMJ*, 26 November 1921, vol. 2, p. 903.

126 *The Lancet*, 6 September 1919, vol. 2, p. 463.

127 The focus for the modernist challenge was the Churchman's Union with its journal the *Modern Churchman*. See also P. Gardner, *Modernism in the English Church*, 1926; Dr W. Pyke, *Modernism as a Working Faith*, 1925; Canon M. Glazebrook, *Faith of a Modern Churchman*, 1925.

128 Conference of Bishops of the Anglican Communion, *The Lambeth Conference, 1930. Encyclical Letter from the Bishops with resolutions and reports*, 1930, pp. 66–7.

129 *Ibid.*, p. 85. For similar statements see Canon T. Guy Rogers, *The*

Church and the People, 1930, pp. 139–43.
130 T. van der Velde, *Ideal Marriage. Its Physiology and Technique*, 1928, p. 111. See also M. Exner, *The Sexual Side of Marriage*, 1932, pp. 98–9; B. Lindsey and W. Evans, *The Companionate Marriage*, 1928; Helena Wright, *The Sex Factor in Marriage. A book for those who are or are about to be married*, 1930. For discussions of women's changing experience of sexuality within marriage see Ellen Holtman, 'The Pursuit of Married Love. Women's Attitudes Towards Sexuality and Marriage in Great Britain, 1918–1939', *Journal of Social History*, 1982, vol. 16, no. 2, pp. 39–51.
131 *The Shield*, January 1913, p. 15.
132 In February 1917 the Home Office introduced a new Criminal Law Amendment Bill. Its clauses included a stipulation that sexual intercourse, or its solicitation or invitation, was a criminal offence for anyone suffering from communicable VD, together with measures empowering magistrates to order the detention of young women under eighteen who were convicted of soliciting. A variant of the bill was reintroduced in 1918, along with the Sexual Offences Bill [H.L.] which covered many of the same concerns, and again in 1920 and 1921. Feminists were divided over the question of the criminalization of VD's transmission, though most women's organizations were nervous about further use of the criminal law. In 1922 Parliament finally passed the Criminal Law Amendment Act, 12 and 13 Geo. 5, ch. 56. The act dropped the contentious clauses on the transmission of VD and the detention of young girls, while including provisions for the abolition of the 'reasonable cause to believe' clause in cases of indecent assault on young persons under sixteen and increasing penalties for brothel-keeping.
133 *The Vote*, 20 April 1917, p. 189. For the shift in feminist strategy away from the criminal law towards sex education see, *The Common Cause*, 11 October 1918, p. 294; *The Vote*, 9 March 1917, p. 137, *The Shield*, February 1915, pp. 20–1.
134 *The Common Cause*, 11 October 1918, p. 294.

Epilogue

1 'Rock "Gave AIDS to His Gay Lovers" ', *The Sun*, 4 October 1985; also 'The Hunk Who Lived A Lie', *The Sun*, 3 October 1985.
2 'The Hunk Who Lived A Lie', *The Sun*, *op. cit.*
3 For reportage which defined gay men as part of the socially undesirable see the coverage of the Brighton boy sex case: 'A Town Without Innocence', *Daily Express*, 22 August 1983; 'Gays In Revenge Terror', *The Sun*, 20 August 1983.
4 For the targeting of high risk groups see: Ministry of Health, *On the State of the Public Health, being the Annual Report of the Chief Medical Officer for 1961*; GBPP 1962–3, XIX, p. 52 and A. King *et al.*, *Venereal Diseases*, 1980, p. 371.
5 Dr R. Wilcox, 'Society and High Risk Groups', in R. Catterall and C. Nicol, *Sexually Transmitted Diseases: proceedings of a conference*

sponsored jointly by the Royal Society of Medicine and the Royal Society of Medical Foundations Inc, 1976, p. 32. Also King, *op. cit*, p. 372.

6 See for example: W. Drew *et al*., 'Cytomeglavirus and Kaposi's sarcoma in young homosexual men', *The Lancet*, 17 July 1982, vol. 2, pp. 125–7 and 'Lifestyle clue to Kaposi's sarcoma', *Medical News*, vol. 14, no. 31, p. 8.

7 A. Pinching *et al*., 'Studies of Cellular Immunity in Male Homosexuals in London', *The Lancet*, 16 July 1983, vol. 2, pp. 126–9. Also *The Lancet*, 12 May 1984, vol. 1, pp. 1053–4.

8 DHSS, *On the State of the Public Health: The Annual Report of the Chief Medical Officer of the DHSS for the Year 1982*, HMSO, 1983, p. 53.

9 The DHSS 'Don't Aid AIDS' campaign was launched with full page advertisements in the national press on 16 and 17 March 1986. For critical comment see *The Guardian*, 14 March 1986.

10 For voices within the gay community which call for a return to monogamy see, in the USA, L. Kramer, '1, 112 AND COUNTING', *New York Native*, 14–27 March 1983, no. 59, p. 1 and in Britain, N. Smith, 'I have stopped being promiscuous', *Capital Gay*, 3 February 1984. For liberal positions see the Terrence Higgins Trust, *AIDS. Medical Briefing*, 1985.

11 The most coherent statement of radical pluralism is in J. Weeks, *Sexuality and Its Discontents*, 1985, chs 9 and 10. See also S. Watney, 'Babbling at the barricades of Pornography', *New Socialists*, June 1986, no. 39, p. 21.

SELECTED BIBLIOGRAPHY

Primary Sources

Primary Sources

I UNPUBLISHED MANUSCRIPTS AND COLLECTIONS

Chadwick Manuscript, University College Library, London.

Josephine Butler Collection, Fawcett Library, London.

Kay-Shuttleworth Papers, John Ryelands Library, Manchester.

Minutes of the National Association for the Repeal of the Contagious Diseases Acts, Fawcett Library, London.

National Vigilance Association Collection, Fawcett Library, London.

Public Record Office, Chancery Lane, London:

Privy Council Papers

Central Board of Health, Minutes, 1831, PC1/101.

Central Board of Health, Minutes, 1831–2, PC1/105.

Papers relating to cholera, 1831, PC1/105.

Central Board of Health, Extract from proceedings, 1831, PC1/2662.

Central Board of Health, Daily report of cholera cases, 1832, PC1/4395.

Public Record Office, Kew:

Admiralty Papers
History and operation of the Contagious Diseases Acts, 1873, Adm/6418.

Board of Education Papers
Dronfield case, ED50/185.

253

Bibliography

Home Office Papers

Criminal Law Amendment Bill, 1884–5, HO45/59343G.

Correspondence, Criminal Law Amendment Act, 1885, HO45/A40683.

Police powers under Criminal Law Amendment Act, 1886–7, HO45/A45364.

St George's Vigilance Society for payments, 1887, HO45/X14891.

Difficulties of police on convictions, 1887–9, HO45/X15663.

Criminal Law Amendment Bill, 1910, HO45/175440.
Criminal law amendment bills, 1908–13, HO45/178486.

Local Government Board Papers

Government Office correspondences, 1873, LGB78178/73.

Miscellaneous correspondence, 1876, LGB58096/76.

Ministry of Health Papers

Central Council for Health Education, Minute Book, 1935–9, MH82/1.

Treasury Papers

Treasury Minutes, 1871, T1/18, 953.

War Office Papers

Venereal disease, army and navy, 1862, WO33/12.

Shaftesbury Manuscript, National Register of Archives, London.

II OFFICIAL PUBLICATIONS

Civil Service

Report on the organization of the permanent civil service; GBPP 1854, XXVII.

Criminal Law

First Report from the Select Committee on the state of the Law relating to the Protection of Young Girls; GBPP, 1881, IX.

Second Report; GBPP 1882, XIII.

Report of the Joint Select Committee on the Criminal Law Amendment Bill and Sexual Offences Bill [H.L.]; GBPP 1918, III.

Health

Copies of Certain Papers relating to Cholera together with the Report of the Central Board of Health thereupon; GBPP 1831–2, XXVI.

Report from the Poor Law Commissioners into the Sanitary Condition of the Labouring Population of Great Britain; HL 1842, XXVI–XXVIII.

Bibliography

Report of the Royal Commission on the Health of the Army; GBPP 1857, XVIII.

Tenth Annual Report of the Medical Officer of the Privy Council, GBPP 1867–8, XXXVI.

Eleventh Annual Report; GBPP 1868–9, XXXII.

Thirteenth Annual Report; GBPP 1871, XXI.

Annual Reports of the Inspector General of Recruiting; GBPP 1901, IX; 1902, X; 1903, XXXVIII.

Report of the Interdepartmental Committee on Physical Deterioration; GBPP 1904, XXXII.

Report of the Interdepartmental Committee on Physical Exercises; GBPP 1904, XIX.

Report of the Royal Commission on the Care and Control of the Feeble-Minded; GBPP 1908, XXXV-XXXIX.

Annual Report for 1909 of the Chief Medical Officer of the Board of Education; GBPP 1910, XXIII.

Forty-Sixth Annual Report of the Local Government Board for 1916—1917; GBPP 1917–18, XVI.

Ministry of Health/Sir G. Newman, *An Outline of the Practice of Preventive Medicine*; GBPP 1919, XXXIX.

First Annual Report of the Ministry of Health for 1919—1920; GBPP 1920, XVII.

Housing
Royal Commission on the Housing of the Working Classes, *First Report of the Commissioners, England*; GBPP 1884–5, XXX.

Industrial Conditions
Children's Employment Commission, *First Report. Mines*; GBPP 1842, XV–XVII.

Marriage and Divorce
Report of the Commissioners on the Law of Divorce, and on the mode of obtaining Divorces à vinculo matrimonii; GBPP 1852–3, XL.

Report of the Royal Commission on the Laws of Marriage; GBPP 1867–8, XXXII.

Report of the Royal Commission on Divorce and Matrimonial Causes; GBPP 1912–13, XVIII–XX.

Police
Report of the Royal Commission upon the Duties of the Metropolitan Police; GBPP 1908, L.

Bibliography

Population

Fourth Annual Report of the Registrar-General of Births, Deaths and Marriages; GBPP 1842, XIX.

Fifth Annual Report; GBPP 1843, XXI.

Venereal Disease

Report of the House of Commons Select Committee to Inquire into the Pathology and Treatment of the Venereal Disease, with a View to Diminish Its Injurious Effects on the Men of the Army and Navy; GBPP 1867–8, XXXVII.

Report from the Select Committee on the Contagious Diseases Act (1866); GBPP 1868–9, VII.

Report of the Royal Commission on the Administration and Operation of the Contagious Diseases Acts 1866—69; GBPP 1871, XIX.

Local Government Board, *Report on Venereal Diseases by Dr. R.W. Johnstone, with an Introduction by the Medical Officer of the Local Government Board*; GBPP 1913, XXXII.

Royal Commission on Venereal Diseases, *First Report of the Commissioners*; GBPP 1914, XLIX.

Final Report; GBPP 1916, XV.

III RULES, REPORTS AND PROCEEDINGS

Brighton Gay Switchboard and Brighton Gay Community Organizations, *AIDS. Some Questions Answered*, 1984.

British Social Hygiene Council, *Empire and Social Hygiene Year Book*, 1934.

Conference of Bishops of the Anglican Communion, *The Lambeth Conference, 1930. Encyclical Letter from the Bishops with resolutions and reports*, 1930.

Gay Medical Association, *AIDS*, undated.

The Girls' Friendly Society, *A Special Report*, London, Hatchards, 1879.

Harveian Medical Society of London, *Report of the Committee for the Prevention of Venereal Disease*, 1867.

International Abolitionist Federation, *Morals and Public Health, Report of the Portsmouth Conference*, 1914.

Ladies' National Association, *Report for the Year Ending 1871*.

The Legitimation League, *Aims and Objects*, undated.

London County Council, *Report of the Education Committee on the Teaching of Sex Hygiene*, 1914, LCC no. 176.

Bibliography

National Birth-Rate Commission, *Youth and the Race. The Development of Young Citizens for Worthy Parenthood. Being the Fourth Report of the Commission 1920—1923*, 1923.

National Council for Combating Venereal Disease, *Annual Reports* 1916–23.

National Council of Public Morals, *Manifesto*, 1910.

National Union of Women Workers, *Handbooks and Reports*, 1909–13.

National Vigilance Association, *Objects, Constitution and Rules*, 1885. Also, *Annual Reports*, 1894–1908.

The People's League of Health, *Second Report for the years 1922–5*.

Terrence Higgins Trust, *AIDS. Medical Briefing*, 1985.

IV NEWSPAPERS, PERIODICALS AND DICTIONARIES

The Adult.
British Medical Journal.
The Common Cause.
The Derbyshire Times.
Eugenics Review.
The Freewoman.
Journal of the Vigilance Association for the Defence of Personal Rights.
The Lancet.
The London Medical Directory and General Medical Register.
National League Journal.
The Practitioner.
Quarterly Record of the Tower Hamlets Mission.
The Shield.
The Suffrage Annual and Woman's Who's Who.
The Suffragette.
The Times.
The Vote.
The Weekly Dispatch.
The Westminster Review.
Women's Dreadnought.

V OTHER PRIMARY SOURCES PUBLISHED BEFORE 1945

Acton, W., *Prostitution Considered in Its Moral, Social, and Sanitary Aspects in London and Other Large Cities, with Proposals for the Mitigation and Prevention of Its Attendant Evil*, London, John Churchill, 1857.

Acton, W., *The Contagious Diseases Act, Shall the Contagious Diseases Act be applied to the Civil Population?* London, J. and A. Churchill, 1870.

Acton, W., *The Functions and Disorders of the Reproductive Organs in Childhood, Youth, Adult Age and Advanced Life Considered in their Physiological, Social and Moral Relations*, London, J. and A. Churchill, 1875.

Bibliography

Anon, *Tabes Dorsalis or, the Causes of Consumption in Young Men and Women*, London, 1832.

Ashley, Lord, *Moral and Religious Education of the Working Classes*, London, John Ollivier, 1843.

Ballantyne, J., *Manual of Ante-natal Pathology and Hygiene. The Embryo*, Edinburgh, W. Green, 1904.

Barrett, Rosa, *Ellice Hopkins: A Memoir*, London, Wells Gardiner, 1907.

Bartlett, Lucy Re, *The Coming Order*, London, Longmans, 1911.

Bartlett, Lucy Re, *Sex and Sanctity*, London, Longmans, 1912.

Bell, W. Blair, *The Sex Complex; A Study of the Relationships of the Internal Secretions to the Female Characteristics and Functions of Health and Disease*, London, Baillère, 1916.

Biggs, T., *The Proposed Extension of the Contagious Diseases Act in Its Moral and Economical Aspects*, London, 1870.

Billington-Grieg, Teresa, 'The Truth About White Slavery', *The English Review*, June 1913.

Blackwell, Elizabeth, *How to Keep a Household in Health. An Address*, London, Ladies' Sanitary Association, 1870.

Blackwell, Elizabeth, *The Human Element in Sex: being a medical enquiry into the relation of sexual physiology to Christian morality*, London, J. and A. Churchill, 1884.

Blackwell, Elizabeth, *The Religion of Health*, London, Moral Reform Union, 1889.

Bloomfield, B., *A handlist of papers in the deed box of Sir J.P. Kay-Shuttleworth*, College of St Mark and St John, occasional paper no. 2, 1961.

Board of Education, *Syllabus of Physical Exercises for Use in Public Elementary Schools*, 1904.

Brougham, Henry, Lord, *Paley's Natural Theology with Illustrative Notes*, London, 1826.

Brougham, Henry, Lord, *A Discourse on the Object, Advantages and Pleasures of Science*, London, 1827.

Browne, F.W. Stella, *Sexual Variety and Variability Among Women and their Bearing upon Social Reconstruction*, London, British Society for the Study of Sex Psychology, 1917.

Butler, Josephine (ed.), *Women's Work and Women's Culture*, London, Macmillan, 1869.

Butler, Josephine, *A Letter to the Members of the Ladies' National Association*, Liverpool, 1875.

Bibliography

Butler, Josephine, *Social Purity. An Address Given at Cambridge*, London, Morgan Scott, 1879.

Butler, Josephine, *Personal Reminiscences of a Great Crusade*, London, H. Marshall and Son, 1896.

Carpenter, E., *Love's Coming of Age*, Manchester, Labour Press, 1896.

Chalmers, T., *The Christian and Civic Economy of Large Towns*, Glasgow, William Collins, 1821–6, 3 vols.

Chant, Laura Ormiston, *Why We Attacked the Empire*, London, Marshall, 1895.

Chesser, Elizabeth Sloan, *From Girlhood to Womanhood*, London, Cassell, 1913.

Cooke, W., *An Address to British Females on the Moral Management of Pregnancy and Labour*, London, 1817.

Cooke, W., *Mind and the Emotions Considered in Relation to Health and Disease*, London, 1830.

Coote, W., *A Romance of Philanthropy. A Record of Thirty Years Work of the National Vigilance Association*, London, NVA, 1916.

Creighton, Louise, *Successful and Unsuccessful Marriages*, London, Longmans, 1916.

Curgenven, J., *The Contagious Diseases Act of 1866, and its Extension to the Civil Population of the United Kingdom*, London, W.W. Head, 1868.

Dark, S., *Five Deans*, London, Jonathan Cape, 1928.

Darwin, C., *The Descent of Man. Selection in Relation to Sex*, London, John Murray, 1871, 2 vols.

Dicey, A., *The Law and Public Opinion in England during the Nineteenth Century*, London, Macmillan, 1905.

Douie, Mary, *How Girls can help towards Social Hygiene*, London, British Social Hygiene Council, 1924.

Dyer, A., *Facts for Men on Moral Purity and Health*, London, Dyer Bros, 1884.

Elderton, Ethel, *The Relative Strength of Nature and Nurture*, London, University College, 1909.

Ellis, H. Havelock, *Studies in the Psychology of Sex*, vol. III, *Analysis of the Sexual Impulse Love and Pain. The Sexual Impulse in Women*, Philadelphia, F.A. Davis, 1903.

Ellis, H. Havelock, *The Task of Social Hygiene*, London, Constable, 1912.

Ellis, H. Havelock, *Little Essays of Love and Virtue*, London, A. and C. Black, 1922.

Bibliography

Exner, M., *The Sexual Side of Marriage*, London, G. Allen and Unwin, 1932.

Gardiner, A., *The Life of Sir William Harcourt*, London, Constable, 1923, 2 vols.

Gardner, P., *Modernism in the English Church*, London, Methuen, 1926.

Gaulter, H., *The Origins and Progress of the Malignant Cholera in Manchester*, London, 1833.

Geddes, P. and Thomson, J., *Sex*, London, Home University Library, 1911.

Girdlestone, C., *Seven Sermons preached during the Prevalence of Cholera in the Parish of Sedgley*, London, 1833.

Girdlestone, C., *Farewell Sermons — Preached in the Parish Church of Sedgley*, London, 1837.

Girdlestone, C., *Letters on the Unhealthy Condition of the Lower Class of Dwellings especially in Large Towns*, London, Longmans, 1845.

Glazebrook, M., *Faith of a Modern Churchman*, London, John Murray, 1925.

Gould F., *On The Threshold of Sex. A Book for Readers aged 14 to 21*, London, C.W. Daniel, 1909.

Green, T. *Lectures on the Principles of Political Obligation and Freedom of Contract*, London, Longmans, 1885.

Greenwood, J., *The Wilds of London*, London, 1874.

Greenwood, J., *Low Life Deeps and and Account of the Strange Fish to be found there*, London, 1876.

Hamilton, Cicely, *Marriage as a Trade*, London, Chapman and Hall, 1909.

Hammond, J. and Hammond, Barbara, *James Stansfield: A Victorian Champion of Sex Equality*, London, Longmans, 1932.

Hartley, D. *Observations on Man, his frame, his duty, and his expectations*, London, 1749.

Hawksley, T., *A Letter to the most Hon. The Marquis of Chandos MP in relation to some of the Extraordinary Powers Assumed by the General Board of Health*, London, 1853.

Health of Towns Association, *Address from the Committee of the Health of Towns Association to the Bishop of London and the Rev. The Clergy*, London, Richard Barrett, 1848.

Hopkins, Ellice, *An Englishwoman's Work among Workingmen*, London, New Britain, 1875.

Hopkins, Ellice, *Work in Brighton*, London, Hatchards, 1877.

Bibliography

Hopkins, Ellice, *The Girls' Friendly Society — An Appeal to the Mistresses of Elementary Schools*, London, Hatchards, 1882.

Hopkins, Ellice, *Village Morality, A Letter to Clergymen's Wives and Christian Workers*, London, Hatchards, 1882.

Hopkins, Ellice, *The White Cross Army, A Statement of the Bishop of Durham's Movement*, London, Hatchards, 1883.

Hopkins, Ellice, *The Power of Womanhood: or Mothers and Sons*, London, Wells Gardner, 1899.

Hopkins, Ellice, *The Early Training of Girls and Boys — An Appeal to Working Women*, London, P.S. King, 1902.

Hume-Rothery, Mrs, *A Letter Addressed to the Right Hon. W.E. Gladstone, M.P. and Other Members of Her Majesty's Government*, Manchester, 1870.

Humphreys N. (ed.), *Vital Statistics. A Memorial Volume of Selections from the Reports and Writings of William Farr*, London, Royal Society for the Prevention of Health, 1885.

Inge, W., *The Diary of a Dean of St Pauls 1911—1934*, London, Hutchinson, 1949.

Johnson, G. and Johnson, Lucy (eds), *Josephine E. Butler. An Autobiographical Memoir*, London, J.W. Arrowsmith, 1928.

Kay, J., *The Moral and Physical Condition of the Working Classes Employed in the Cotton Manufacture in Manchester*, London, James Ridgway, 1832.

Layard, D., *Directions to Prevent the Contagion of the Jail — Distemper Commonly Called Jail Fever*, London, James Robson, 1772.

Layard, D., *Hints Respecting the Prison of Newgate*, London, 1794.

Liddle, J., *On the Moral and Physical Evils resulting from the Neglect of Sanitary Measures. A Lecture*, London, 1847.

Linsey, B. and Evans, W., *The Companionate Marriage*, London, Bretano's, 1928.

LNR [Ellen Ranyard], *Life Work; or the Link and the Rivet*, London, 1861.

LNR [Ellen Ranyard], *London and Ten Years Work in It*, London, 1868.

Lombroso, C. and Ferrero, W., *The Female Offender*, London, T. Fisher Unwin, 1895.

London, J., *The People of the Abyss*, London, Isbister and Co., 1903.

Marchant, J. (ed.), *Public Morals*, London, Morgan and Scott, 1902.

Marchant, J., *Aids to Purity*, London, Health and Strength series, 1909.

Marchant, J., *The Master Problem*, London, Stanley Paul, 1917.

Maudesley, H., *Body and Mind — An Inquiry into their Connection and*

Mutual Influence, specially in reference to Mental Disorders, London, 1870.

Maurice, F. (ed.), *Lectures to Ladies*, Cambridge, 1855.

McCulloch, J. (ed.), *A Statistical Account of the British Empire*, London 1839, 2 vols.

McDougall, W., *An Introduction to Social Psychology*, London, Methuen, 1908.

McDougall, W., *An Outline of Abnormal Psychology*, New York, C. Scribner, 1926.

Macrosty, H. and Bonar, J., *Annals of the Royal Statistical Society 1834— 1934*, London, Royal Statistical Society, 1934.

Mearns, Rev. A., *The Bitter Cry of Outcast London*, London, James Clarke and Co, 1883.

Miller, E., *Counsel to the Young. The Substance of a Sermon Preached at Putney Chapel*, London, 1833.

Newman, G., *Infant Mortality. A Social Problem*, London, New Library of Medicine, 1906.

Newman, G., *The Place of Public Opinion in Preventive Medicine*, London, Ministry of Health, 1920.

Newsholme, A., 'Infant Mortality – A Statistical Study from the Public Health Standpoint', *The Practitioner*, October 1905, pp. 489–500.

Newsholme, A., *The Declining Birth Rate. Its National and International Significance*, London, New Tracts for the Times Series, 1911.

Newsholme, A., *The Moral Aspects of Social Hygiene*, London, NCCVD, 1924.

Newsholme, A., *The Evolution of Preventive Medicine*, London, Baillière, 1927.

Newsholme, A., *Fifty Years in Public Health — A Personal Narrative with Comments*, London, G. Allen with Unwin, 1935.

Newsholme, A., *The Last Thirty Years in Public Health. Recollections and reflections on my official and post-official life*, London, G. Allen and Unwin, 1936.

NVA, *Pernicious Literature. Debate in the House of Commons. Trial and Convictions for Sale of Zola's Novels with Opinion of the Press*, London, 1889.

NVA, *Work Accomplished by the Association*, 1907.

Pankhurst, Christabel, *The Great Scourge and how to end it*, London, E. Pankhurst, 1913.

Parent-Duchâtelet, A., *De la prostitution dans la ville de Paris, considerée sous le rapport de l'hygiène publique, de la morale et de l'administration*, Paris, 1836.

Pearson, K., *The Problem of Practical Eugenics*, London University College, 1909.

Pearson, K., *The Scope and Importance to the State of the Science of National Eugenics*, London, University College, 1909.

Pearson, K., *Darwinism, Medical Progress and Eugenics. The Cavendish Lecture. An Address to the Medical Profession*, London, University College, 1912.

Pearson, K., *Eugenics and Public Health. A Lecture delivered at the York Congress of the Royal Sanitary Institute*, London, University College, 1912.

Percival, T., *Medical Ethics, or a Code of Institutes and Precepts adapted to the Professional Conduct of Physicians and Surgeons*, Manchester, 1803.

Plarr, G., *Lives of the Fellows of the Royal College of Surgeons of England*, London, Royal College of Surgeons, 1930, 2 vols.

Platt Elspeth, *The Story of the Ranyard Mission 1857—1937*, London, Hodder and Stoughton, 1937.

Pringle, J., *Social Work of the London Churches. Being some Account of the Metropolitan Visiting and Relief Association 1843—1937*, London, OUP, 1937.

Rentoul, R., *Race Culture, or Race Suicide? A Plea for the Unborn*, London, 1906.

Rogers, T., *The Church and the People*, London, Sampson Low, 1930.

Ryan, M., *Lectures on Population, Marriage and Divorce*, London, 1831.

Ryan, M., *The Philosophy of Marriage, in its Social, Moral and Physical Relations; with an account of the diseases of the genito-urinary organs*, London, 1837.

Saleeby, C., *The Methods of Race-Regeneration*, London, New Tracts for the Times Series, 1911.

Scharlieb, Mary, *Womanhood and Race Regeneration*, London, New Tracts for the Times Series, 1912.

Scharlieb, Mary. *The Seven Ages of Women. A Consideration of the Successive Phases of Woman's Life*, London, Cassell, 1915.

Schofield, A., *Continence*, London, 1909.

Seligman, E. (ed.), *Encyclopedia of the Social Sciences*, London, Macmillan, 1930–5.

Sibly, F. and Scharlieb, Mary, *Youth and Sex Dangers and Safeguards for Girls and Boys*, London, The People's Books, 1912.

Bibliography

Simon, Sir J., *English Sanitary Institutions Reviewed in the Course of their Development and in Some of their Political and Social Relations*, London, Cassell, 1890.

Simon, Sir J., *Personal Recollections*, London Spottiswoode, 1894.

Sims, G., *How the Poor Live in Horrible London*, Chatto and Windus, 1883.

Smellie, K., *A Hundred Years of English Government*, London, Duckworth, 1937.

Smith, F., *The Life and Times of Sir James Kay-Shuttleworth*, London, John Murray, 1923.

Social Purity Alliance, *Schoolboy Morality. An Address to Mothers*, London, 1884.

Southwood Smith, T., *Treatise on Fever*, London, 1830.

Squire Sprigge, S., *The Life and Times of Thomas Wakley MD*, London, Longmans, 1897.

Stansfield, J., *Speeches ... on the Contagious Diseases Acts*, London, National Association for the Repeal of the Contagious Diseases Acts, 1875.

Stead, W., *The Maiden Tribute of Modern Babylon. The Report of the 'Pall Mall Gazette's' Secret Commission*, London, 1885.

Stopes, Marie, *Married Love: a new contribution to the solution of sex difficulties*, New York, Critic and Guide, 1918.

Stopes, Marie, *Contraception — Its Theory, History and Practice — A Manual for the Medical and Legal Professions*, London, J. Bale, 1923.

Swiney, Frances, *The Bar of Isis; or, the Law of the Mother*, London, Open Road Publishing, 1907.

Swiney, Frances, *The Mystery of the Circle and the Cross; or the Interpretation of Sex*, London, Open Road Publishing, 1908.

Swiney, Frances, *Women and Natural Law*, London, C.W. Daniel, 1912.

Tait, W., *Magdalenism: An Inquiry into the Extent, Causes and Consequences of Prostitution*, Edinburgh, 1840.

Taylor, C., *The Statistical Results of the Contagious Diseases Acts ... showing their Total Failure from a Sanitary Point of View*, Nottingham, Stevenson, Bailey and Smith, 1872.

Thomas, H. Preston, *Work and Play of a Government Inspector*, London, Blackwood, 1909.

Tilt, E., *The Serpentine 'as it is' and 'as it ought to be'. And The Board of Health 'as it is' and 'as it ought to be'*, London, 1848.

Toulmin Smith, J., *Centralization or Local Representation? Health of Towns Bill. An Address by a Citizen*, London, 1848.

Bibliography

Tristan, Flora, *Flora Tristan's London Journal*,. trans. D. Palmer and Giselle Pincetl, London, George Prior, 1980.

Tuke, H. (ed.), *Dictionary of Psychological Medicine, with the symptoms, treatment and pathology of insanity and the law of lunacy in Great Britain and Ireland*, London, J. and A. Churchill, 1892.

Velde, T. van der, *Ideal Marriage. Its Physiology and Technique*, London, Heinemann, 1928.

Walker, A., *Women Physiologically Considered as to Mind, Morals, Marriage, Matrimonial Slavery, Infidelity and Divorce*, London, 1839.

Walter, J., *Practical Observations Concerning the Cure of Venereal Disease by Mercurials*, London, 1765.

Wardlaw, R., *Lectures on female prostitution; its nature, extent, effects, guilt, causes and remedy*, Glasgow, 1842.

Wilkinson, J., *The Forcible Introspection of Women for the Army and Navy by the Oligarchy Considered Physically*, London, 1870.

Wilson, Rev., J., *Sins of the Flesh. A Sermon Preached in Clifton College Chapel*, London, Macmillan, 1883.

Wright, Helena, *The Sex Factor in Marriage. A Book for those who are or are about to be married*, London, Noel Douglas, 1930.

Secondary Sources

I   Unpublished works

Brand, J., *The British Medical Profession and State Intervention in Public Health, 1870—1911*, unpublished dissertation for the PhD degree, London University, 1953.

Hodgkinson, R., *The Medical Services of the New Poor Law 1834—71*, unpublished dissertation for the PhD degree, London University, 1950, 2 vols.

II   PUBLISHED BOOKS AND ARTICLES

Abrams, P., *The Origins of British Sociology 1834—1914*, Chicago, University of Chicago Press, 1968.

Altman, D., *AIDS and the New Puritanism*, London, Pluto, 1986.

Ashton, T., *Economic and Social Investigations in Manchester, 1833—1933*, Hassocks, Harvester, 1977.

Bailey, V., and Blackburn, Sheila, 'The Punishment of Incest Act 1908: A Case Study of Criminal Law Creation', *Criminal Law Review*, November 1979, pp. 708–18.

Ballhatchet, K., *Race, Sex and Class Under the Raj. Imperial Attitudes and Policies and their Critics, 1793— 1905*, London, Weidenfeld and Nicholson, 1980.

Bibliography

Banks, J. and Banks, Olive, *Feminism and Family Planning in Victorian England*, Liverpool, Liverpool University Press, 1964.

Bland, Lucy, ' "Guardians of the Race" or "Vampires upon the nation's health"?: Female sexuality and its regulation in early twentieth-century Britain', in Elizabeth Whitelegg *et al.* (eds), *The Changing Experience of Women*, Oxford, Martin Robertson, 1982.

Bland, Lucy, 'Marriage Laid Bare: Feminists Take Issue with Marital Sex, 1880–1st World War', in Jane Lewis (ed.), *Labour and Love*, Oxford, 1986.

Bloomfield, B., *A Handlist of papers in the deed box of Sir J.P. Kay-Shuttleworth*, College of St Mark and St John, occasional paper no. 2, 1961.

Bloomfield, B. (ed.) *The Autobiography of Sir James Kay-Shuttleworth*, Education Libraries Bulletin, supplement 7, 1964.

Brand, Jeanne, *Doctors and the State: The British Medical Profession and Government Action in Public Health, 1870—1912*, Baltimore, John Hopkins, 1965.

Bristow, E., *Vice and Vigilance: Purity Movements in Britain since 1700*, Dublin, Gill and Macmillan, 1977.

Caterall, R. and Nicol, C. (eds), *Sexually Transmitted Diseases: proceedings of a conference sponsored jointly by the Royal Society of Medicine and the Royal Society of Medical Foundations Inc*, London, Academic Press, 1976.

Clark, G. Kitson, 'Statesmen in Disguise': Reflections on the History of Neutrality of the Civil Service', *The Historical Journal*, 1959, II, 1, pp. 19–40.

Cominos, P., 'Late-Victorian Sexual Respectability and the Social System', *International Review of Social History*, 1963, no. 8, pp. 18–48, 216–50.

Cullen, M., *The Statistical Movement in Early Victorian Britain*, Hassocks, Harvester, 1975.

Davidoff, Leonore, 'Class and Gender in Victorian Britain. Arthur J. Munby and Hannah Cullwick', *Feminist Studies*, 1979, vol. 5, no. 1, pp. 89–133.

Davin, Anna, 'Imperialism and Motherhood', *History Workshop*, 1978, no. 5, pp. 9–65.

Dyhouse, Carol, 'Working-Class Mothers and Infant Mortality in England, 1895–1914', *Journal of Social History*, 1978, vol. 12, no. 2, pp. 248–67.

Finer, S., *The Life and Times of Sir Edwin Chadwick*, London, Methuen, 1952.

Finlayson, G., *The Seventh Earl of Shaftesbury*, Eyre Methuen, London, 1981.

Foucault, M., *Discipline and Punish. The Birth of the Prison*, London, Allen Lane, 1977.

Bibliography

Foucault, M., *The History of Sexuality, Volume I: An Introduction*, New York, Pantheon books, 1978.

Fowler, W., *A Study in Radicalism and Dissent: The Life and Times of Henry Joseph Wilson 1833—1914*, London, Epworth, 1961.

Freeden, M., *The New Liberalism: An Ideology of Social Reform*, Oxford, Clarendon, 1978.

Gorham, Deborah, 'Victorian Reform as a Family Business: the Hill Family', in A. Wohl (ed.), *The Victorian Family. Structures and Stresses*, London, Croom Helm, 1978.

Hall, Catherine, 'The Early Formation of Victorian Domestic Ideology', in Sandra Burman (ed.), *Fit Work for Women*, Oxford, Oxford University Press, 1979.

Hall, Ruth (ed.), *Dear Dr Stopes — Sex in the 1920s*, London, Deutsch, 1978.

Hamer, D., *Liberal Politics in the Age of Gladstone and Rosebery: a study in leadership and policy*, Oxford, Clarendon, 1972.

Harrison, B., 'State Intervention and Moral Reform', in Patricia Hollis (ed.), *Pressure from Without in Early Victorian England*, London, Edward Arnold, 1974.

Harrison, Rachel and Mort, F., 'Patriarchal Aspects of Nineteenth-Century State Formation: Property Relations, Marriage and Divorce and Sexuality', in P. Corrigan (ed.), *State Formation and Marxist Theory*, London, Quartet, 1980.

Hart, J., 'Nineteenth-Century Social Reform: a Tory Interpretation of History', *Past and Present*, 1965, vol. 31, pp. 39–61.

Hay, D., *et al.*, (eds), *Albion's Fatal Tree. Crime and Society in Eighteenth Century England*, Harmondsworth, Penguin, 1977.

Heasman, Kathleen, *Evangelicals in Action. An Appraisal of their Social Work in the Victorian Era*, London, 1962.

Heyck, T., *The Transformation of Intellectual Life in Victorian England*, London, Croom Helm, 1982.

Holtzman, Ellen, 'The Pursuit of Married Love. Women's Attitudes Towards Sexuality and Marriage in Great Britain, 1918–1939', *Journal of Social History*, 1982, vol. 16, no. 2, pp. 39–51.

Hudson, D., *Munby Man of Two Worlds. The Life and Diaries of Arthur J. Munby 1828–1910*, London, Abacus, 1974.

Humphries, Jane, 'Protective Legislation, the Capitalist State and Working Class Men. The Case of the 1842 Mines Regulation Act', *Feminist Review*, no. 7, 1981, pp. 1–34.

Bibliography

Hussain, A., 'Foucault's History of Sexuality', *m/f*, 1981, nos. 5 and 6, pp. 169–91.

Hyde, H. Montgomery, *The Other Love: a historical and contemporary survey of homosexuality in Britain*, London, Mayflower, 1972.

Ignatieff, M., *A Just Measure of Pain. The Penitentiary in the Industrial Revolution*, London, MacMillan, 1978.

Inkster, I., 'Marginal Men: Aspects of the Social Role of the Medical Community in Sheffield 1790–1850', in J. Woodward and D. Richards (eds), *Health Care and Popular Medicine in Nineteenth-Century England*, London, Croom Helm, 1977.

Jeffreys, Sheila, *The Spinster And Her Enemies. Feminism And Sexuality 1880—1930*, London, Pandora, 1985.

Johnson, R., 'Educational Policy and Social Control in Early Victorian England', *Past and Present*, November 1970, no. 49, pp. 96–119.

Johnson, R., 'Educating the Educators: "Experts" and the State 1833–9', in A. Donajgrodski (ed.), *Social Control in Nineteenth-Century Britain*, London, Croom Helm, 1977.

King, A. *et al. Venereal Diseases*, London, Ballière Tindall, 1980.

Lambert, R., *Sir John Simon 1816–1904 and English Social Administration*, London, MacGibbon and Kee, 1963.

Lewis, Jane, *The Politics of Motherhood: Maternal and Child Welfare in England 1900—39*, London, Croom Helm, 1980.

Lidderdale, Jane and Nicholson, Mary, *Dear Miss Weaver. Harriet Shaw Weaver 1876—1961*, London, Faber, 1970.

Longmate, N., *King Cholera. The Biography of a Disease*, London, H. Hamilton, 1966.

Marcus, S., *The Other Victorians. A Study of Sexuality and Pornography in Mid-Nineteenth Century England*, Weidenfeld and Nicholson, 1966.

MacDonagh, O., 'The Nineteenth-Century Revolution in Government: A Reappraisal', *Historical Journal*, 1958, ii, pp. 59–73.

McGregor, O., *Divorce in England. A centenary study*, London, Heinemann, 1957.

McHugh, P., *Prostitution and Victorian Social Reform*, London, Croom Helm, 1980.

Morris, R., *Cholera 1832*, London, Croom Helm, 1976.

Mort, F., 'The Domain of the Sexual', *Screen Education*, 1980, no. 36, pp. 69–84.

Mort, F., 'Purity, feminism and the state: sexuality and moral politics,

Bibliography

1880–1914', in Mary Langan and B. Schwarz (eds), *Crises in the British State 1880—1930*, London, Hutchinson, 1985.

Morton, R., *VD and diseases transmitted sexually*, London, Corgi, 1971.

Nead, Lynda, 'Seduction, Prostitution, Suicide: *On the Brink* by Alfred Elmore', *Art History*, 1982, vol. 5, pp. 310–22.

Nield, K. (ed.), *Prostitution in the Victorian Age: Debate on the Issues from Nineteenth-Century Critical Journals*, Farnborough, Gregg International, 1973.

Noble, R., *Sexually Transmitted Diseases: a guide to diagnosis and therapy*, London, Kimpton, 1979.

Pelling, Margaret, *Cholera, Fever and English Medicine 1825—1865*, Oxford, Oxford University Press, 1978.

Peterson, M. Jeanne, *The Medical Profession in Mid-Victorian England*, Berkeley, University of California Press, 1978.

Prochaska, F., *Women and Philanthropy in Nineteenth-Century England*, Oxford, Clarendon Press, 1980.

Richards, P., 'State Formation and Class Struggle 1832–48' in P. Corrigan (ed.), *Capitalism, State Formation and Marxist Theory*, London, Quartet, 1980.

Rose, N., *The Psychological Complex. Psychology, Politics and Society in England 1869—1939*, London, Routledge, 1985.

Rowbotham, Sheila, *A New World for Women: Stella Browne — Socialist Feminist*, London, Pluto, 1978.

Schwarz, B., 'The Language of Constitutionalism: Baldwinite Conservatism', in *Formations of Nation and People*, London, Routledge, 1984, pp. 1–18.

Searle, G., *The Quest for National Efficiency: a study in British politics and political thought. 1899—1914*, Oxford, Blackwell, 1971.

Searle, G., *Eugenics and Politics in Britain 1900—1914*, Leyden, Nordhoff International, 1976.

Shapiro, Rose, 'Britain's Sexual Counter-Revolutionaries', *Marxism Today*, February 1985, vol. 29, no. 2, pp. 7–10.

Shorter, E., *The Making of the Modern Family*, Glasgow, Fontana, 1977.

Stedman Jones, G., *Outcast London. A Study in the Relationship Between Classes in Victorian Society*, Harmondsworth, Penguin, 1984.

Stone, L., *The Family, Sex and Marriage in England 1500—1800*, Harmondsworth, Penguin, 1977.

Summers, Anne, 'A Home from Home – Women's Philanthropic Work in the

Bibliography

Nineteenth Century', in Sandra Burman (ed.), *Fit Work for Women*, Oxford, Clarendon Press, 1980.

Tagg, J., 'Power and Photography: Part One. A Means of Surveillance: The Photograph as Evidence in Law', *Screen Education*, 1980, no. 36, pp. 17–55.

Taylor, Barbara, *Eve and the New Jerusalem. Socialism and Feminism in the Nineteenth Century*, London, Virago, 1983.

Turner, G. l'E., *Historical Aspects of Microscopy: papers read at a one-day conference held by the Royal Microscopical Society at Oxford*, Cambridge, Heffer, 1967.

Vaughan, P., *Doctor's Commons, A Short History of the British Medical Association,* London, Heinemann, 1959.

Walkowitz, Judith, *Prostitution and Victorian Society. Women, class and the state*, Cambridge, Cambridge University Press, 1980.

Walkowitz, Judith, 'Male Vice and Feminist Virtue: Feminism and the Politics of Prostitution in Nineteenth-Century Britain', *History Workshop*, 1982, no. 13, pp. 79–93.

Walkowitz, Judith, 'Science, Feminism and Romance: The Men and Women's Club 1885–1889', *History Workshop*, 1986, no. 21, pp. 36–59.

Watney, S., 'Babbling at the baricades of Pornography', *New Socialist*, June 1986, no. 39, p. 21.

Weeks, J., *Coming Out. Homosexual Politics in Britain from the Nineteenth Century to the Present*, London, Quartet, 1977.

Weeks, J., *Sex, Politics and Society. The regulation of sexuality since 1800*, London, Longmans, 1981.

Weeks, J., *Sexuality And Its Discontents. Meanings, Myths and Modern Sexualities*, London, Routledge, 1985.

Wohl, A., 'Unfit for Human Habitation', in H. Dyos and M. Woolf (eds), *The Victorian City. Images and Realities*, London, Routledge, 1973, 2 vols.

Wood, Nancy, 'Prostitution and Feminism in Nineteenth-Century Britain', *m/f*, 1982, no. 7, pp. 61–78.

INDEX

Acton, William, 70, 71, 77–9, 82, 185, 186
Addison, Christopher, 202
admiralty, 69
adolescence, 174, 186, 190–1, 193–4, 204
advertising, 134, 177; *see also* popular culture
age of consent, 103, 134, 142
AIDS, 1, 2, 9, 211–9
alcoholism, 172
Alison, Dr, 39–40
amateur prostitute, 188, 190, 199
Analysis of the Sexual Impulse (Freud), 186
anglicanism, 32, 70, 175, 204–5, 206
Aniss, Inspector, 125
Annual Report of the Chief Medical Officer of the DHSS (1982), 215
anti-statism, 34
aristocracy, 17, 43, 73, 84–5, 88, 103, 113, 131–2, 167, 176
armed forces, 22, 69, 75–6, 165, 166–7
Arnold, Inspector, 127
Ashley, Lord, 34, 35, 37–8, 54, 88
Asquith, Herbert, 143–4
Association for Moral and Social Hygiene, 180, 208
Association for Promoting the Extension of the Contagious Diseases Acts to the Civilian Population, 70
Association for the Promotion of Social Science, 75, 76, 88, 92

Association of Medical Officers of Health, 81
Astor, Nancy, 203
Astor, Viscount, 200

Baden-Powell, Sir Robert, 194
Ballantyne, Dr John, 169
Band of Hope Mission, 112
Banks, F.C., 97
Baptists, 30
Barclay, Dr, 75
Bartlett, Lucy Re, 138–9, 140
Bath Preventive Mission and Ladies' Association for the Care of Friendless Girls, 127
Bedborough, George, 147
Bentham, Jeremy, 27
benthamism, 35, 107, 196
Berwicke, Alice, 98
Besant, Annie, 82
Bevan, William, 80
Bible, the, 139–40
Bible Society, 57
Biggs, Thomas, 88
Billington-Grieg, Teresa, 145
Biological Education Congress, 204
biometry, 171
birth-control, 192, 201, 203, 206
birth-rate, 44–5, 169–71; *see also* motherhood; population
Births, Marriages and Deaths Registration Act (1836), 45
Bitter Cry of Outcast London, The, 105

271

Index

Blackwell, Elizabeth, 110–11, 116–17, 122, 185

Bland, Lucy, 190

Board of Education, 168, 184, 199, 200

Board of Health, 14, 16

Boer War, 166–7, 194

Bonwick, Miss T.E., 197

Booth, Mrs Bramwell, 104, 117, 130

Booth, Charles, 166, 171

Booth, William, 129

Boy Scouts, 194

Boys' League of Honour, 112–13

Bradlaugh, Charles, 82

Bradwell, Mr, 158

Bright, John, 91

Bristow, Edward, 118

British Medical Association, 72, 171–2, 176

British Medical Journal, 76, 106, 163, 172

British Women's Temperance Association, 137

brothel-keeping, 103, 106, 142, 144

Browne, Stella, 148

Buchanan, Sir George, 109

Burroughs, Inspector, 134

Butler, Rev. George, 91

Butler, Josephine, 7, 87, 89, 91, 95–6, 98–9, 120–1, 126–7, 138

Carpenter, Edward, 139, 147

catholicism, 140

Chadwick, Edwin, 7, 26, 29, 33, 34, 35, 39, 51–2, 61, 65–6, 74, 107, 178

Chalmers, Rev. Thomas, 21

Charity Organisation Society, 72, 81

Chartism, 74

chastity, 111, 122, 137; *see also* continence; self-control

Chesser, Elizabeth Sloan, 187, 191–2, 193

child assault, 141; *see also* white-slave trade

children, 38, 48–9, 122, 124, 160, 161, 162, 165, 197; boys, 48–9, 103, 193–6; child pornography, 84; child victims, 103; girls, 104, 115, 127, 153, 157, 158, 159, 189–93

Children's Employment Commission (1842), 26, 48–50

chivalry, 115–16

cholera, 8, 13–18, 20–1, 25, 28, 30, 34, 43, 214; *Cholera Gazette, The*, 16

Christian Socialism, 66, 110

Church Lads' Brigade, 113

civil service, 74, 107–8, 165–6, 215; *see also* government; Northcote-Trevelyan Report

Clancy, Dr Reid, 13

Clapham Sect, 54

Clapham Vigilance Association, 131

collectivism, 133, 165, 199

Common Cause, The, 141, 143, 144, 208

Communicable Diseases Centre, 215

Congregationalists, 30, 32, 80, 90

conservative governments, 129, 131, 215–16

contagious disease, 28; *see also* cholera

Contagious Diseases Acts, 8, 68–76, 86, 88, 106, 110, 118, 131, 149, 179, 216

continence, 43–4, 111, 115, 119, 122, 138–9, 148, 181, 218

Cooke, William, 31, 44

Coote, William, 104, 112, 130, 132, 136, 143, 204

Cowper, Lady, 88

Creighton, Mandel, 175

Crimean War, 55, 69, 72, 75

criminal law, 104–5, 112, 122–3, 129, 149, 163, 174, 207–8

Criminal Law Amendment Acts: (1885), 105–6, 126–30; (1912), 143–5

Criminal Law Amendment Bills: (1909), 142; (1917–22), 207

Cullwick, Hannah, 85

Index

Index

Inter-Departmental Committee on
Physical Deterioration, 172
International Abolitionist
Conference, 179
International Abolitionist
Federation, 137
International Congress of Geneva,
89
Introduction to Social Psychology, An
(McDougall), 189
inversion, 148
Irish, the, 36
Islington Dispensary, 77

Jeffreys, Sheila, 118
Jewish Association for the Protection
of Girls and Women, 142

Kaposi's Sarcoma, 1
Kay, Dr James Phillips, 7, 18–22,
27, 28, 29, 30, 35, 36, 43, 51–3, 61,
212, 213
Kay, Janet, 52–3
Kell, Elizabeth, 95, 97–8
Kennedy, John, 51
Kennedy, Rachel, 51–2
Kingsley, Charles, 66, 110
Kitchen, Nancy, 14
Koch, Robert, 164

Labouchère, Henry, 129
Ladies' Association for the Care of
Friendless Girls, 112
Ladies' National Association, 87, 93,
94, 95, 98, 135, 137, 142, 143–4,
145, 180
Lamarck, J.B., 171
Lambert, John, 107
Lambeth Conference, 206
Lancet, The, 14, 17, 28, 43, 45, 70–1,
82, 83, 105, 106, 108, 185, 205,
211–12, 214
Lane, Sir Arbuthnot, 205
Layard, Daniel, 23
League of Isis, 140
Legitimation League, the, 147
lesbianism, 148

Lettsom, John Coakley, 24
Liberal Party, 90–1, 94, 112, 132
libertarianism, 136–7, 146–9, 218–
19
Licensing Act (1872), 76
Liddel, Sir John, 70
Liddle, John, 30
Lingen, Ralph, 108
Liverpool City Council, 135
Llewellyn-Smith, H., 133, 167, 171
Lloyd George, David, 143, 203
Local Government Act (1871), 106–
7
Local Government Board, 106–7,
109
Logan, William, 80
Lombroso, C., 188
London Bible and Domestic
Mission, 58
London City Mission, 54
London Committee for Suppressing
the Traffic in Young Girls, 126
London County Council, 190, 199
London, Jack, 105
London, moral state of, 136; *see also*
Haymarket
London Women's Christian
Association, 127
London Working Men's College, 55
love, 53, 80, 91, 111, 137, 139, 140,
155, 188, 192–3, 206
Lyttleton, Rev. Edward, 175, 193,
195

McDougall, Professor William, 189
McGair, Dennis, 15
McKenna, Reginald, 133, 144
Mahony, Dr, 15
'Maiden Tribute of Modern
Babylon, The' (Stead), 103
Malthus, Rev. Thomas, 45
Manchester Statistical Society, 44
Manning, Cardinal, 110
Marchant, Rev. James, 173, 175
marriage, 45, 46, 77, 80, 122, 139,
163, 170, 172, 205, 206, 208; and
the middle class, 52–3

275

Index

nurses, 55

obscenity, 104, 134, 135
Ormiston-Chant, Laura, 117
Outram, Miss, 153, 156, 183–5, 187, 197

Paley, Archdeacon William, 32
Pall Mall Gazette, 103, 126
Palmerston, Lord, 88
Pankhurst, Christabel, 7, 139–41, 181, 183
Pankhurst, Emmeline, 145
Pankhurst, Sylvia, 145
parenthood, 156, 163, 186–8; *see also* the family
Parnell, Charles, 130
Pasteur, Louis, 67, 164
Paul, St, 40
Pearson, Karl, 170, 171
Pease, Joseph, 162
People's League of Health, 177
Percival, Thomas, 24
permissiveness, 213
Personal Reminiscences of a Great Crusade (Butler), 138
philanthropy, 22–5, 35, 36, 46, 71, 81, 104, 118, 135; and women, 53–60, 95–9, 119–20, 122, 123–6; *see also* rescue work
photography, 83–4
physical training, 168
Plymouth City Council, 76
pneumocystis pneumonia, 1
political discourse, 87–9, 91, 132–3, 201–3
Poor Law Board, 106–7
popular culture, 76, 114, 177, 188, 202, 204; *see also* advertising
popular press, 105, 113–14, 211–13
population, 20, 44–5, 167, 169–72; *see also* race; statistics
pornography, 84, 134
pregnancy, 44, 169, 191
Pre-Raphaelites, 79
Priestman, Mary, 91
Pringle, John, 22

prison reform, 22–3, 24
Privy Council, 16–17, 20
Privy Council Medical Office, 65–6
prostitution, 69–70, 76, 77, 79, 81, 84, 98, 106, 135–6, 144, 199; *see also* amateur prostitute
Prostitution (Acton), 77
Provincial Medical and Surgical Association, 27
psychology, 146–7, 148, 189; *see also* freudianism
Public Health Act (1848), 33
public order, 76, 106, 131
purity, 103, 109–14, 120, 134–5, 174–5, 185, 198, 203–9; and feminism, 117–19, 123, 125–6, 132; and the state, 126–30

Rabelais Picture Gallery, 134
race, 157, 169–73, 181, 193, 196; racial instinct, 163, 186; racial poisons, 170
radical pluralism, 218–19
Ragged Schools Union, 54
Ranyard, Ellen, 56–9, 95, 96
Ravenhill, Alice, 181
Reform Act, 109
regulationists, 70–3, 75–83, 86–7, 125, 179; *see also* Contagious Diseases Acts
Relative Proportion of Male and Female Population, The, 44
religion, 14, 20, 22, 30–6, 42, 50, 55, 89, 92–5, 110–11, 115–16, 118, 120, 138, 139–40, 153, 173, 175–6, 206; evangelical, 19, 23, 25, 30–1, 34, 40, 54, 60, 80, 90–1, 112, 128, 175, 178
Rentoul, Dr Robert, 171, 182
repeal campaign, 86–99, 118, 124, 125, 131, 179
Report from the Poor Law Commissioners into the Sanitary Condition of the Labouring Population of Great Britain, 26, 38–40
Report of the Royal Commission on

277

Index

Index

Social Purity Alliance, 94, 115
Social Science Congress, 87
Society of Friends, 126
sociobiology, 213
Southwood Smith, Thomas, 27, 28, 33–4, 178
speaking out, 114–17, 183, 185
Spencer, Herbert, 169, 182
spermatic plethora, 43
spinsters, 138, 139, 161
Sport, William, 14
Spring-Rice, T., 17
Standard, The, 113
Stansfield, James, 89, 91, 107
state, the, 5, 35, 104–5, 118, 123–4, 130–6, 140–6, 149, 201–2; *see also* civil service; government
state medicine, 5, 16–18, 26–7, 32–6, 45–6, 65–8, 70–2, 86, 99, 106–9, 149, 163–9, 174–5, 176–8, 208, 215–16; *see also* medical profession
statistics, 170–1
Stead, W.T., 103, 104, 126, 129, 132, 212
sterilization, 171
Stevenson, Frances, 203
Stopes, Marie, 192–3, 203
Stuart, James, 128
Suffragette, The, 138, 157
Sunday People, The, 211
Swiney, Frances, 139–40, 181–3
Symons, Jelinger, 48, 51, 52, 83

Talbot, John, 80
Tanner, Margaret, 91
Tansley, A.G., 195
Taylor, Barbara, 93
Terre, La (Zola), 113
Terrence Higgins Trust, 217
Thomson, J.A., 182, 188
Times, The, 65, 107, 129
Tory Party, 70
trade-unionism, 104, 105, 128
treasury, 108, 201
Treatise on Fever (Southwood Smith), 28–9

Tristan, Flora, 84–5
Twining, Louisa, 66

unfit, the, 167, 170–2
Unitarians, 73, 80, 90
urban poor, 105–6

Van der Velde, Theodore, 207
Vaughn, Robert, 80
venereal disease, 69–76, 77, 156, 172, 178–9, 190, 199–200, 213–14; *see also* Contagious Diseases Acts
Vigilance Association for the Defence of Personal Rights, 125, 128
Vote, The, 141

Wakley, Dr Thomas, 17, 19, 27
Walkowitz, Judith, 77, 118
'Walter', 83–4
Ward, Lord, 72
Wardlaw, Ralph, 80
war office, 69, 168
Webb, Beatrice, 133
Webb, Sidney, 133
Webster, Sir Richard, 134
Weekly Dispatch, The, 161
Weeks, Jeffrey, 118
Weismann, August, 171
welfare state, 209; *see also* government; state
Westminster Review, The, 16, 70
White Cross League, 115–16
Whitelaw, Lord, 216
white slave trade, 126–7, 145
Wilberforce, William, 54
Wilcox, Dr R., 214
Wilde, Oscar, 113–14
Wilkes, Anna, 129
Wilson, Helen, 91, 180, 186, 197, 199
Wilson, Henry, 91, 126, 132, 135
Wilson, Rev. J.M., 115
Wolstenholme, Elizabeth, 91–2
women, 4, 7, 8, 44–6, 66, 77, 79–83, 86–7, 92–9, 104, 116–26, 127, 135,

279